ALSO BY JOHN MUNDER ROSS

Father and Child (edited with S. H. Cath and A. Gurwitt)
Tales of Love, Sex and Danger (with Sudhir Kakar)
New Concepts in Psychoanalytic Psychotherapy (edited with W. A. Myers)
The Oedipus Papers (edited with G. H. Pollock)

The MALE PARADOX ...

John Munder Ross, Ph.D.

Simon & Schuster
New York London Toronto Sydney Tokyo Singapore

SIMON & SCHUSTER
Simon & Schuster Building
Rockefeller Center
1230 Avenue of the Americas
New York, New York 10020

DESIGNED BY BARBARA MARKS
Manufactured in the United States of America

10 9 8 7 6 5 4 3 2 1

Library of Congress Cataloging in Publication Data

Ross, John Munder.
    The male paradox / John Munder Ross.
        p.   cm.
    Includes bibliographical references and index.
    1. Men—United States—Psychology.   2. Gender
identity—United States.   3. Sex role—United
States.   4. Masculinity (Psychology)—United
States.   5. Femininity (Psychology)—United States.
I.Title.
HQ1090.3.R67   1992
155.3'32—dc20   92-21639
                                                  CIP

ISBN: 0-671-70517-2

The Male Paradox is dedicated to the two people I love most:

my beloved Barbara Fisher

and

my dear son, Matthew Ross

I would also like to thank those who were instrumental in helping me develop the project and in working on the evolving manuscript: My agent, Suzanne Gluck, my editors, Bob Asahina and Laura Yorke, and my assistant, Keith Bradley, were critical presences at every stage in the book's production. In addition, there were the dear friends who helped inspire my ideas and refine my prose: Barbara Fisher, Vicky Traube, Skip Ascheim, and Sudhir Kakar. And I can't begin to name all those whose ways of thinking and whose life stories have influenced my understanding of "the male paradox": the teachers and analysts, patients and research subjects, parents and children, theorists and artists, and along the way, friends and lovers.

Contents

Preface:
About This Book
About Men

The Male Paradox is not a book about fairy tales, dreams, or rituals of any kind. It's not a book about men getting back to themselves. It's a book about men in real life—about men and women, and children, bosses, parents, and lovers.

The Male Paradox will tell you just how unpredictable, how unstraightforward, how mysterious men are every day of their lives. And it will then explain why.

Consider Hal Goldsmith. For three years he worked like a man possessed, up to sixteen hours a day, just to become the managing director of his division. But when he finally got the promotion, Hal came back from the office party, got on his bike, and fell and broke his hip before he even got to the park, laying himself up for three months.

A coincidence? Too much champagne?

Jim Bonner was utterly in love with Jane. After wooing and winning her, three weeks past their honeymoon, Jim began an affair. She was the first woman he had slept with since laying eyes on Jane five whole years earlier.

Bill Minelli, a pediatrician and former camp counselor, had

always wanted kids of his own. For two years, he and Susan tried to get her pregnant. They were just about to adopt when at last it worked. Now Bill savors that swelling belly as if it were his own. But when he tries to celebrate with Susan by making love together, he usually goes limp. He even has strange thoughts, ones he'd never anticipated—impulses, for example, to bang his fist against Susan's stomach.

Why do these men—men like those you know or live with—act the way they do? Why do they sabotage themselves? What do they want and why are they afraid of getting it?

To begin to answer these "what" and "why" questions, I'll tell you a variety of different stories about men and women. The characters you will meet in the pages that follow are real people. They're based on patients and research subjects I've known over the years, on cases that have been presented to me in my professional travels across the country—though I've taken pains to disguise their identities.

You will happen upon unexpected connections among the many characters in these stories. Like us, they like to believe that others' lives are much simpler than their own, not fathoming the actual similarities. Far from such insight, men especially project onto others the ideals or stereotypes they can't measure up to. But people, I will show, are never what they seem. What men have in common, ironically, is most often the individual secrets they suffer in silence.

Some of these characters will seem familiar. We've all known guys with marital or potency problems, people who've slept around too much or with the "wrong" sex, men who've been sick or gotten fired or had kids with serious difficulties. Maybe we or our husbands have been in a similar fix ourselves.

Other characters may seem strange to you, capable of feeling or doing things you think you never dreamed of. Well, you say, *maybe* you can accept a man's dropping out for a while or fleeing the coop or even, as a kid, being fascinated in a peculiar way with women's underwear. But how could a guy have sex with his daughter or beat his son?

Yes, men do these things—we've heard the TV reports and read the statistics. Still, they seem so alien to a normal way of life. Yet if you stop and look hard enough at yourself even as you make your way through the stories of their lives, perhaps you'll find just a little bit of them in you. Maybe "monsters" such as these can begin to tell us some unwanted truths about all men.

In all these accounts, then, it's my aim to take you into the most foreign, but ever-present, territory of all—the unconscious mind. This world within us is powerful but like the ocean depths, unknown and hard to fathom.

There the past, our forgotten childhood, lives on as if there were no such thing as the passing of time. Consequently, everything a man does in his adult life, I will show, is influenced not only by current realities but by the ghosts of his past—by the unexpected wishes and fears accompanying a little boy's first steps into an exciting but also scary world, a universe that adults can no longer easily comprehend.

Introduction:
Marlboro Man Meets
Mr. Mom

By the time he's grown into manhood, a boy has learned to cover up his childish confusion about what it means for him to be male. Most men try to simplify matters of masculinity for themselves.

Like the kid he once was, the boy enamored of his superheroes, even the most sophisticated of adult men still cleaves to unrealistic and two-dimensional models of manhood. In the fifties, there was the Marlboro Man, that hypermasculine caricature of the lone wolf, a tough guy who needed nobody—certainly not a woman. That was before the Surgeon General's report and before the Vietnam War. Nowadays a hypersensitive Mr. Mom is touted as the "new man" for real men to emulate. Give up your aggression, your independence, and ambition, men are now exhorted— give up your machismo in favor of the softer, and yes, more feminine, side of life. "Yeah, that takes real balls," and that's the way to the truth.

There's even a certain continuity here—a thread I'll return to later. Like the Lone Ranger, the heroic Househusband, having made himself like a woman, doesn't seem to want women around either.

Neither of these icons offers a viable alternative in real life; something's missing in each extreme. Indeed, in recent years researchers have been challenging most of our preconceptions about what is invariably male, what female. Sex differences, they've found, reside very much in the eye of the beholder.

The trouble is, most men—and certainly the boys they once were—haven't kept up with modern psychology. Along the line, aspiring to be that perfect man, whatever he may be, they've gotten some pretty fixed notions about what it means to be "masculine" or "feminine."

Men's male ideals express a measure of their heartfelt longings and aspirations. Yet they also prevent them from fully knowing their hearts. And since so much of what they feel and want doesn't really fill the "masculine" bill (for reasons we'll soon discover), men are constantly at war—with themselves and with those, such as the women in their lives, who call their masculinity into question. Men pretend that they are stronger or at least more straightforward than women to cover up, or compensate for, the wrenching paradoxes inherent in their sexual identity. Their changing male stereotypes help keep men from acknowledging the sense of conflict and mystery at the core of their maleness.

> · · ·

Men want to be men, of course, and there's a lot of pleasure accompanying being and acting "like a man." Yet, this book will show, it's not so simple as all that.

First of all, men also wish to be like women sometimes, or rather how they see women—soft, more emotional, child oriented, passive at times, sexy and sensuous . . . feminine. But women's womanliness can seem "catching" to many men, especially if they're exposed to it for too long. In fact, be with a woman, men feel and fear, and you may become her. So if you don't want to be like women, don't want to join them, then beat them in one way or another. Or better, beat it. And fast.

These doubts and fears have their origins in men's boyhoods. Boys are mostly brought up by women—their mothers. The first "significant others" in their lives, their first role models for being a person, are female. These caretakers and their female aura, their style and their rhythms, thus leave a deep "imprint" on their sons' psyches.

Even their male sexuality reveals not only men's virility but along with their power to conquer, their longings to get back to their origins in a mother's arms. In the presence of women, men secretly yearn to recapture a time when they felt united with their mother and all that will later become defined as her compelling femininity. All women present this allure and specter to men. And ironically, therefore, they threaten to unman them.

On the other side of the coin, these same men feel terrified of the potential violence that also goes along with being male—the inherent destructiveness that comes with asserting (and assuring themselves of) their masculinity.

There's a basic biology to this continuous "self-masculinization," one that is echoed in a man's psychology. Men *need* to aggress. Nature has endowed males in ways that are different from females. They're bigger; they're stronger; they don't carry babies; they were made to fight. Indeed, being aggressive for most men means being male, and they use their competitiveness to reassure themselves that they are.

Before they know it, however, this, too, can get out of hand. Since a man also feels moved to fight just to "prove" himself a man, innocent bystanders, even his own kids, can sometimes become targets of unfocused hostility that has an even more hidden agenda: the basic fear that he may be more woman than man after all. Or at least he may become sexually ambiguous and infantile, a mama's boy at best. And so, almost reflexively at times, men have to resort to violence to empower their maleness. Working beneath the surface and sometimes erupting in explosive behavior, impulses such as these act to sabotage the integrity of the family as well as a man's pursuit of success on the work front.

Yet, as decent citizens, grown-ups, men don't like resorting to violence. They like to think of themselves as good, solid, true-blue guys, ready to stand up for what they believe in and to take arms if necessary to protect their communities and serve the common good. And these days Marlboro Men have added to the mix Mr. Mom's nurturing and tenderness, qualities hitherto associated with women. To these mature men, their naked aggression can seem childish and uncivilized—reminding them of a kid in the playground, squabbling, bloodying other boys' noses and skinning his own knees.

Indeed, a man defines himself in opposition to three polarities: child, woman, and beast. Because he has the attributes of all of these within him and fears "becoming" any one of them, he remains perpetually on his guard.

So it's not so easy being a man—a man's man—as men themselves and even some professional psychologists would like us to think. Men's self-deceptions to the contrary, along with women's collusions in taking these at face value, make it all the more difficult to get a handle on the unruly and frightened little child who haunts the lives of most adults. In subtle and more overt ways, this confused little boy tends to dictate and subvert adult relationships, wounding women as he makes the grown man he's supposed to be flee from love. It is with these ritual myths and shared misconceptions about men, and the need to acknowledge the essential vulnerability behind men's posturing, that the book begins.

From there I will turn to the problems posed by the unexpected stresses that come crashing in on most men's lives.

In Sections II, III, and IV, I will follow men as they negotiate the abiding personal problems, unexpected detours, and external calamities at least one of which most of us will suffer during a lifetime: the currents and storms of making a commitment to one woman, homosexuality, and persistent sexual failure; extramarital affairs and being divorced; getting fired, suffering a major illness, and ruing a disabled child. In so doing I hope to show how easily misstep or misfortune is interpreted as a frontal assault on a man's masculinity. Experiences of incapacity and near disaster force a man to regress. They expose his ever-present terror of being effeminized and unleash the rage and violence that are mobilized to defend an imperiled manhood.

Stories like these, concentrating as they do on adult lives, only deal with the boys these men once were in retrospect. In the next series of chapters, I will look at one man's childhood as it actually unfolds.

Section V follows this man's story from infancy to midlife. In the process, we will look at the role of all players in the developmental dialogues of this life: mother, father, siblings, and grandparents; coaches, teachers, friends, and interlopers; friends and girlfriends; wives, children, and others yet to come. Throughout this narrative we will follow the interweaving of the book's two threads that pursue a male from cradle to grave: the powerful impact of a man's feminine origins on his basic identity and the aggression entailed in forever asserting his masculine integrity. Beset by these opposing forces, a man must make an effort to construct a life of purpose, decency, and productivity. It's in the assumption of fatherhood, real and metaphorical, that the solution to the male paradox is found.

Others are not so lucky in developing a sense of themselves as generative and paternal men—men whose work bears fruit for others and who become caretakers to the subsequent generation. In these men, intrusion and hostility, the defining characteristics of male aggressivity, emerge unfettered in more or less desperate and unthinking attempts to gird their loins in the face of impingements from within themselves on their sexual identity. It is to an understanding of the terror that impels their excesses that the last two chapters on child abuse are devoted.

Baffled by his female patients and colleagues, Sigmund Freud once asked his disciple and benefactor Princess Marie Bonaparte, "My God, what does woman want?" Men, we now know, are no less mysterious. It's just that most of the time they don't admit it.

Running Scared: Men's Flight From Themselves

Men and women have some pretty fixed notions about who a man is and what he should be, images often at odds with what he actually does. In contrast to women, who are caricatured as dependent creatures ruled by unruly emotions and confused about their sexuality, men are said to be independent minded, straightforward in what they want, and undaunted in going after it. Men are men, and women something else.

Neither women nor men nor the culture as a whole seem to see men—again in contrast to women—as having psychological conflicts. Both sexes retreat from recognizing the essential ambiguity and fragility of men's manhood; at the same time, they downplay the danger, the destructive potential, that is activated when they act aggressively to establish their virility. And the tensions between these forces, between a man's feminine yearnings and hypermasculine strivings, are even harder to handle.

These days, in the wake of the so-called New Man, many of us like to think that we've given up our sexist stereotypes—at least in our personal lives. Yet scratch the tender surface of even the most sensitive of males, and you'll find Marlboro Man lurking at the next layer—a wolf in sheep's clothing.

Moreover, from the Lone Ranger to Mr. Mom, our shifting masculine ideals have yet another feature in common. They help us pretend that men don't need or want women.

As I've noted, it's when men are around women, in fact, that untoward desires and anxieties come into play, prompting them to behave in unpredictable ways and calling their oversimplified views of themselves most into question. In the presence of women, the confused little boy comes out of hiding—the child unsure of himself and of his sexual identity, fighting one minute and fleeing the next, the kid within who gives the lie to a man's illusions about himself.

From the female point of view, men's behavior toward women baffles and bothers them. Mostly they see it as *mis*behavior, proof positive of how callous or selfish men are. Or else women take it personally, as a reflection of something mysteriously but basically wrong with them. It's only when a woman can dispel her self-doubts, uncertainties rooted in the ways men have responded to her throughout her life, that she can begin to see that the men in her life are running scared.

What she may not be able to see even then is that these big boys have brought a host of other characters into the drama taking place between them. Not only have other women surreptitiously entered the scene of their relationship. But also mothers and fathers, brothers and sisters, schoolteachers and coaches, all the men and women these guys have been with or aspired to be; and yes, all the heroes, villains, and fools that ever were in the whole wide world haunt their life together. To glimpse *these* scenarios, real and imagined, and the major players in them, you have to get inside a man's mind.

In this first section of the book, then, I'll tell two stories about our more time-honored misconceptions about what it means to be a man, what they desire and what they fear. In Chapter 1, I'll show how even the most savvy of women finds herself stupefied by men—at a loss to contend with what they do to her much less to figure out what they want. Only when she begins to feel better about herself can she free herself to see more clearly and to ask the right questions: not "What's wrong with me?" but rather "What's going on in him?" Having asked the right questions, women will find themselves in a unique position to find out what it is that their men want and don't want and to help their partners gain insight into themselves.

Having posed these questions from the women's point of view, in the second chapter I will present the unfolding inner world of one man from adolescence to middle age. There's a little boy inside him, I will reveal, who has come along for the ride of his adult life. What he and this inner boy want—to be with a woman they love—is also what scares them the most.

1
...

The Men in Their Lives: What *Women* Have to Say

Maybe it's not so true anymore, but it used to be that women far outnumbered men as consumers of books on self-help and psychology as well as of actual psychotherapy. Of course, women, single women, feel they outnumber men—period.

It's usually the little boys who are referred to mental health clinics for children, getting into trouble in school more than girls do and thus calling attention to themselves, their problems, and their greater emotional vulnerability. But when it comes time for adults to seek such help, it's the women, far more than the men, who come to practitioners' offices.

And what do these women patients talk about once they're in the consulting room? Men. At least for the most part. True, feminism has changed women's sensibilities, moving them to ponder not only their love life but their work life as well. And lots of women are bitterly angry that men matter so much to them.

But they do. Even in the professional arena, men—husbands, bosses, colleagues, and subordinates—figure prominently in their consciousness. Women tend to be fairly obsessed with their bosses and with their fathers' expectations of them—or most often, the lack of them. And everywhere women find themselves dealing with the problems men pose, including the parts they play in either impeding or facilitating their careers.

How many men, in contrast, complain of sexism in the office? Though nowadays some of them may make professional choices and geographic moves based in part on a wife's career and her other needs—how many men consciously consider their mothers' role in having stimulated or discouraged their future pursuit of independence and success?

And even the most successful women, whose work lives are in place despite the misogyny that continues to dog their credibility and diminish their incomes, find themselves mostly complaining about men. About how they fail women in what should be their more intimate encounters. About "men who can't commit," who are hard to "keep faithful" or "monogamous," and who don't seem to love enough the "women who love too much." The popular books for women about men capture women's most pressing preoccupation: how to keep men from running away.

Having been stung in so many ways, left in the lurch often without a word, some of the most accomplished, attractive, and desirable of women can't help taking men's treatment of them personally. They find themselves repeatedly hurt by men because more often than not they are absolutely convinced that in the end, just because they are women, they are worthless—in their own eyes. Either this, they think, or men are inherently cruel and selfish. Guys are out to use and misuse women, who, being who they are (drubs, doormats), can expect no more out of them.

These beliefs have resonances in women's conscious and unconscious fantasy lives, which in turn have roots in their earliest childhood disappointments and distortions. Life begins with daddy. And the childhood history in which he played so central a part has a way of repeating itself in adulthood.

If or when she is freed from this past, and thus from the stereotyping of both sexes, a more "emotionally liberated" woman will sense that she has become the target of anxieties and hostilities that should be directed elsewhere. It is she who receives the brunt of a man's fear and guilt at the mere fact of his loving her. It is she who is the recipient of resentments that have to do not with her as a woman but with other men. It is she who takes men away from other men and into her world, the world of women. And so she sets conflicts in motion that, when a man is alone with her, he tends to take out on her person.

It's in understanding herself that a woman can discover her power then to comprehend and confront the men in her life. For all her smarts, it took my patient Jackie Faracci years—years of life experience and psychotherapy—to arrive at this simple realization.

• • •

"For thirty-eight of my thirty-nine years," Jackie exclaimed, pounding the couch, "for my whole life I've been trying not to take these guys 'personally.' Before that I didn't know better because I didn't *know anything*. And now you tell me to do the same damned thing I've been trying to do all along! Anyway, Doctor R, how would you know about men? You're a man!

"You know," Jackie continued, "even when they manage to stick around, most men are emotionally 'dyslexic.' They can't read feelings—their own or anybody else's."

Nearing forty, Jackie is still childless, and no longer married. According to her estimate, derived from a *New York* magazine article some years back, she has as good a chance of being "killed by a terrorist as of finding a husband again." Not to mention a baby.

This is not to say that Jackie is by any means a wallflower. Athletic, a former ballet and jazz dancer who switched careers in her late twenties, becoming editor in chief of *The Movies* after a mere eight years in the magazine business, Jackie Faracci is simply beautiful. Thin, elegant, sensuous, she is the sort of woman who, in the vernacular of her mother's or grandmother's eras, should have been "grabbed up" years ago.

What's more, though they may mystify her, Jackie loves men—adores them, body and soul, hungers for sex with them, and is among the elite 30 percent of women (maybe fewer) who, according to Shere Hite, regularly reach orgasm during intercourse. Jackie never anticipated being without men at this point in her life, just as she never predicted she'd have ended up so *mad* at them.

When she thinks about it, however, especially in her psychoanalysis (with a "man—I just couldn't have gone to a woman, not then"), the seeds were there from the beginning. "All along men have been making me hate myself. I hadn't been able to figure out how or why . . . and I have to now. To see, I guess, that my problem is their problem."

She knew I'd like this, Jackie continued, because it was

"straight out of Freud," but the second man she made love with reminded her of her father. It was February, the second semester of her freshman year at Bennington, when Professor Golden began coming on to her. . . .

He was teaching Elizabethan drama and poetry in what the college referred to as an "intimate seminar situation." Forty or so, smelling of tweed and corduroy, with accents of pipe tobacco, his temples graying and brow furrowed, crinkles forming under his eyes and crow's-feet beside them, the whole of him rough-soft, rumpled—Dick Golden was the walking opposite of smooth-skinned Billy, the high school boyfriend with whom she had broken off during her Christmas vacation. Dick—"just call me Dick"—had black hair on the top of his hands and prominent veins like what might be seen, she mused, on an Italian Renaissance sculpture. Golden was writing a book on the dramas of Christopher Marlowe, Shakespeare's rakish contemporary who died young after being stabbed in the forehead in a tavern brawl. Golden directed plays with undergraduates in them. His wife was no longer living with him. Golden, Dick, was very attractive.

He had a certain reputation, which was always getting forgotten.

"Miss Faracci." Jackie had lingered after class, shuffling papers before turning to leave. "Your last two papers were truly superb."

He meant it actually.

"Thanks."

He paused, taking in the picture before him—long, loose brown hair, bangs, jeans, suede jacket, large chestnut eyes, that way of drifting leggily through everyday space—the Bennington girl, the dancer.

"You ever act?"

"No." She swallowed.

"You have a feel for verse. A sense of cadence."

"Oh, I get very nervous when I have to speak to large groups. I choke, and my voice hits a register that is—uh—high, grating to say the least." Jackie's heart was pounding just then. And her throat drying up into a desert within her, she could hear her voice cracking indeed.

"Too bad. I'm casting *The Trojan Women*." He seemed not to have noticed. "You would be good for Cassandra or"—now he cleared his throat—"maybe, Helen."

Again they paused, looking at each other.

"I dance though."

"Really."

"Yeah, that doesn't bother me." Jackie wondered all of a sudden whether she was lying. "Just moving."

Sweeping past the next possible lull, she continued, "In fact I have a performance next week with the Dance Ensemble Group. Maybe you'd like to come. . . . It might give you some ideas for your chorus."

"Sure."

That was simple enough, she thought to herself, closing the classroom door behind her. But then she caught herself. The piece was so obvious. The erotic reverie of a virginal bride. Oh, shit. Why, Stella had wanted her to perform naked until she objected and they compromised—Jackie had never been one for all that disgustingly pink "nudity on the stage," which was just then in vogue. Suppose everything got messed up—Golden, the concert, everything.

On that fateful Saturday a week later, Jackie found herself staring at her face and body in the mirror as she applied the final blush to her right cheek. She was pretty naked under the nearly diaphanous, cream body stocking, further enveloped by some Isadora-type scarves. Her father wouldn't have approved, though her mother might, and Billy wouldn't understand. Jackie felt her flesh shrivel a little, grow hard and tight in places, as she imagined Golden somewhere out there in the darkened house.

"Hokey but sexy," she said, giggling at her reflection as she wrapped the final strand of gauze around her ponytail before tossing it like a horse swatting a fly.

Rising from her seat in that row of chairs in the collective dressing room, Jackie made her way to the wings, the black velvet wings, it seemed. She waited for her cue and then leapt into the ball of white light flecked with yellow, which, enveloping her, guarded her concentration. Even so, she couldn't help congratulating herself as she began to dance: "What an elevation—what an f-ing elevation!"

That night, after the show, Golden and she went out for drinks at Carl's together. The next week they went to bed.

"Let me look you over," Dick said.

Nude now, Jackie positioned herself in front of the window so that rays from both the moonlight and streetlamps fell on her form. She could feel the little whistle of cold air catch her behind and waft through her legs, brushing her pubic hair. Chilly as the wind was, her crotch was fiery, sending up jolts of desire.

Jackie could barely contain herself. She forced herself to savor this moment, however. There she was naked, being admired by this gorgeous, brilliant man—not boy—himself undressed and aroused beneath the mound of sheets. So she paused to take it all in—the books strewn about, the typewriter, tobacco pouches, Dick's hand draped over the sheet. Her father had hands like Dick's, Jackie caught herself thinking, with a further little twisting of desire and apprehension. But he never let himself look at her like that. Of course not.

When she had turned fourteen, and her breasts seemed to burst forth at last, her legs lengthening at the same time, Jackie's father had started to turn away. She had felt ungainly. Sometimes she'd even thought her menstrual flow made her smell.

He'd never cared all that much about what she did, preoccupying himself with the achievements of her three brothers. But her father had always liked the way she looked. Or rather he liked to have her body adorned with frills, party dresses and tutus, but then seemed to reject the body itself. Jackie shuddered at how he would have reacted to the sexuality she kept to herself, the thoughts of the night.

Thank God, in this world of boys—all three would become doctors like Dad, unlike their "artsy" sister (whose SATs were a good hundred points better than any of theirs, though nobody seemed to notice)—thank God, she could find an ally in her mother and something of a soulmate in Rich, a year older than she and the youngest of the brothers.

Jackie and her mother would talk for hours as they did the "women's work" of the household. They'd think together about boys and men and their roles as women. They'd ramble on about women's bodies, how they look and change. Jackie's mother's had grown fat—abused by the family's ceaseless demands and a little too much to drink in the evening, and at the same time, unused, like the law degree lying somewhere in the bottom dresser drawer. Now and then, Rich would join them, his muscles pumped up from a workout or practice, guzzling whole milk, teasing these two women he loved with courtly comments, and listening.

Rich, destined to become chairman of Psychiatry and then Dean at Emory Medical School, always went to watch Jackie dance. Once or twice they nearly "fooled around," stopping themselves just in time—but that's another story, and not so terrible as it might seem. Mom and Rich were always there, next to the vacant third seat the Faraccis had reserved.

Rushing from hospital or office, her father succeeded in making only one of the ten concerts during Jackie's junior and senior years. Breathless and puffing, he caught her second solo. But he was there in the audience for this one curtain call, raising his hands in applause so that Jackie, homing in on them and the smiling face they framed, found herself shivering with delight, as if graced by God. . . .

Now she rushed into Golden's expectant arms. She'd had her fantasies about sex, but never had she imagined being touched like that. At seventeen, inevitably Bill had been clumsy at first and quick to come, tender but rather inept. She'd had to find out about herself and teach him at the same time. This man, in contrast, knew just where everything was—knew, too, what Jackie wanted and was willing to give it. So, the first weeks, as they raced back and forth from campus and class to Dick's apartment— "chambers," she whispered to herself, "Professor Golden's chambers"—were wonderful. Jackie luxuriated in the sex and the languorous fatigue it left behind.

Looking back, Jackie couldn't recall just how long it lasted: the "honeymoon" and what she came later on to foresee as the inexorable waning of passion. Maybe it was a month, but Dick became uninterested. No, that wasn't the right word, really. It's that he seemed to become less interested in her than in himself.

As the book deadline he had set for himself approached, he seemed to want less of her sexually but more of her time. The typewriter she had admired in his apartment was in her room now day and night, as Jackie found herself burning the midnight oil, not to do her work, but to crank out page after page of her lover's manuscript. When it was completed, he took off for two weeks, canceling his classes and leaving Jackie to water the plants. Could she call him? No, he'd be traveling and would have to call her.

It was there, in that apartment, while spraying the avocado tree, that Jackie saw the note from Mrs. Golden: "Okay, 'meet me in St. Louis,' You Dick." He'd gone to see his wife.

When Dick came back, alone, she confronted him. Sure, he said, he'd had to figure it out, had to go full circle. It was over though, okay?

But it was over with them, too. First the sex disappeared. They even fought a little, but Jackie had almost stopped caring. They had one more night together before the summer, which was all right. But Dick didn't call her in the fall.

One October night at Carl's, Jackie saw Golden with another freshman.

Like Jackie, many women feel lousy about their bodies—not all, but a good number nonetheless. According to Freud, their feelings of defectiveness derive from so-called penis envy and from the wish to be a man or at least have what he has, his "phallus" and thus his patriarchal power. Indeed, for many years psychoanalysts believed that these motives underlie a woman's wish to marry and make babies as substitutes for her missing male genitals. If you can't *be* him, they reasoned, join him!

Thanks to the feminists, later practitioners came to abandon these chauvinistic views and to grant women their due. They spoke now of a "primary femininity." After all, most of the major theorists after Freud were women themselves.

Still, though the process is different from the one Freud suggested, from the very beginning men and their evident attitudes toward the opposite sex have a lot to do with how a growing girl comes to feel about her body and her self. Quite early on, I've found both in my observations of children and in my women patients' recollections, a daughter turns from her mother to her father for something different. She wants to bask in being admired, to feel that she is beautiful, whole, unique, and separate from her mother. She wants to be loved. More often than not, however, her father is bound to fail her, withdrawing his attention from his daughter's overtures in what seems to her to be indifference, disapproval, or disgust.

Not yet aware that a parent has his own psychological conflicts to contend with—his own wishes, fears, and *self-deceptions*—she takes his repeated rebuffs, yes, personally. There must be something wrong with me, she reasons, with my body, its private parts, my thoughts, my very essence. He's rejecting me, not because he's uptight, but because I'm a girl!

Unable to get beneath or beyond what psychoanalysts call these "manifest" or surface interactions and communications, the little girl grows into womanhood stung to the very core of her femininity. She ends up feeling deflated and embittered, resenting her dependence on men's presence and attentions to feel just a little bit better about herself.

Other psychological factors come into play, of course, but one alternative to feeling terrible about herself is for a girl and then a woman to become increasingly disgusted with men. So she may come to see *them* as the culprits, as base and callous brutes who seduce and abandon. How much better as people women are than the men who have repeatedly wounded them, such women now comfort themselves. And how much better off they'd be without them!

Women such as these collude with men's need to present themselves as superior, even sadistic, in order to keep their emotional distance and secure their masculinity. They reenact and thus vainly try to master the deadening childhood traumas of their fathers' apparent and repetitive rejections of them. They're holding on to the past, you see, and the people in it for fear of finding anything new. They're afraid of those things—a man, a relationship—that might move them to let go and in so doing, show them how wrong they have been their whole lives. About themselves, their bodies, and other people, about men in particular.

· · ·

Jackie Faracci's later relationships, in college and after, seemed more complete, more real, less an enactment of fantasy. Even so, she had the sense somehow that after a while her intensity, emotional and erotic, drove men away. Some seemed to wilt with her and ended up looking elsewhere for something easier. Others put her on a pedestal and became shocked at her more "imperfect" desires, needs, angers. Still other men simply never called back.

" 'Was it me?' I'd keep asking myself. What had I done or not done to please him? Even when I sensed the guy might simply be scared, I found myself torturing myself with questions like these. Just like adolescence, I'd even wonder whether there was something wrong with me physically, though, frankly, I knew how attractive I was. I'd stare at myself in the mirror, wondering whether I was getting fat like Mom. I'd rerun the fights, the sex that failed, all of it. Had I been too forward, too aroused, too much to handle, too smart, etc., etc.? I'd keep turning it back on myself."

When she was doing psychological research, Jackie remarked, former Radcliffe president Matina Horner discovered that women often fear alienating men by being more successful than they are. As students and later as workers of one sort or another, they therefore try to undermine themselves in order not to lose a man's love. This same fear may also be present in sexual encounters, where many women prove not only more orgasmic than their partners but a good deal less inhibited, better as lovers. Their greater sexual capacity, many women sense, can intimidate their men.

"Maybe I was oversexed," Jackie wondered at first. " 'Non-sense,' I told myself after each aborted relationship. They, the individual 'theys,' were the defective ones. Uptight, emotionally limited. So I'd try again, hoping to find a man who wanted something from life, who wanted me. But the same thing kept happening."

• • •

Even the most accomplished and experienced of women can get into trouble with men when she takes her dealings with them at face value. And no matter how smart they are or how hard they try to do otherwise, most women, women such as Jackie, do end up taking men *personally*, and literally. Taking it, and them, again and again!

Nor do the problems come to an end when an adult woman gets involved in a more or less exclusive, more or less committed relationship. Anticipating indifference or criticism on the part of the man in her life, who often seems all too willing to accommodate her expectations, she finds herself caught up in self-fulfilling prophecies. Afraid both of each other and of feeling bad, of having their self-esteem assaulted or of being burdened with guilt, women and men play out their preordained roles in vicious circles of mutual miscommunication and recrimination. It becomes increasingly difficult for either sex safely to tell the other what she or he truly feels, and wants. A woman's or man's expectation of suffering and the testiness that comes with guarding oneself and one's boundaries undermine their capacity for sustained innocence. A defensive hostility, drawing from their shared history and from more ancient pasts known to neither of them, erodes the lovers' love for each other.

• • •

Jackie was thirty-one when she got married—old by her mother's standards, par for the course among today's women. She and Henry had been living together for two years, trying to decide—to get married, to have kids, on being with each other. Jackie Faracci became Jackie Burrows, somebody else at last.

A chronic tendinitis in her knee, the recognition that she might really have to support herself after all, maybe a preparation for nesting and settling down, for a life with regular hours and income, had converged in Jackie's decision to abandon her dancing. Then again, if she was around more, her presence becoming more predictable, maybe then the men would be there, too—though she hated to acknowledge this concession as a factor in the decision.

Having advanced from junior editorial assistant to assistant editor within her first year at the *Media Magazine,* she had met Henry, a reviewer and free-lance writer, at a screening. They dated, made love, and gradually began to live together de facto, splitting the time between each other's apartments. Henry was fun, puckish in his humor and appearance, a decent lover, not easily roused to anger. Pretty soon they decided to consolidate space, time, and money, and Henry moved his books and belongings into her place.

Six months later Jackie proposed to him, noting that time was passing and she might very well want to have a baby. Things between them were going well, after all. Henry thought about it for two weeks and then said yes. The wedding date pretty much coincided with Jackie's promotion to senior editor.

So there they were married, and pretty soon "things" began to change. Henry, free-spirited Henry Burrows, got more and more cranky. Maybe good ol' Matina was right, Jackie reflected, maybe she shouldn't have been so successful.

While Henry stayed "stuck in the fuckin' rut" of third-string reviewer—and not for the *Times,* either!—Jackie's career seemed to start soaring. First, articles editor, then an offer from *The Movies* to take over for Helen Gable as managing editor—the ladder had extended itself before her. And she had only to climb. And how competent she was: Jackie still did that "women's work," making dinner most nights at seven, stocking the refrigerator, cleaning up over the weekends, throwing out the kitty litter while Henry found his time to write or play squash.

The trouble was, this wasn't all she wanted. At thirty-three, she mused, Christ had already died, and she had yet to have her baby. She didn't quite know how she would work out her hours, but it could be done. She could drop out for a while, maybe free-lance edit at home, relying more on Henry's income, reentering the full-time fray when "everybody at home was ready. Everybody."

Sure, it would be tight for a while. Sure, she was now earning twice as much as her husband. But they'd manage.

Here as in other spheres in her life, she wanted to be above average. The average American household now has only 2.6 people in it, she'd read—down from the fifties when the mean was five. Jackie's home then had a grand total of six, not to mention cats, dogs, and visitors. Just like her parents, she mused, she wanted to be better than the norm. But that wasn't it really. It came from inside her.

She told Henry it was time. He balked, wasn't "really ready," he said. All right, he'd "give it a try."

Three months later he quit his job on the paper. Otherwise, he averred, that damned book would never get written.

Six months, nine, a year—and the periods kept coming, regular as ever. While her womb lay fallow, Henry now puttered about the apartment, spending an hour or two at the word processor, then turning his attentions elsewhere. The book was hard going, he complained, but at least he had the free-lance magazine pieces to distract him (not a few of these via his wife) and to make up a portion of the lost regular income.

Jackie decided it was time to consult with the gynecologist. She told Henry he might have to be examined as well. Muttering something about "jerking off for posterity," he grumbled an "if necessary" assent. Fortunately—and how odd it was to think of the news as good in any way—the problem turned out to be hers, not his. Henry was off the hook, perhaps in more ways than one, because it was Jackie who wasn't ovulating. She started taking chlomid. Sex was to be scheduled now in a regimen to which Henry once again grudgingly agreed.

"Do you have to stand on your fuckin' head every time we screw?" he rasped.

Jackie had found herself tuning Henry out, as if filling her ears with white noise to drone out, however softly, the constant murmur of her husband's irritability. But then, another six months into the impregnation process, she found herself unable any longer to overlook his failure to cooperate with her. She found out that Henry was having an affair.

She had happened to be having lunch with a colleague, Susan Bowles, an agent whose writers were published in her magazines. Not at a midtown restaurant as usual, but at the local Sarabeth's Kitchen where for some time she and Susie had been meaning to have that delicious tomato soup. She had glanced up and through the plate glass window onto the street just as Henry walked by hand in hand with Rachel Avery.

In that instant, a great void—here and now, their future, the wasted years—descended on Jackie. It seemed to separate her legs

from her torso, and sitting there in Sarabeth's, she no longer knew
how and if she was put together, where the different parts of her,
the whole of her, began and ended. In a cliché out of some movie,
some New York story, Jackie, graceful Jackie, dropped her spoon.
It thudded into her soup, splattering her and Susie with salmon
red before careening out again and clattering onto the floor.

"Arghhh!" she exclaimed on that analytic couch a half dozen
years later. "Even then I wondered what was wrong with me. Had
I made too many demands on Henry—poor whimmy, wimpy,
drivelly, selfish Henry! But I caught hold of myself that very
afternoon.

"I realized I hadn't respected or loved him for some time.
Henry couldn't handle it. Not me! *He* didn't know what he wanted.
And I deserved more.

"You know, a woman will go along with a man, it seems like
forever, until in a kind of quantum leap, it just gets to be too
much, and at long last she's had it. I wasn't gonna drag this guy
along through my life forever. I confronted him that night, and his
confession gave me the excuse I needed to tell him to leave. . . .
'What,' I wondered, 'what in the hell had I been doing?' "

• • •

The first job a woman has, in psychotherapy or elsewhere, is *not*
to take it personally. Only then can she begin to see both herself
and men for who they really are.

Once she's conquered many of her own fears and defenses, she
will then see that men run from her not because she's weak and
"drivelly and yukky," but rather, as they say, because she's *awesome*—awesome just because she's a woman! Most men are deeply
and incorrigibly afraid of her, a more mature woman comes to
understand, because they are overwhelmed by her beauty, her
difference from them, her touch, the pull of the sensuality con-
necting their skins. And they are frightened as well by her insides,
the inner reaches whence they came, the hold she still has on
them. They're scared she'll eat them up alive. They wriggle free,
and that's why they act tough and mean.

It's too bad that the onus falls on women, unfortunate perhaps
that they are entrusted with first reading their own and other
people's feelings. But if she doesn't do the job, who will?

More often than not, men are too threatened by emotions—
theirs or anybody else's—to play the peacemaker by seeking the
truth. By training and perhaps by disposition, it's a woman who

first makes sense of a little child's tumult of sensations, putting emotions into words. It's she who has long been the "interpersonal diplomat" and "emotional soothsayer" in families, in couples, quite possibly in the community at large.

Then, too, being a woman, she has the power to make a man forget himself, to defy the demands his peers make of him. To trap him. She moves him to compete for prizes—love or fatherhood, for instance—that only seem to take him away from the pursuit of independence, material ambition, and worldly success.

What can a woman do then to make a man feel secure? It requires patience, tact, detachment, resolve, and a certain toughness in the end, but perceiving herself clearly and thereby seeing beneath the surfaces of men can permit a woman to know them and let men know themselves in surprising new ways. There are many men—the egotistical Dicks and babyish Henrys—who just can't rise to the occasion, so unsure are they of their adult masculinity, so fearful of making it either in the real world or with a real woman. Yet there are others, she learns, whom a woman can draw out of themselves.

There are men like Vasily Kurmani.

• • •

If at first she doesn't succeed, a woman with will will try again. In those years after Henry, among so many things undertaken on her own, Jackie Burrows started going to dance classes again. A certain low-keyedness, a disheartened calmness of mind, but calm nonetheless, settled over her. Taking the barre, doing her pliés, Jackie fixed on her mirror image and reminded herself how well put together her body in fact was. Now and then she visited her widowed mother, whose diabetes had called a halt to evening scotches and who seemed thinner, too. She visited Rich and his family in Atlanta. She even toyed with the idea of becoming a "single mother by choice."

Then Jackie met Vasily, "Wahseely," the Romanian contractor who was doing the renovation of *The Movies'* offices, over which Jackie F. Burrows now presided. He had strode into her particular space, his behemoth reflection in the plate glass window startling her before she pivoted in her chair to greet him. They discussed the schedule of reconstruction—though Jackie never believed contractors' promises regarding deadlines.

Vasily proved her wrong. Over the next months he revealed himself to be reliable to a fault. What's more, he developed a habit of appearing in her office at the end of each working day.

He told her about himself—how he, a Jew, had been a phys-
icist in Bucharest, slated to take over the university's professorship until he left behind it and a fiancée, who, he said, was
unwilling to emigrate with him; how he was now "no longer
professor but rich, heh, heh!" And Vasily began, "Iee em so
sahree—I am so sorry—pryingg into Jackie's pershonal life—but
how come no man!"

He also began walking her home. Once Vasily seemed to get
jealous when another man, Bill Sabatini, picked her up. Soon after
this, Jackie and this 230-pound Eastern European were going out.

They would make love, and the next day, a few hours after
Vasily had heaved out of bed at six A.M. to begin his twelve-hour
day, silver roses or rubrum lilies, which Jackie had said were her
absolute favorites, would appear at the office he'd finished redoing
some months earlier. He'd call, the sounds of saws and drills
humming in the background, and whisper tender, muffled obscenities.

"How silly we all are," said Bear in his still "breaking" English. "Here you are so smart and so beautiful, and you don't
know it. Until me, Bear, you choose only men who are too tiny to
love you. They are frightened of your mind and your woman's
body. You need a big fat peasant with a bald head to keep up with
every inch of you—a man too beaten up already to be scaredy-
cat."

Jackie felt loved at last, loved and protected. Still she resolved
to be careful, not simply to sink into something and let it carry her
along aimlessly and into emptiness.

Besides, Vasily *was* afraid despite what he said.

"The trouble is," she told analyst and friends alike, even her
mother, "every time I hint at children or marriage, especially after
a sumptuous weekend, I can see the big guy starting to pull
away—just like the rest."

All of a sudden, reliable Vasily began to flag. The "one more
time before Monday morning" might end up a dud, though not
because it was "too much fer an ol' boyee," as Vasily would at
such moments like to claim. And his work schedule couldn't suddenly have become so crammed that they couldn't find time to get
together on Tuesdays as usual.

No, Vasily—Old World, family-oriented but still bachelor Vasily—was, at forty-nine, still running scared. He wasn't used to
lying hour after hour on Sundays in that king-size bed of Jackie's,
being caressed, massaged, and not infrequently, made love *to* by
her.

• • •

"I'm working on it. When this man retreats, it's him, not me, I realize. He truly feels my love, and that's just a little too much for a lion who's had to tough it out across the globe. Why, once in my bed, and he might never want to get up and out again. . . . How did Othello put it?—'She loved me for the dangers I had passed, And I loved her that she did pity them.' "

"Not good enough!" Susan interrupted her. It was a Wednesday, and again they were sipping soup at Sarabeth's. Once more, she told Jackie, feckless men were running roughshod over her. Then again Susie, Bennington graduate herself, was also a veteran of the Dick Golden amour wars. (It had taken three years of working a friendship before they'd discovered this exact little fact! Small world.) Jackie was like the cliché the feminists had long been lambasting, Susie went on, the woman who only needs a man to make her happy, no matter what the costs and conditions, no matter how lacking his knowledge of her, no matter what his terms.

"But he does, he does understand. He's just a person—frightened like everybody, or like men at least."

"Not good enough," Sue Bowles repeated. "What about you? What *do you* want! . . . "

• • •

"When I started wearing short skirts"—it was her Thursday session, and Jackie was remembering her teenage years—"when I put on makeup and then started dating, my father went bullshit . . . oops, I, uh, mean 'apeshit.' "

She'd made a Freudian slip, and now, patient that she was, Jackie thought about it.

"I guess, I still take him literally—as if my sexuality got him mad, offended him. As if I were odious somehow. But that was a show, a blustering show, I'm saying to myself. Yes, I'm whispering to myself to protect him, so he won't hear, my becoming a woman turned him on. My body scared him. What I read as disgust, contempt, disapproval, was my father's excitement and fear. I wanted to be admired and loved, and he just ran away. Like any other man, I guess."

With a woman close upon him, she now mused, a man lets down his guard. He comes out of hiding before her very eyes, revealing himself and discovering in himself wishes, sensations, illusions, and facts of life that he would never have recognized or at least acknowledged in the company of his fellow men.

Knowing him with his pants down, so to speak, a woman can find out just how intensely, whatever his protests to the contrary, a man wishes to be with her. With luck, she and he can then come to realize that they want many of the same things—passion, love, union, tenderness, babies, all of those life goals typically ascribed to the one sex alone, female, and resisted by the other, male obviously, yet realized only as a function of their mutual agreement and achievement as a couple.

• • •

Six days later it was Vasily Kurmani who was lunching with her at the same restaurant, augmenting with a sour-cream-and-caviar omelet the soup she'd told him to order. He'd wanted to take her there after hearing the Henry story the week before.

"I bin tinkin', Ms. 'Freud' Faracci-Burrows. You are as smart about me as I am about you. I *am* scared. I never thought I'd be able, how you say it, to settle in anywhere. Guys like me got used to keep moving. I bin tinkin' dat we give it, how you say, 'a try.' . . . That is, if President Ceausescu didn't sterilize me at birth."

"Give it a try," Jackie repeated to herself before dismissing the echoes.

He chuckled and zupped and then stopped himself to look at Jackie as she glanced down. "Oh, yah, I mean it. You know your Bear, he's there when he says he's there. I might even stop eating so many eggs an' stuff so I stick around even longer."

She looked up and gazed at Vasily. Yes, he was really proposing to her. She wondered what her father would have thought of this "Turk," how Vasily would look in black tie at the next Ambrose dinner for editors-in-chief, and why they, of all "odd couples," could be so straight with each other.

Reaching under the table, she gave a quick squeeze to the flesh above his knee. Vasily purred.

"You so much of woman," he murmured across the noise, "you make even the Bear feel like a pretty pussy."

• • •

A woman's *first* step toward intimacy, and toward the acceptance of her capacity to take the initiative in the arenas of both work and love, is to get herself and then a man to look at least into his own heart.

Since much of what he finds there is disconcerting, disquieting, hers is by no means an easy job. In fact, it's rather like that of the therapist, male or female, who must chip away at their male patients' formidable defenses, both hypermasculinizing and moralizing, until a clinician's hand and sometimes his heart begin to ache with the effort.

But this touches on our next story. And in the meantime, you still have your lingering doubts about this one, don't you?

Too good to be true, you say, too much the happy ending? Besides, a woman shouldn't have to count on a man but should find her own way? And how—coming from so divergent a culture—could he possibly understand her?

Well, to answer the last question first, love works in mysterious ways. It is true that most of the time it takes a lot more effort for a woman to be known by a man than the other way around. It's a far more difficult accomplishment on both sides, given a woman's tendency not to intrude and instead to subordinate herself to a man, to listen mutely to him and to cover herself up in the process while he in turn closes up his ears, fearing his receptivity to her and making himself as if deliberately impervious. But pressed by the passage of life, Jackie and Vasily are no longer so young and foolish that they have to pretend not to know themselves and each other. For one thing, both now realize, both of them successful loners, life for the one feels unfinished, incomplete, rather cold without the other. Whatever their protests to the contrary, somehow men and women seem to need each other.

Nor is the story over. It's just begun in fact—the grinding struggle to make it together and to make something together. To keep the fear, self-hatred, and resentment at bay.

That's anybody's story—the story of Dave Feigelman, another patient of mine, and a man.

2
···

Running Scared: How Men Talk About Themselves

Diffident in their lovers' arms, most men come even less willingly to the therapist's office. Seeking such help is seen as an admission of failure, a sign something's wrong with their manhood. Men, men think, don't give in or acknowledge weakness and confusion much less neediness. Consciously at least, they choose not to dwell on their skittishness in love, reluctance to make commitments, or difficulties expressing feelings. And they hate feeling nervous— fearing fear itself.

Nor do men readily submit to another person's intrusions on their psychological privacy. Women are used to surrendering up their secrets, to being penetrated and probed, to bearing and owning up to the pain and threat that often come with being exposed. So sitting in a shrink's office doesn't fit men's images of themselves. Once they're there, opening up and letting somebody else "in" further threatens their masculinity. It's usually under duress, then, that they'll start talking about themselves—a process that men find scary in its own right.

Moreover, the impetus to seek counsel usually has to come from the outside. Often it's the women in their lives who demand

that men take a good, hard look at themselves, sometimes threatening to leave them if they don't follow through. Or else men are
moved to seek insight of this kind because they find their initiative, ambition, or penis flagging, because they want to *do* better.
Men are goal oriented. They play for results. And when their
objectives are interfered with, then they may simply feel forced to
seek psychotherapy.

And once in it, men bring their male bias to the treatment
itself. Their first instinct is usually to get better fast, without much
messing around. But the patient has to do his share of the work,
cutting away his emotionally dead skin without anesthesia, challenging the tried and true defensive maneuvers that keep him from
knowing himself and that no longer quite work. This takes a
different sort of guts, and just as in their relationships with women,
so with their doctors men find themselves running scared.

When it comes to choosing a therapist, most men look for
other men. Skeptical perhaps about the sort of guy who sits around
all day while people "pour their guts out," doing a *woman's* job,
just listening, these men also want father figures. When their trust
has been secured and they don't flee right away, soon enough they
endow their analyst with an almost oracular authority. Their
"shrink" now fills in for fathers who were either too lacking or too
busy to fit the bill. (See Chapters 4 and 5 for more on father
absence.)

Pretty soon they want to win the therapist's approval just as
in the past they sought to please their dads. In treatment now they
want to do a good job.

So it's their fathers in all their past and present incarnations
who occupy these men's therapy at first. They think about being
and not being the kind of men their fathers wanted them to be;
about being *conditionally* loved and half-abandoned; about how
their dads tyrannized them; about how hard they are on themselves as a result. It takes time for them to get their fathers out of
their systems, to get down to even more basic "basics," to put into
words men's feelings about their mothers and what they have
meant to them.

Thus, like women when they talk to psychotherapists, men
also start out talking mostly about men. Women—their mothers,
wives, lovers, daughters, sisters, coworkers—tend to enter the picture later, often enough at a therapist's prompting. Even when it
comes to sex, men begin their introspection leaving their partners
out, first calling attention to themselves as men. They rate their

performance. They may dwell on their guilt. And so on, until they are enjoined by their therapist to ponder the person with whom they have shared their pleasures, mishaps, and anxieties and to plumb the deeper levels of communion involved.

Not that they're necessarily prudish. Men just don't have the words to express what they want from women and why this scares them. Scares them even more than their fathers did.

• • •

Take David Feigelman, a former Olympic athlete and a forty-nine-year-old writer at an ad agency. Broad shouldered and square jawed, looking like one of the jocks in his own commercials, he initially sought psychoanalysis with me because of his "excessive perfectionism, inhibitions at work, lack of sexual interest, bouts of the blues, and parenting problems."

So obsessed was he with getting it just right that David couldn't finish editing his writing. The pressure of deadlines at work forced him to complete copywriting assignments, but when it came to the fiction that was so important to him, he found himself utterly at a loss. Short story after story lay pencil-marked but unsubmitted in the drawers of his study desk.

He felt paralyzed at the prospect of client presentations and tried his damnedest to avoid them. Sex with his sexy wife, Jean, had dwindled to a trickle—intercourse occurring maybe once every six weeks, and then without much passion, or for that matter, sensation. And David was constantly at loggerheads with Josh, their teenage son, whom he loved dearly but criticized constantly.

"It's time," Jean had said after the last family blowup. "I just can't take it anymore. You need to find some peace so we can get some."

Easing into a four-day-a-week psychoanalysis had been a fitful process for David. He'd even worn, almost inexplicably, a jock strap underneath his chinos and boxers for his first session on his back. David had been seized with fear as he had contemplated lying there supine on the couch, unable to see the man behind him. Irrationally, he'd felt he had to protect himself—from what he didn't know: himself maybe.

He hadn't admitted doing this until many months later, when David had gotten more and more intrigued with what he was learning about himself, willing to wade through the anxiety and confusion to get to his wishes. It was as if the process were another "meet" to be won, another "account" to be garnered. His performance in the process mattered to him more than the state of his "self." Once engaged, he forced himself to be open and flexible. Indeed, he became hell-bent on contemplating what was inevitable in his life and what was a function of misapprehension, on clearing away the debris and changing.

His various and increasingly ingenious efforts at evading his feelings having been concertedly confronted, David began to remember. He'd never been one to admit how much he missed people, especially to a "professional," and a man to boot, such as "Dr. R." But David had started to write again—memoirs mostly —especially during his "shrink's" proverbial August vacations.

And so, on the Tuesday after Labor Day, three years to the date of the commencement of the analysis, he entered and silently handed me his journal entry for the month of August. David lay on the couch in silence, anticipating a response. Like a schoolboy or college kid waiting for his blue book to be handed back, he tingled with anticipation.

It was 1955, and I'd made the Charleston High swim team. I was proud but also relieved because now I felt my father would be satisfied that at last (I was fifteen!) I had achieved something he could understand.

Pop always put down what I did do—for my "own good," just to "push" me. He wanted a lot out of me—"It wasn't easy being Jewish down South then—pretty lonely," he told me over and over. He needed to "prep me for the tough world." Shit, I remember all the pronouncements, all the criticisms. What do you call it? "A father's unconditional love"? Well, I never had it. And I guess I thought there was something wrong with me. Like I wasn't a real man.

He'd told me I had no competitive flair in academics, so I should concentrate on athletics instead. But it became clear to Pop that when I tried playing the hot corner at third—I did have a great arm—the baseball scared the living shit out of me.

And he was right. I remember I would hear that thwack and see the white thing sizzling toward me. And in that awful moment of expectation, I couldn't help imagining it skipping and arcing off the dirt right up into my balls or else smashing my teeth into irretrievable smithereens. So I'd do a little sidestep and shimmy, backhand the ball when I didn't have to—trying to look great the whole time, like Fred Astaire walking on the walls, but bobbling or letting it slip through my dancing legs. The humiliation was horrible.

Well, racing was pretty solitary, exposed, nobody else to lose but me, but still I couldn't get hurt. Besides, by then I had what my son, Josh, calls a good bod, pecs and all.

And—this is so hard to say, I could never tell you in person but I gotta confess—I got turned on wearing the silky nylon suit. Here I was macho man, Abraham Feigelman's son, staring at the girls in their racing suits and the nipples caressing their nylons, but getting excited thinking about myself and my mother's panties.

Oh, yeah, I'd opened her drawer once when I was twelve or so and there they were. I still shiver when I remember taking them out, smelling them, imagining her in them, caressing my cheek with them, and staring at my face in her dressing-table mirror before returning them to their proper place. A real Dixie-boy Portnoy!

Actually, and this is even harder to acknowledge—again I could never tell you in person, never—I did this more than once. I'd come home from baseball practice on those afternoons when nobody was home, or so I thought. Her smell was everywhere, and you know, her indentation was there in one of those pink—how d'you call 'em?—demi-chairs, you know, with the stubby arms, women used to use to sit up in bed to watch TV, smoke, drink scotches.

It was dark in that room with all its heavy folds of drapery and needlepoint. And I'd light up the triptych mirror with the little lamp on the dressing table and brush her panties across my cheek, yeah, like some "fairy."

Encircled by my own reflections, I'd think to myself, wonder what it would be like to be a woman and just look lovely and be looked at. It was as if women didn't have to do anything, as if they didn't have to perform to be beautiful and admired. They could lie back and be stroked just for being themselves. I'd imagine what not having a dick would feel like, being ogled and loving it and never giving away the telltale sign of your excitement. Mom always seemed so composed, so charming, unruffled.

I thought once about actually trying them on—I remembered lurching about in her stiltlike heels when I was maybe three. Surrounding myself with her. Being her. But then Cornelia, our cook and my old nanny, hollered upstairs for Mom—"Mrs. Feigelman, you thea?"—and she tore the veil of darkness.

I got real scared and shoved the stuff back into the drawer, slipping out and down the hall into my own room. I wondered whether I was queer.

Now I strode up to the block, out there in front of all those people, in front of Mom and Pop, like Tarzan—or like Jane, maybe. In front of the crowd, I was terrified of getting a hard-on, first of all, and after that, losing. It was so weird—only me, no team, almost no clothes even. I'd look at the guy next to me, with his dark shadow, as if he were dressed in his beard. I'd think he never had perverse thoughts like mine, he never fondled his mother's underwear!

Up there nearly naked in front of everybody, and my prick drew itself back up into the perineum, my scrotum creased, wrinkled tight as if there were nothing to it. I'd crouch and shut out everything, staring at the watery tunnel

*ahead, concentrating at last. Bang, and I'd vault from the block into the air,
slicing that membrane of H_2O as if the heels of my hand were fucking sabers!*

That was the time I began to win things.

*I dunno, but it all came together then—my defiance, my sensuality, my
power to win. It was exhilarating, complete. Like I'd overcome so much, as
they say, in one stroke. And I'd done it alone. Back to the womb, I figure
now—that's how I became a Super Jock at last.*

*But, you know, for all those highs, still Josh is luckier. Times have
changed, I guess, and he doesn't have to try so hard to make like a man. I
envy him his comfort in his own skin.*

Because all along I stayed scared, scared and alone.

Thus began David's narrative of his extraordinary career as a
freestyler. Within three years of beginning to swim in earnest, he
had won the state championship. The practice regimen was excruciating—four to five hours in the pool daily, before and after
classes. His coach and his own conscience drove teenaged David
to that brink of "No more." Exhausted, he found himself vomiting
when he left the pool, heaving the dry heaves in the locker room
stalls, depleted but tightened, the palms of his hands puckered as
if they belonged to an old man, the rest of him reeking of chlorine.
Deferring to the sport, David reversed the natural order of things,
shaving off his hair for the winter competitions (his brush cut
looking more like a bunch of dusty blond flies fixed into his scalp)
and letting it grow a little longer for the summers.

He wanted to win.

Among his teammates, all nearly bald in their flannel wind-
breakers with the oversize *C*s front and back, he stood out as the
best. The girls sashayed up to him, but Dave didn't quite know
what to do with their overtures.

Still, he found himself injected with new confidence. Despite
the long hours swimming demanded, his average rose. He had
become a sure bet for his father's alma mater—Yale, the jock
school among the big Ivies in those days, renowned especially for
its swim team.

His father, himself a former football and baseball standout at
college, was now entirely pleased, he said, with his son's accomplishments. He added, though, since it didn't have to do with
balls, and since girls did it, too, at first he hadn't quite understood
or respected swimming. At least David was lucky, he wouldn't
have to suffer what Abe did his senior year when those four Cornell linemen had twisted his leg—two on the thigh, two for the

calf—and torn the ligaments in his knee, permanently crippling the "kike upstart."

"Yeah, Pop made a whole lot out of that leg of his—a whole lot. Like he was some cowboy with an Indian arrow in him. A veteran of the race wars . . . a cowboy."

· · ·

In the fifties, all red-blooded American boys aspired to be cowboys. Even so, many of them encountered their icons of masculinity in the most unexpected circumstances. For Davy Feigelman, it was on his cousin's bed.

Beth Hannah, his mother's brother's daughter, lived two blocks down the road from the Feigelman house. She was the closest thing he as an only child had to a sister, and a big sister, to boot.

Once or twice a week, Davy would visit Beth's to watch TV for the hour or two he'd allotted himself. He'd plop down on his teenage cousin's canopy bed, tolerated for the time being by Beth and the girlfriend or two she might have over. He was a kind of mascot, they said.

They'd all be sipping Cokes and helping themselves to leftovers as they gazed at television. Now and then Davy would get up at the girls' bidding to play with the rabbit ears or steady the rebellious vertical hold. And once or twice, doing so, through the bathroom door left slightly ajar, he caught sight of Beth's crinolines, splayed out and drying, and a torpedolike bra draped lazily over the edge of the tub.

"Look at those hands," sixteen-year-old Beth used to say of the cowboy in the TV ads that had seduced kids her age into smoking, "great hands." Hairy, firm, callused, well-heeled, they dropped to the horn of the saddle after he had sucked in the obligatory drag against the Western landscape.

Moments later, the opening sequence of "Gunsmoke" came on. Big Marshal Matt Dillon squared off against some stubble-faced, drawling lowlife, ready to draw the Colt from its sleek holster. Dave zeroed in on the gun. Alas, his female companions had their eyes elsewhere. Right on Matt's ass.

"What a rear," Dave's cousin's friend chimed in, "what a fanny."

"Yeah, what a heinie!" Beth giggled. She had, she said, been waiting all week to catch sight of the giant's flat buttocks.

"James Arness doesn't have a 'heinie,' for chrissake. A big guy like that barely has a rear end," the boy had thought to himself. As a twelve-year-old of the times, anticipating the gunplay to erupt momentarily, Dave felt both offended and intrigued. The hero's privacy had been invaded by all these girls. Yet he couldn't help enjoying all this vaguely prurient banter about things to come later in life when the sexes, he dimly realized, would be getting together.

"Butt," David Feigelman interjected. "Matt's ass is a butt."

But Beth and the other girls simply ignored him. For his part, Davy Boy forgot these first encounters with the sexual models that he and his boyhood buddies would one day aspire to emulate. It was the heroes and their guns that stuck in his mind.

• • •

David and his cronies might find their hearts warmed by "good Joe" family men such as Disney's Fred MacMurray or wise Robert Young of "Father Knows Best." But it was the tough guys, the cowboys, the loose cannons, and the rolling stones who captured the imagination in America's 1950s, embodying everybody's ideal of solitary nonconformity at a time when conformism was at its height.

Smoking himself to death maybe, Marlboro Man was a loner. Either he was a Lone Ranger who did his leaving early on, riding off into the sunset while the women he left behind wept in awe as well as sorrow, or else, like Gary Cooper in *High Noon,* he learned to do without women and their less than honorable demands. Though they might snare him in the end, returning after temporarily forsaking him or settling the lone wolf down to a life on the ranch, his "darlings" merely drifted through his landscape for the time being—whether in the guise of prim Easterners or as more sage women of the world, whose ancient calling was not made explicit in those days. Because pine as they might for him, Marlboro Man didn't require women for his well-being.

He didn't mind loss. He didn't need love. He took us away from ourselves. Away from women.

• • •

David's diary continued:

It's so odd, though, how our lives unfold, how we hide behind its phases. Here I had to make like a stud, and I didn't really have sex till I was a junior in college. Petting, wet kisses, and dry humps, lots of hard-ons, spilt seed, gooky underwear, and just as many lies to my roommates about how far I'd gone with so-and-so—but no intercourse, no penetration, nada! We were just coming out of the fifties—the gum-chewing, dirty-bucked fifties, and to me at least, girls seemed so strange. So clean. So unapproachable. "Look but don't touch!"

In fact, socially, yeah, sexually, the first two years of college were filled with different kinds of "lost weekends"—weekends in the pool, "washouts." Training, shaving parties maybe—but no time for the real thing. Not at least until I had made it to Rome and back.

The Olympics! I have the team's bronze for the relay in my night-table drawer to prove it—I was there. No individual golds, not even medals—not with stars like Don to compete with, but I still got two solo fourths there in the Eternal City. That was enough to make me and even Pop happy—enough to let me go home, hang up my Speedo, let my hair grow, and start smelling human again.

I remember the last night there, a foretaste of visions to come. The meets were all over, and a bunch of us, guys and girls, got into the pool to celebrate with cases of beer. Here, we'd gone months, years it seemed, without the brew, unlike almost everybody else our age, and all we could get was some Italian Mickey Mouse stuff—not Bud, but birra.

This one girl from Australia, Donna, silver medalist, started to slug them down one after the other, taking bets and drinking two of our guys under the bleachers. Then she swaggers over to the side of the pool, strips off her sweats, peels off her suit, and turns her bare ass to the rest of us before diving in. She streaks out to the center and stops, waving those powerful arms at us, biceps and deltoids big as mine, and starts shouting for us "blokes" to come on in and join her. It's dark in the hall, remember, and the pool's lighted up like turquoise.

We're all sitting and staring, stone silent after all the belly-laughing and backslapping. So Donna swims back to the side of the pool and hoists her body out, frontwise first this time.

And there she is, short-cropped hair and all, built like a boy. But in the center of all those man's muscles, her breasts disappearing into her chest, she's got a bush just like any other woman's, big and brown and dense and lit from beneath. And every guy in the place—Americans, Aussies, Italians, Orientals—winners and losers from all nations—every one of us staring right at it.

Right then and there I tasted that same acid taste I used to feel right before the gun went off, the same sudden aroma of fear and excitement I did the time Cornelia's cry burst in on me in my parents' room when I was fiddling with Mom's lingerie. My heart stopped. I could've died.

"What's the matter with you pussies!*" she taunts us.*
For the moment nobody stirs. We all just let her stand there.

*Winning was what I was supposed to want. But looking back, I real-
ized even then that wasn't it. There was something else. Things Pop didn't
want me to want. I couldn't quite figure it out. Had I known it at the start,
well, who knows what I would have done.*

*It's ironic, I guess, but only after I stopped being a jock and a Big
M.O.C. did the girls begin to get interested in me. What Josh calls "vibes"
probably did it.*

*I began to get near them for real now. No more just looking. Maybe I'd
had to prove myself as a man beforehand. Or I just had time to relax now.
Or it could be that I smelled better. But they weren't so off limits, and my
body could be used for other things than beating other guys to the finish
line—I could take some pleasure in it.*

*You and I've talked a lot about how sex with girls meant and still
means, deep down, breaking taboos. And we've also said it was like betraying king and country, deserting my buddies, the team, even Dad.*

*But there's also something more to it, I realized this summer lying in bed
with Jeanie for two whole days—yeah, we did it, no kids around, no work,
nothing. There's more to the myths of saltpeter and Marvelous Marvin
Hagler not foolin' around before a fight. It's as if a woman's femininity
might be contagious.*

*Anyhow, my junior year, Susie Bowles was my first one. Her smell is
etched into my memory forever, and I thought I'd be lucky even to remember
the "chick's" name. We'd met two years earlier at a freshman mixer, though
I took my time asking her out. That Friday night after her poetry reading—
imagine, I didn't have a meet the next day—we got into bed and she unzipped
my fly before I could lay a fumbling hand on her.*

*"No," she'd said, laughing, looking me over, "I never saw you swim,
Davy. I don't like sports, remember?" The Bennington girl, of course.*

*Anyhow, I still remember her finger tracing the veins in my cock and her
sucking, slithering all over my glans. Nobody had ever touched me like that.
It was unbearable, the voluptuousness was so intense. I felt her all over me,
and it was as if I were bursting out of myself. I completely lost control—how
did Vladimir Nabokov put it?—I dissolved in a "puddle of pleasure" the
minute I entered that slippery warmth of her vagina for the first time, the soft
cave under her hair.*

*Two or three times later, I managed to hold on. We could talk now, and
I began to feel close. But it wasn't the way I'd expected. I didn't take charge.*

*Susie knew me. She taught me about my responses and saw right through
my uptightness, playing with parts of my feelings and my anatomy I'd seemed*

*to have forgotten. It was thrilling and embarrassing, yet soon enough I
yielded up my sex to her and let myself sink into my senses and lose control.*

*But I had to learn from her about pleasuring her body—she told me what
to do—such as not to retreat when her clitoris did. Yes, I got to share her
excitement. Sometimes she rode me like some sex sorceress, laughing, throwing back her head and howling as if I were her thing.*

*All along I'd told those pathological lies to friends about how I'd done
it to so-and-so, to the point that I just about believed them myself. And
without knowing what sex with a woman felt like! And now here I was
on my back with this literary she-wolf striding me, rubbing my nipples in
my dark little college room and loving it, talking her Virginia Woolf stuff
when she rolled off and over into the wrinkled sheets. And here I was
loving it!*

*And Susie helped me start writing. First, poetry like hers, which was
sort of okay. Then short stories, which she, I, and then my writing teachers
began to say were pretty good—damned good. I credit her with my first
awakenings—even if they didn't last.*

*It was I who aborted them. When I also started going out with Abby—
beautiful, blond, leggy Abby.*

*"Screw yourself!" Susie said. "If that's your type, you're not mine."
And she walked right out of my life—all five feet two inches, black hair, and
almond eyes of her—only coming back as a friend now and then to admonish
me about my various forms of dishonesty.*

*My trouble is, like everybody else, I had a father and mother. And she
was also something more than real.*

So concluded David's August diary.

Until this juncture, in the treatment sessions themselves, he'd
dwelled on the former: the hard, defined presence of his father.
He'd ruminated about his struggles to please Abe, and now me,
and wondered how, no matter what, he'd always come up short.
He'd tried to figure out the hidden agendas on both sides. Did he
love his old man or hate him? Did Abe Feigelman really want his
son to win rather than lose?

And often to his chagrin, sometimes to his horror, David had
discovered that he was reenacting these primal battles and acting
his father's part, as he now tried to contend with his son Josh's
coming into his own. "The times, they were a-changin'." Men
were seen differently now. He had vowed to let Josh be his own
person, and here David found himself coming down on the boy
continually just for being different. Just as his father had done to
him.

• • •

The upheavals, revolutions, and disaffections of the sixties—the nonviolence of Martin Luther King and Gandhi before him juxtaposed with the dizzying images of martial manhood gone awry in Vietnam—changed men's sensibilities and aspirations. Or so it seemed. They brought in their wake the ascendancy in the seventies of the New Man. He was a guy, a heterosexual to boot, who was unafraid in truly his own way—able to forgo his male posturing and his work ambitions for the joys of nurturing. He wasn't scared of being called a sissy! Names couldn't hurt him! In fact, women's work proved damned hard to do for men thrust upon the newly laid daddy track.

By the 1980s, movies had given us *Kramer vs. Kramer, Three Men and a Baby,* and *Mr. Mom.*

Men didn't have to be on the make all the time, the plots and characters of films such as these told us. Babies were more important in life, along with some TLC. It didn't matter to the moviegoer that the men making such quiet little blockbusters—the stars, producers, agents—had tapped into a popular sentiment, and market, adding to their track records and bank accounts as a consequence.

Now this New Man also suffered an interesting twist of fate; sex roles had been reversed in more senses than one as a result of the women's movement. Where Marlboro Man had cast his women by the wayside, Mr. Mom had often found himself left behind by them. Either they'd never been there in the first place, or else these women deserted and divorced him later on in search of wider horizons—at the very least reentering the job market for large segments of the working day.

De-aggressivized, pretty soon Mr. Mom, having identified with women, became desexed as well. Nor, administering all that care and cuddling, did he find much time to be mothered in turn.

The New Man had started out taking women a little more seriously, and he soon learned just what skill and effort are required to perform the duties of domestic life. But ultimately, having identified with the woman's role, he, too, came to manage on his own. Thus, like his virile predecessor, the "androgynized male," as he came to be called, didn't seem to need women either.

The two successive opposing stereotypes thus shared a common ground—actually on two counts. More than not "needing" women, neither of these "perfect" men has much time to *long* for them and the feminine aura they bring into men's lives. In fact, women loomed as Eve-like temptresses, luring men into a less than ideal state. So, better to do without them.

Second, no man could possibly live up to either standard. Nor when it came down to it would he wish to. A life alone, a life without women, is an empty and hard life indeed.

Initially, the New Man generation had protested against the harshness and emptiness of the virilized ideals set before them. Yet these self-styled change agents had come up with equally superficial, unattainable, indeed lonely, expectations of themselves as men. Like their fathers and predecessors, they also denied men's incompleteness in the absence of the opposite sex.

Woman is in fact banished from all our modern-day myths of the idealized man. Her presence and what she invites in the way of feeling and desire are reminders that a mere mortal man's dependency on her, on her very womanliness, lingers in life. Even his male sexuality, supposed testimony to his virility, derives from a man's sense of yearning for sexual completion and emotional surrender.

No wonder, then, the female sex is excluded from the iconography of the self-sufficient male. Otherwise she might be there, whispering incessantly to him, telling him again and again what it is that he truly wants, fears, and can't forget: love. Her, herself. And nobody, nothing else—nothing can get in the way.

But for all its limitations, the advent of *Mr Momism*, of the acknowledgment of male nurturing and tenderness, has allowed young men, adolescents such as Dave's New York nineties son, Josh, to find the female in themselves. Unlike his father a generation earlier, a boy such as this is able to accept his more stereotypically feminine qualities as natural. Discovering the woman within, he's then freer to find her in the world outside.

• • •

Priorities are different, in fact, for Josh. Josh doesn't swim—it's not so easy in New York City in 1990. He does play tennis for his private school (second doubles) and soccer, mostly warming the bench. Steeped in environmentalism from an early age, Josh now organizes summer mountain traverses for younger boys and girls, some of whom he used to baby-sit for.

Though his father would like Josh to apply to Yale, continuing the tradition, Josh has his sights set on Oberlin, where he hopes to pursue his interest in the viola and composition.

Unlike his father, then, Josh seems unabashed in pursuits once considered sissy stuff. According to David's perspective at least, his son can own up to having not just goals but soul. Ironically, it is he, not his father, who seems to have had the wherewithal, the "balls," to "make it with a woman" long before anything like an official coming of age. David has not been apprised of his son's sexual secrets, but he infers that at seventeen Josh has had intercourse with his girlfriend, Jenny, whom he met on an Outward Bound excursion two summers ago. Josh isn't scared of girls, it seems. With all the matter-of-fact nudity in movies nowadays, "ogling a titty is no big deal, Dad," and "girls are just people to guys like me."

In his father's idealized version of matters at least, the son seems to have been spared the submission that so tortured him. But digging a little deeper, David finds himself envying his boy, with his young body, the less effortful adventure of his adolescence, his outward peace, the precocious sexual union with a woman not seen from afar but first known as a peer, playmate, partner, and friend, even his "androgyny." Despite himself, he begrudges Josh the very future that he, David, has worked so hard to secure and expand.

As he reflects back on *his* father's inability to understand him, David fears seeing his son not in his skin but skin-deep. Maybe that's why he can't quite get it, can't quite accept Josh's lack of interest in the sports that were his very life as a teenager. Maybe that's why David is compelled to bug him about the dangers of AIDS on Sunday mornings after he's heard the boy pull into the driveway at midnight—a decent enough hour after all—and slip into the house after "studying" with Jen—a decent girl. And certainly, he comes to realize, that's why he hounds him about actually studying harder when, taking after his mother, Josh has garnered grades and SATs already better than his father's were at the very same age. Maybe, too, he's afraid of being a father—the kind of father he never had.

"Leave him alone, damn it," Jeanie had exclaimed in frustration again and again. "Leave yourself alone."

David was now learning that there was a history behind all this. It wasn't a linear story, however, this inner life of his, but rather a narrative cast in concentric circles, the center of which was never quite to be found. One of the circles, David had found, came from the reflections cast by that mirror on his mother's dresser—the discovery of himself in her. Another belonged to Abe and the real-life conflicts he'd passed on to his son and he, in turn, to his. Though he was easier to define and felt more like a square, Abe, too, was everywhere. And still another circle had to do somehow with the history beyond and around him.

Senior year at Yale and after Abigail, David had met Mary Jane. Eileen and Abe especially had loved this blue-blooded girl, fresh out of crinolines, the deb from Charlottesville. And so, despite the loss of possibility, the novelty cut short, despite the fact "Mae Jae" and "Davy Boy" never quite connected, he married her.

The couple moved to L.A. where Abe's old teammate from the class of '29 had gotten David a position in the West Coast branch of a brokerage firm. Along with the marriage, the job lasted five years.

Jeanie then swept into his life—woman cardiologist, assistant professor at UCLA, a medical miracle with hair of flax and eyes like emeralds. Married woman, two years older than he. Yes, they committed adultery, and Abe and Eileen, finding them out after the fact, were appalled. But it was Jeanie who helped David "say no to all that."

Pretty soon they were remarried—to each other, though Abe had been, to put it mildly, skeptical it would last "that long." Dave had started writing copy at Drake Advertising, with a story and poem or two on the side, again to his father's consternation. Three children soon followed, the oldest of them a son, whom they named Joshua after an uncle of Jean's. When Jeanie was offered a tenure-track appointment at Columbia, they moved to the East Coast and bought a Tudor house in Riverdale.

Slightly eclipsed by his wife's brilliant star, still Dave was doing quite, quite okay. He was making a bundle at Drake's New York office. More than his father had ever seen, he remarked to himself. The house and the children were gorgeous, his wife a Super Mom—defter by far, more competent across the board, than the genteel lady who had brought him up. And then Dave was promoted to vice president—maybe three rungs below the very top.

He'd invited his parents to visit and celebrate, to see Drake's offices, to hear an award lecture Jeanie was scheduled to give, to admire the house and all that he had made of himself. The table was set, the champagne on ice, as they waited that morning for the flight from Charleston.

Abe and Eileen never arrived, never crossed that threshold

into their son's world. On the way to the airport, Abe's chest had
begun to tighten and then to erupt in pain. The cab was redirected
to the hospital emergency room instead.

There in Mercy Hospital, moments after arriving, Abraham
Feigelman expired. In the corridors of the building where Eileen
had given birth to the son who awaited her up north in Riverdale,
Abe died.

"The motherfucker up and died on me!" David remembered
growling to himself. "It was just too much for him—I was too
much for him."

Dave now felt two contradictory forces converge on him. On
the one hand, he found himself wanting more, wishing to be even
less his father's son and more his own man. On the other, some
heavy but invisible door seemed to have slammed shut on what he
already had, on his ability to enjoy life before moving on through
it. He was locked in a chamber somewhere in his mind. He groped
in the darkness to find the key to a future before it was his turn to
get into the grave.

And that's when it began again: the unfinished writing; the
terror of presenting work to clients on whom, he later came to see,
David now superimposed his father's critical image; the constant
riding of his own son; the dullness and alienation from Jean; the
unremitting worry.

"I was running scared, but the trouble is, the ghost of a conscience is harder to escape than a man in real life. . . . And you
know, I did love him, too."

　　　• • •

The story never concludes, David realized; its circles never close.
Even after he understood what Abe had meant to him, he had to
keep going back, back. Or as his kids might say nowadays, "Back
to the future!"

The night after that first September session, David and Jean
made love. They'd been doing more of that lately. In bed afterward, David told her about the diary, about what he was learning
about himself as a man with a woman. He even let her read what
he'd written, which he'd not done before.

And he mentioned that he'd sent off some old stories he'd also
been tinkering with to his old flame Susie Bowles, now a big agent,
for a "quick diagnostic." He hoped this didn't jinx him—telling
her.

Jeanie closed the folder and smiled. "No wonder you've been

so scared of what you want, sweetheart." She paused. "Did you know men actually begin life as women?"

"No kidding." David rolled over and reached for the Diet Coke that had long ago replaced the proverbial cigarette of a generation past. He took a swig and gazed back into his physician lover's green eyes.

"Yes, my dear dove. The male embryo has labia just like mine and a clitoris, too." She patted herself through the sheet. "All it takes is a few male hormones, androgens, and those lips fold into a scrotum." She sighed triumphantly. "And then that clitoris grows and grows—just like Pinocchio's nose—and bam, before you know it, you have a penis."

"Do tell, Doc." David tried to exhale with supreme nonchalance, but then squirmed and giggled as, cackling and burrowing, his wife reached for his balls.

"Ready or not, here you come!"

• • •

All right, he's a jock and a family man. But his mother's *underpants?*

That's too weird, you say. Men don't fool around with that sort of thing!

He's a weirdo, a fairy all right!

Then what about the years strutting his stuff, bragging he'd been making it with girls long before the first event? Isn't that sort of thing more familiar to most of you—to the men recalling their adolescence and the teenage girls who suffered it?

No, this is all so perverse. Normal guys want to sow a few wild oats and then settle down to love and marriage. And that's the way it is.

Well, then, what about all those men who frequent topless bars, patronize peep shows, slip into massage parlors: guys who gaze at Channel J into the wee hours or gladden Hugh Hefner's or Bob Guccione's hearts and bankbooks with their subscriptions to *Playboy* and *Penthouse;* husbands and surreptitious johns who add to Bloomingdale's revenues by livening up their bedroom lives with a garter belt, an oddly scalloped pair of panties for the wife now and then—not to mention the famed Frederick's of Hollywood. (Remember now, *men* buy these women's things.)

This is all garden-variety deviance, guys, the perversions of everyday life. They are a part of the sex life of the vast majority of our culture's males, making pornography, like baseball, a national pastime. They govern a good deal of the relations between the sexes, leading to the objectification and sometimes exploitation of women. They're diversions, deviations, decoys, expressions of ever-present fear—and of desire.

The manufacturers and retailers, magazine publishers and moviemakers know what men want. They know what their society pretends not to. Men wish for what they fear the most. They want something different from what the macho myths portray.

Men want to feel what women feel. If pornography and more subtle forms of sexual exploitation objectify and subvert women as individuals, they also allow the male onlooker to identify with the "disembodied" female body.

The mixed messages are coming from everywhere. From within and without. Whisperings from childhood paradoxes, from a collective past.

Men try to adhere to what their fathers have demanded of them, forgetting that the older generation of men has its own often hostile and self-serving agenda, its illusions, its need, therefore, to foist on sons the safest of stereotypes and most comfortable of aspirations. Whether their sons win that conditional love or not, fathers are themselves mortal and limited, destined to die. Confused by their own conflicts, other men don't have the answer. Measuring up to their notions of manhood doesn't work.

As we've seen, it's women who can best tell men what they want—love, immersion, languor, oneness, nothing at all. And men just don't want to know what they want—not this sort of thing, not unless they have to. But this takes us to the symptoms, stresses, and calamities that compel men to look into their hearts, and to the next series of chapters.

What Men Don't Want, I

Sex Symptoms

Men and women such as David and Jackie are lucky. Despite some hiccups along the way, their love and sex lives are largely in place. They've been able to have fulfilling sex lives and seem capable of cementing relationships, building careers, and creating families. They're overachievers, even superstars.

Others are less fortunate. They may succumb to sexual restlessness and compulsive betrayal and can never settle down. Or they can't find any erotic satisfaction with women and must seek sex with other men. And even when they are happily married, sexual gratification may prove elusive. Rising from within, these imperatives and limitations dog these men throughout their lives.

It's in these abiding sexual problems—Don Juanism, homosexuality, and sexual dysfunction—that a man's conflicts with women, the terror of losing themselves in a woman's love, are most clearly revealed. And not only do men's fears of merger and effeminization surface in their broken sex lives, but also their conflicts of loyalty toward other men. Many of these men displace their hostility toward rivals of the same sex onto the woman who is the object of the competition. And pushing her away, they further hurt themselves in the process. The sex symptoms—the compulsions, deviations, avoidances, and inhibitions—expose, as nakedly as the act itself, men's most unwanted wishes.

3

Womanizing: Sex and Sexual Identity

To know another's heart, an individual must know his or her own. And often enough neither party really wants to know — himself, herself, the other. Whenever men and women get together, they engage in emotional dialogues whose various elements are partly obvious and clearly stated, partly silent and complicit and very much subtextual or (as psychologists say) unconscious.

In such instances, ignorance is bliss—temporarily. It means that two people can go on doing what they're doing. They can remain protected by the illusions they've maintained together from revelations about personal responsibility and choice, from the sort of self-knowledge that demands change.

In the case of the womanizer, it is the woman who's said to suffer. It's she, not he, who is unsettled by the discovery of her man's misbehavior. But then again, maybe it's not as simple as that. Consider, for example, Nissa, twenty-seven, and Don, her older man.

. . .

"Singin' in the rain," Nissa sang to herself, even though the day was dry.

61

There was still a chill in the light gray air left over, she guessed, from April. She felt warmed by the arm that lay across her back and clasped her shoulder. Maybe its owner's eyes seemed elsewhere, but his arm warded off the breeze as they strolled together. Its touch spoke of love.

Nissa glanced at his face and neck, the tan flesh stretching and easing above the contrasting white collar. And the whole of it— the sensations and the idea of them together like this—turned her on.

"Merry," Don Cummings hummed to himself, "oh, so merry is my month of May." The spring heat had brought the girls out, warming their thighs, Don mused on, in anticipation of his coming.

Lowering his hold, now he cradled Nissa's waist as they strolled overlooking the Seine's embankment. Paris in the springtime, and he knew she was ecstatic. For seven months she'd been asking her lover to take her there the next time he passed through en route to business in the Middle East, and this time he'd consented. Every now and then Don turned to wink and briefly snuggle with his pretty young friend.

But yes, his eyes *were* elsewhere. On the ladies. "Ooh, la, la! Zee pretty little French girls!"

Why is it, he wondered, that a woman's state of undress is such a relative matter? Here were all these girls thawing out from winter, shedding their furs and flannels. Yes, that night he'd be making love to Nissa, spreading her legs, twirling her clitoris, probing in search of the cervix. But here he was transfixed by the pink signal of the crease of a bobbing breast peeping out at him from behind a T-shirt, as its owner swung her arms in the tempo of her stride. As she passed, Don would swing around to catch the outline of her bikini panties visible through the seat of "les blue jeans" stretched so very tightly across her bottom.

He'd once read in a women's magazine a piece on "How to Get Rid of That Nagging Panty Line." How foolish—how little they knew! The ridges and creases made a V pointing to the spot—to the dark mystery of a crotch he had not gained permission to see and feel and most likely, might never find access to. Yes, V, not X, marks the spot! Delta Venus! Venus' Delta!

As the details of this one's outline disappeared into the blur of the distance, Don's attention was seized by another "filly." She was a sweet sixteen-year-old locked in lilting French conversation with her schoolmates. Her books were evidently heavy, and she'd taken advantage of a serendipitous bench to help her prop them up. She stood there, foot on the bench, chattering and giggling.

So another V seized Don's gaze, the one made by her leg where the underside of calf and thigh conjoin below the knee. No longer swathed in some stretchy dark fabric to ward off the winter wind, the bareness of her quivering leg invited him upward toward the plaid, pleated mini-mini skirt that carelessly guarded the girl's inner thigh from view. Staring, Don caught, as the mademoiselle laughed, a quick glimpse of her rear end, which had been momentarily exposed by the little convulsion of glee. A flash of flesh, that was all, a hint of taupe panties, the elastic digging gently into this flesh of hers, and he inferred, the mesh of her pubis palpable through the Swiss cotton. He imagined beads of excitement, like dew, on the curls of hair underneath. Oooh, how he, at forty (almost forty-one), could drive a girl like that crazy!

Nissa seemed to sense his distraction and tugged him back toward her. Don sighed. Releasing his gaze, he let his hand drop from her waist for a moment, patting her rear end, and nibbling quickly at an earlobe as if grazing before pressing on.

He wanted them, he wanted them all. . . .

"Does he want me?" Nissa found herself forever asking herself. "I mean really want me, me, want me around all the time?" Of course, she had to conclude that no, Don didn't.

Still no man had made Nissa, at twenty-seven, feel the way he did. No one had made her so beautiful, and such a woman. Yes, *made* her. Ambiguous as their relationship was, everything about him seemed so emphatic.

Don was like a drug, the mere sight of him making her throb with fear and excitement. "Anticipation" as Carly sang it. It was as if each of their urgent encounters might be the last, and she had to "get it—him—while she could." To borrow from Janis this time. And put up with him, too—with his repeated admonitions that she not be jealous, with the empty midweeks without phone calls.

Her kid sister, Sylvia, good "Solid Syl," shrink-to-be, had tried to warn her off him in her typical way of reversing the big- and little-sister roles. But what did she know about a man like Don? Her life was so predictable.

Nissa hoped she was growing on him. "Growing on him" was an interesting way of putting it, she reflected, the image being, maybe, Don's worst fear. Paris was a good sign, a minimiracle maybe. Still she knew she couldn't push him too far too fast. And she dared not count on him, this man who made her knees turn to jelly, who fooled around and who often seemed to suffer her nearness to him, as if she were a supplicant, no matter what he said.

• • •

Don Cummings is one of those "incorrigible" bachelors. He is a modern-day lady-killer like his legendary namesake, Don Juan, immortalized in the poem by Lord Byron, who, sharing his protagonist's appetite for erotic conquest, found himself in a continual flight across the globe, pursued by the irate husbands whom he'd cuckolded. And there was Casanova, of course.

What makes these men so hard to settle down, such loose cannons?

The conventional wisdom has it that it's not in the male nature to be monogamous. After all, 50 to 75 percent of married men are reported to stray from their domestic pastures, even after they've been brought to the altar.

Men are said to be like other male studs in this respect, sowing their wild oats and spreading their seed among a population of females, who must stay put in order to bear and then rear the fruits of their libidinal labors. Competing with other potential impregnators and getting first dibs on many women become points of honor—proof the dominant male's germ plasm has priority in the gene pool. The "more the merrier," in other words, the more the man.

Conventional wisdom, however, sometimes makes for convenient rationalizations. People are different from lesser animals. The size of their neocortex, the higher brain, and their long dependent childhoods mean that they are able to *learn* rather than being preprogrammed to react. And this allows them to replace predetermined instinctive responses with personal choice and free will. (See also Chapter 15 for the problems this poses as men try to deal with their inborn aggression.)

Whatever a man's myths to the contrary, women don't go into heat like the females of other species. They emit pheromones at certain points in their fertility cycle, we now know. But still the human female does not have anything like what students of animal behavior call a discrete "estrus" period, a limited time when she is receptive to copulation and when she gives off scents and other signals that release complementary sexual responses in males. Instead, she's potentially ready and willing at any time, independent of her ovulation, and so is her partner. It's her choice. Besides there are animals—gerbils, pigeons even—who do mate for life.

Of course, there are "instincts" in human beings—a biological push behind sex and the desire for it as well as tendencies to produce and care for the young and guard our territories from competitors and marauders. However, male and female impulses do not come to people in the form of obligatory actions, behaviors without meaning and awareness. Instead, they're experienced as complex wishes serving many different functions—not only biological but social and psychological.

Moreover, as the sex researchers have shown, males don't crave sex any more than females do. Men may be quicker to rouse themselves erotically than women. Their penises are less complicated organs than the larger, more extensive, and mysterious female genital system—simpler than vulva, clitoris, vagina, and womb, and more "up-front." Once energized, however, a woman is capable of more orgasms than her hapless bedmate, who, "having shot his wad," must wait for his neurons to get activated and the blood and semen supplies to flow back again basically into one place. Given her potential at least for those mythic "multiple orgasms," it's by no means clear how, physiologically speaking, one woman could readily be satisfied by one man.

Indeed, in the wild, once those dominant older males have had their due, dismounting and searching out another female who might happen to be in heat, often enough the other males, lower down in the hierarchy, set to the receptive female. Once nature has ensured that the "best" sperm and genes have gotten to her egg first and done their job in natural selection, she is free to "humor her fancy" before settling down to pregnancy and motherhood. Often enough it's the female animal who, at any given point in time at least, has the greater number of sexual partners.

So much for the biology of male promiscuity—what about its sociology?

Is a man's philandering a variation on the age-old theme of polygyny, where the male can marry many wives, again ensuring that it's his genes that predominate? Certainly, this is a far more common practice than polyandry, where a woman possesses more than one husband.

Yet we're not talking about multiple *marriages*, in which reproduction is a central objective, but rather a multiplicity of purely sexual unions whose aim, more often than not, is to *avoid* making babies. At all costs.

Indeed, like the analogy to the "male animal," the equation of a modern with a tribal man also breaks down. With birth control, sex has been liberated from the dictates and burdens of procreation. From Casanova on—who perfected its manufacture as well as its uses—the condom, along with other devices and stratagems, has freed men (and women, too, of course) to do what they will.

Like women, then, men can be monogamous or promiscuous. And like women, they can put off love, marriage, and parenthood indefinitely. And in this avoidance, not only desires but hidden fears come into play, conflicts once again at the very core of their maleness. More than any lustful impulses that go along with being male, it is his fear of his masculinity that interferes with a man's capacity for commitment.

• • •

It seemed like a dream to Nissa, that night at L'Hôtel Verlaine— "the charming little restover in Le Quartier Latin." She'd listened to Piaf the whole week before, and now here she was with her "beloved . . . in Paris."

It was the third time in two and a half hours that they'd made love, burning off the calories from their dinner—crayfish and foie gras—at Pré Catalan in the Bois du Boulogne. Their bellies, slightly distended still, but oiled now with their shared sweat and secretions, bounced and slithered toward climax. Nissa had already had her two orgasms for this go-round, deep, inverted tidal waves that had begun innocently with the button of her clitoris but which, with Don's sure tongue and uncanny sense of her, of what she felt, then seemed to pound in and out of her as if drawing their inner worlds together. And now they were entwined and getting deeper into each other.

Nissa marveled at his energy, Don's staying power. She had sensed his starting to fade, his penis softening for a moment, only to have her lover find his reserves again. He straightened himself out, driving into her as if to pinion her soul. Beside herself with expectant pleasure, Nissa trembled with the joy of gratitude. . . .

"Three fucking times," Don muttered somewhere inside himself. His eyes half-closed, he'd groaned and looked down at the woman beneath him. Yes, Nissa was beautiful, with her full lips and lapis eyes. But it was as if, and he thought less of himself for thinking this, she was draining from him the last drop of his manhood. Taking it, making herself a woman, not girl, with it, pulling off his dick even. He felt sucked out of himself.

It was at this point that the head and shaft of his penis had gone numb, threatening to wilt into mush. Don had closed his eyes then, calling up an image of the girl from the river. Now, deep in the mind's eye, he was with her.

It was her room, her parents were out for the *après-midi,* and Don was maneuvering her toward the bed with its pale cream cover and stuffed bears left over from a childhood just past. He reached up her leg, gently cupping the V beneath that knee, caressing her peach fuzz, reaching toward her inner thigh. "I wanna see you," the girl moaned. *"S'il vous plaît?"* Don thrust the pelvis toward her and invited the virgin to unzip his fly and pull out his cock. "Oooh," she added as the purple priapium confronted her gaze and his, as the two of them stared at Don's hard, definite dick.

Don found himself growing erect again, able once more to pump away at Nissa. He hated himself for the imagery that took him from the moment, for the internal distance, for being fearful of reality, for the confession of failure in his recourse to scenes merely imagined. But he did need it. He needed pictures, needed to start over, over and over.

The girl grabbed his cock and pointed it toward the shadow below her skirt. And heaving forth the very last of him, Don came again at last, ejaculating somewhere into the woman under him.

And under him, greeting his gift, Nissa sighed and groaned in delight. Reverberating with the pulsing of the organ and man she loved so, she sobbed in thankfulness and at the thought that it, and he, might ever leave her.

• • •

As we inch our way into Don's mind, we begin to see that his womanizing has a complex psychology. Its nature can only be plumbed by an in-depth analysis of the conflicts that motivate it.

If the sex drives of women are no less pressing than those of men, men are no less prone to the fears and compunctions that come with straying from the fold. To think otherwise is simply to relocate Marlboro Man from the prairie to the bedroom.

Fear of loss, jealousy, and the forces of guilt are dangers to be reckoned with—no less peremptory than the power of desire itself. Monogamy is an institution whose functions have been to protect individuals from being abandoned, to guard against rivalry, and to ensure the stability of the society in which they live. Even more to the point, whatever they may make themselves think at the time, desire alone does not move men to become promiscuous. Fear does—fears of other men and of women, fears of one's own feelings.

• • •

Having deposited Nissa on her flight back to Boston, Don Cummings then made his phone call.

Finished, he placed the receiver down with a prolonged click followed by the discharge of change somewhere inside the box. He then strode out the glass door and into a taxi. He didn't need to stop at the drugstore—the chemist. She'd have her own.

Lily would. It was she who now awaited him.

She was thirty-five or so and sold advertising space for the *Herald Tribune*. Lil was separated from her most recent husband and had two little mulatto kids, a boy and a girl, from a previous one who had died. They were usually asleep when Cummings was around. He didn't care much for children and often thought about the mess his brother Roger, who had married late, was having with the two sons he and his wife, Pud, had adopted.

Anyhow, Lil did some choreographing during off-hours for a modern-dance group. She also wanted to act, she said. She was quite pretty with curly, dirty blond hair, blue eyes, fleshy lips, and a lingering Georgia drawl. Her breasts were a little too flat for her body, small maybe, and she had crinkles on her upper thighs and around her waist. But she was very passionate, and after sex she liked to give Don a bath and feed him amoretti.

Lil would wake him at five and drive Don to the airport in time for his eight-twenty A.M. flight.

Don pictured his departure the next morning and rested his cheek against the taxi's window panel. Tired, he thought. His eyes burned—from the exhaust.

He was breathing into the pane, he noticed, making little O's and more diffuse impressions on his mottled image, like a puffing dragon. "Growl." The glass tasted bitter, the way it had when he'd been a kid.

• • •

Yes, men like Don Cummings wander not only out of desire but out of fear. They need to deny love and must minimize the relationship with the woman with whom they make it. After adolescence at least, indiscriminate sex results as much from inhibition as impulsivity. Don Juans evade their lover's hold, fleeing into the arms of another woman. There they "score"; they hit and run; they get in and out "like a shot," as one of my male patients once put it. Or as a woman patient of mine phrased it, they treat their women "like pit stops" on the fast lane of their love life.

It sounds like a comfortable cliché, but it's true. For all his technical sophistication and worldliness, the womanizer is still sexually immature. He "womanizes" because, feeling like a kid, he's afraid of being "womanized." In more ways and for more reasons than one. Let me explain.

There are, to be sure, some such men who are so deeply into themselves and so cool, even chilly, so impervious and unmovable when it comes to another person (male or female), that they are in effect incapable of love. Maybe once upon a time the potential was there, but by the time they've reached adulthood, the flame has long been extinguished. Guys like this can do just about anything without worrying about it. It's themselves they pleasure—or rather some perfect picture of themselves.

Others, however, are more easily stirred. A man like this, such as Don maybe, resents a woman *because* she wants him and warms him. She invites his tenderness, rouses his deeper desires, and offers to soothe him and fulfill his trust. Falsely, he thinks.

He imagines she will leave him.

Many (not all) womanizers were their mother's favorite during their infancy, or sometimes an aunt's or grandmother's, only to be supplanted quite abruptly or absolutely by a tyrannical father, by another adult lover of hers, or even at times by a sibling of one sex or the other—or by the mother herself, by *her* narcissism. Overindulged and overstimulated, they found themselves abruptly cast aside and left out in the cold. Seduced and abandoned.

Each later romantic encounter harks back to childhood days, reviving this man's Oedipus complex—his incestuous love for his mother, the rivalry that goes with it, his view of himself as a little boy (see Chapter 12), and his mother's reneging on her *seeming* promise of exclusivity. Now, he imagines, this beautiful adult woman, who has taken his grown penis and manly heart into her body and soul—she, too, will betray him in the end. So, angry at the start about the fate he foresees, he gets his revenge in advance by doing to her what he feels was done to him. And he gets while the getting is good.

A man like this acts mean and calls the shots completely because he feels vulnerable to hurt and inadequate to the conflict—to the struggle to win and then sustain a woman's love. Acting cavalier and invincible, he in fact underestimates his staying and lasting powers. He can't compete in the long haul. Like other men, he runs scared.

Furthermore, a nagging and irrational sense of guilt also comes into play and for related reasons. Repressed perhaps, nevertheless it does its powerful work in the corners of the mind. Ironically, such guilt, which usually has nothing to do with present circumstances, leads a man to do immoral deeds.

Not only does he hurt because he's been hurt and fears further injuries, the womanizer also acts to destroy the object of temptation. Feeling imperfect and therefore unworthy of being loved by a woman, like a "bad boy" indeed, the unfaithful lover does his best to nip the conflict in the bud, and bed. He destroys love at the root, calling it quits before it can flower.

Such a man makes a *show* of being entitled to do exactly what he wants. But in the process, he ends up provoking others to mistrust, dislike, and finally to reject him so that he can count on nothing from them in turn. He feels awful about being selfish and meanspirited and so ups the ante in his behavior. He *acts* as if he were clearly undeserving and thereby gets himself punished in advance.

Plumb a lady-killer's mind even deeper, and you will discover the hidden and usually unconscious sources of this, his half-acknowledged guilt. It is the guilt left over from the Oedipus complex once again, the emotional punishment that all of us, men and women, inflict on ourselves to expiate our sins of the heart.

Thinking he's proving his masculinity, the womanizer unmans himself. Scared of a father he experienced as both absent and oppressive, he is afraid to usurp his parent's place. Symbolically, the womanizer evades his patriarchal rule and "outdoes" him only to find that all along he has been doing to himself what he fears his father will do to him. Each time he ejaculates into the void, the Don Juan effectively castrates himself.

A Casanova skirts the felt dangers and sustained excitement that come with growing up. Settle down, win a woman's loyalty forever, father her child, and he fears truly offending God the Father, of whom there can only be one. So he plays around, taking a thousand little chances just to prove he's not a sissy, after all, even if he hasn't the heart for the ongoing concerns and worries that go with building a life with another person. Like the sky diver or any other daredevil, the Don Juan beards the lion in his den just to prove a point—namely, that he's not as terrified as he truly is. The thrill of a new and genuinely risky encounter obscures a deeper if more irrational dread of commitment.

Unlike the sexually deviant male, he is able to get an erection, penetrate, have intercourse, and ejaculate. And he's capable as well of fulfilling a woman's need for sexual pleasure. But the Don Juan stops short of creating anything of value from these masculine feats and of experiencing what he happens to produce. He deprives and effectively "sterilizes" himself without knowing it. He's afraid of the challenge that comes with commitment.

When the married man and father strays, he's denying the rest of his life in these ways. For a moment or two at least, each time he does so, like the incorrigible bachelor he becomes a kid again.

But why should a man be any more willing than a woman to expose himself indiscriminately, to give his body to a person or persons unknown? Promiscuous sex degrades men just as much as it does a woman, whatever the social conventions say to the contrary. He humiliates himself and as we'll see, lets himself be used. The womanizer is like an unclothed little child who makes his body everybody's business and whom nobody takes too seriously.

But there's more to this inner story. . . . Later in his life and work, Freud had some interesting things to say about the underpinnings of "castration anxiety," some subtle twists on an otherwise obvious theme. Most men think of their penises as visible proof that they are men—independent, forceful, able to get away and make it on their own, anything but little mama's boys. However, as Freud reminded his readers, without a penis a man couldn't get into a woman's vagina—and symbolically at least, back to the womb.

Behind the sexual urge in men, he implied (and as I've tried to suggest in Chapter 2), lies their longing for paradise lost. Through sex men can return in fantasy and feeling to a time long past when they were protected from the rigors and harshness of the world outside the mother's sphere. All men would like to languish there forever, inside and beside her, mother, woman. And up to a point, the womanizer-to-be has had a measure of this miraculous immersion.

It is this dependency, along with the sacrifices real and imagined that go with it, that he continues to long for yet strives to escape. Since he can't get away from himself, he tries to run from her instead. The danger? Once more, being *womanized*. Especially so, that is, since deep down he's more unformed boy than mature man.

Not only does he fear his father's retribution (castration), the womanizer fears being "unmanned" in the sense, one, of being simply overwhelmed by a woman, and two, of being effeminized by her. The longer any man stays close to one lover, the more that man's childlike need and sensuality come to the forefront, and the more he identifies with her. (You know how it is—how couples get to *look* more and more alike the longer they live together?) Since he already feels like a little boy whose masculinity is tenuous, the man we're talking about fears that he'll *lose himself* in intimacy. Unending love threatens to take away not only his more adult freedoms, autonomy, and privacy but also his separateness, his identity, his manhood, his balls.

And one way to prove that you still have balls—penis and testicles—and that they are big enough and function okay is to see them in use. In contrast to intercourse itself, where these disappear from view, sexual conquests usually involve a good deal of foreplay centering on looking, showing, and touching from something of a distance. The compulsive conqueror thus has much in common with an exhibitionist who flashes at women, getting a response from them to it in order to prove that his penis is still there. Removing himself, stepping back, he avoids uniting with his lover for too long and crossing the boundaries between self and other, male and female.

Indeed, not a few seducers prove to be unsuccessful as lovers once they've gotten their conquest into bed. They succumb there to those sexual malfunctions that can plague any man (premature ejaculation or impotence, the subject of Chapter 5) but that, with a would-be Don Juan, make for a particular letdown. Such men are all hype and no delivery. Men such as these are even more deeply afraid of women and what they can "do" to them. For them, not only closeness but also empathy pose a threat to their sexual identity.

Other such practiced "lovers" are truly sexy—as so many of their women assert. Their appeal derives not only from good looks but from the fact that they seem to know just what to do. Having savored his mother as a child, this kind of Don Juan understands women implicitly. He has a sixth sense about them in fact. His charm lies in his feminine intuitiveness, in his uncanny empathy for a woman and what turns her on. Hence, ironically, his male charisma.

But this is also a felt liability. His boundaries feel permeable. He dares not dally for *too* long, but must tear himself away to reestablish his manhood.

. . .

Compulsive promiscuity in men, as in women, has much in common with addictions. Sex is like a drug in a way, except that it's women and not inanimate substances that are being abused. The sex addict can't do without it. He's hooked. A woman crosses his path and he wants her. No, he must *have* her. The physical sensations—the arousal accompanying foreplay, the brief moment of orgasm—are highs. Their intensity wipes away personal worries and the sorrows of the world.

But the analogy breaks down because people are not substances, first of all, and secondly, because all good sex, with friend *or* stranger, can serve such purposes. In point of fact, womanizing has even more in common with perversions. Yes, when looked at psychologically, "screwing around" resembles flashing, as I've already noted with Don, as well as the voyeuristic escapades of the Peeping Tom, as I've also implied. Above all, it has much in common with fetishism.

Psychoanalysts have defined perversions as activities leading to climax that either substitute for or must accompany sexual intercourse with a member of the opposite sex. Essentially, because of some of the fears just described, the pervert deflects his attention from women as dynamic sexual partners, turning it to himself and/or to some inert object instead, both of which prop up his masculinity and enable him to come. In fact, it's his own penis that excites him most, concretely or in symbolic form. And it is the absence of this in a woman that above all terrifies him. Afraid of the difference, turned off by it, the pervert ends up making love to himself.

Isn't the compulsive conqueror just such a "narcissist"? Yes, unlike less fortunate men, he can perform with a woman. He can "do" it—at least most of the time. And in all fairness he *is* turned on by her, drawn to that which is womanly about a woman. Still, he, too, retreats from immersing himself in her for too long. At that very moment when he might sink into her, he defensively preoccupies himself with himself instead—seeing himself in the act, envisioning not only his next conquest but himself as conqueror.

Partly, a woman's erotic passion rivets his attention because the compulsive lover sees in her arousal his own. But he differs from the true romantic in resisting this kind of surrender of self for very long. And shifting the emphasis, he finds in her responsiveness a demonstration of his power—and that of his penis—to excite her, indeed to drive her *crazy*. A woman in the throes of *ecstasy*, a woman outside herself, becomes an extension of his own dynamic masculinity. She becomes a living, breathing, thinking, feeling, female fetish—not a person, but a fetish.

He just can't let himself get away from himself! And he has an accomplice in his self-absorption. Indeed, she's not only a sex object in this drama of exploitation. All the while the womanizer's woman has been using him.

· · ·

Orly had scared Nissa.

She'd told Don how when she was twelve, she and her sister, Sylvia, had arrived there on their own en route to meet her parents on their second European family vacation. They'd gotten lost for nearly an hour before the Cushmans caught up with them. She returned at twenty with a backpack and yes, a Eurailpass, with Ed James and Sammie (Don Cummings's cousin, who'd introduced them later) the summer after their sophomore year.

But she'd never gotten used to all the signs and figure eights in the access road, and the French themselves. And Nissa still couldn't quite use the public telephones, either. Anyway, Don had to put her on the flight back, installing her in the business-class section this time—he'd had plenty of upgrade awards. They had drunk coffee, chatted, read the *Tribune,* and looked at *Le Monde* in the Clipper Lounge. And they kissed at the last security gate beyond which only passengers can go.

Don's plane for Riyadh, where he marketed his surgical staples, left the next morning. Poor dear, what would he do alone. . . ?

Staring out the window of the plane as it parted sideways at first from the beige accordion attaching it to the terminal, Nissa smiled at her conceit. She imagined Don inside its bellows, his raincoat flaring behind him as he hurried down the long corridor. He was horribly good fun. And she could still take her time, she reckoned. It was his that was passing. It was he who had "nothing left to lose."

· · ·

Nissa's quieter, cannier than most in her position. Typically, the womanizer's conquest complains, justifiably, of having been seduced and abandoned. She rails at having been relegated to a harem whose other members remain hidden from view but who, she imagines, are sisters in suffering. Nor, since their lover has been so assiduous in maintaining his right to privacy and ingenious in his wanton duplicity, can his secret women get together to commiserate with one another.

The truth is that many of these women either know from the start or learn soon enough that they are being misled and mistreated. And they deceive themselves when it comes to the active part they have been playing in the drama being enacted.

Like Dracula's paramours, the lady-killer's ladies are, at least in part, his willing victims. Without quite allowing themselves to admit it, more often than not they have either unwittingly sought him out or stuck with him because being used and betrayed is also what they want.

Well, maybe *want* isn't exactly right. There's a difference between our various *wishes*, which are often unconscious because they are indeed unwanted, and what we consciously strive for, what we think and hope we want. As with most men, so with most women: people don't want what they wish! It's too scary.

Because of fantasies left over from childhoods, the womanizer's women can play right into his hands. How many young women, after all, especially during the adolescent prelude to real-life romance, have dreamed or even daydreamed about ravishment? What about those Valentino and other old movies in which the "Sheik of Araby" sweeps in in black robes, entrancing his victim, abducting her, having his way with her, maybe selling her into white slavery or leaving her, like the heroine of Paul Bowles's more modern novel *The Sheltering Sky,* to wander the dunes and sink into the degradation of the caravan camp follower?

The wish to be violated by a man is an inescapable by-product of a little girl's earliest understanding of love and sex. It's a childish misconception that she later brings to her dealings with men.

A little girl imagines her parents having sex. Or she sees animals locked in what looks like the combat of coitus. Maybe she glimpses her father's penis or that of some large dog or horse. Looking at her own little vulva—and remember, she doesn't have breasts yet and is ignorant about the extent of her vagina much less the existence of her womb—she can't for the life of her figure out how that big thing gets into such a tiny place.

Thus, when it comes to intercourse, such a girl imagines a violent meeting, with men beating and boring into women, skewering them, tearing them apart, making holes maybe—all before finally going away. Psychoanalysts call these notions of hers, destined to influence her love life in so many ways, her "sadomasochistic fantasies about the primal scene."

Whatever pleasure might be associated with getting hurt in this erotic way is further compounded by a woman's guilt—left over from *her* Oedipus complex this time. Like most conflicted people, she's guilty about getting anything good out of life, associated as this is with forbidden fruit. If you get what you want—sex with your daddy (or any man), for instance—you must get punished for it. At the same time, in fact. Indeed, crime and punishment become one and the same. So she ends up impelled and compelled to get "screwed" by men.

At some point, women do shed their naïveté and desire more from a lover than being conquered and otherwise hurt or exploited. Whatever their unconscious wishes, women *want* to make something out of their lives and themselves—career, marriages, children. And when it comes down to it, most women must take the initiative to induce their men to go along with these ambitions. It's just that for many, what they don't know (about themselves) *can* hurt them.

Women aren't alone in their "masochism," of course. As I shall show later on (Chapter 7), men are also moved to surrender to "cruel mistresses" who toy with and withhold from them. (Indeed, this is sometimes one of the wishes a philanderer struggles to deny, covers up, and inevitably enacts in his overtly sadistic but also provocative behavior toward his lovers.) Yet until recently at least, being, as they say, "pussy-whipped" was anathema to the stereotype of masculinity whereas getting "fucked over" by a man provided a common bond for soul sisters. Women have greater permission to suffer so.

In fact, both actors in an unhappy love affair hurt and get hurt, the roles remaining surprisingly muddy and interchangeable. Aggressors are partly "seduced" into acts of aggression, as one psychoanalyst put it. Dracula's victims become infected with his "bloodlust," converted by him into vampires themselves.

There's another irony here, which women have to watch out for. Being misused salves the conscience, and women can exploit being exploited in order to deny what they themselves get out of a Don Juan's joyride. Indeed, some women, without admitting it, are also in it for that ride—the pure fun of uncommitted sex. If men, we learn, don't necessarily divorce sex from love, women similarly have needs for sexual gratification and experimentation. And if they have to pay for it, they tell themselves fleetingly, so be it. The heaven's worth the hell.

A woman *also* grows and learns from erotic encounters, in which a deft lover instructs his partner, who may be still a novitiate, in the ways of the flesh. The practiced lovemaker helps her discover her body and its responses. If he is seasoned and somewhat older, the incestuous overtones of this erotic mentoring add spice to their trysts. (See Chapter 1.)

And not only does this inevitable desertion on his part, a trauma that she may very well have anticipated, serve as a sop to her conscience, providing the punishment she needs if she's to enjoy herself in the moment. It also places a limit, a time frame, on their encounter, absolving her of any responsibility for seducing and abandoning *him*.

A woman like this may not be ready herself for a lasting relationship. Or if she's having an affair outside her marriage, she may have mobilized her desires in order to call that primary relationship into question or to make up for what she's missing in it. Aware of being used by her Casanova, such a woman can't quite let herself recognize that she's been using him as well.

Yes, Mr. Valentino, it "takes two to tango."

＊ ＊ ＊

10 P.P. Ten years post-Paris—he never thought it would be so important, that trip—and Don Cummings had turned fifty.

"Happy Half Century" had been the inscription on the gateau St.-Honoré that Karen, his latest, had ordered for him from "Le" French Bakery. Now it was Don's turn to return the favor since Karen's birthday—a considerably lesser number to be sure—was fast approaching. And it was with this mission in mind that he found himself strolling along Palm Beach's Worth Avenue on a sunny Wednesday afternoon in January and gazing into the windows of its expensive boutiques.

What would this young woman, who unlike him had already been married once, divorced now—what would she want?

The Missoni shop now occupied his interest. Standing, his weight, he noticed, more on the right than the left foot, to compensate for the tendinitis that had curtailed his weekends on the tennis court, he surveyed the array of psychedelic bargello knits.

Sweaters, sweater dresses, and ties melded together in unisex fashion, now the one, now the other framing the inquiring face reflected in the picture window of the man who was looking at them.

Don's focus shifted to the image of himself, of the ever-grayer hair that framed his still tan, still handsome face. The hairline had receded ever so slightly over the years, but the gray had overtaken him suddenly, almost overnight it seemed, maybe eight years earlier, just after "she" left him.

It was then, just then ironically, that he saw her. Don's eye had wandered back from his image to the muted kaleidoscope of clothes in the window before him. And there she was, another mirror image in the shadows of these serious colors, but Nissa nonetheless.

She had cut her hair short, as "a woman in her thirties should," according to another of his ex-lovers. She seemed rounder, shorter, her breasts fuller, more womanly, he thought, until he further realized that Nissa was holding a child.

A towheaded boy, maybe three years old, was sliding down the side of her body and across Nissa's jutting hip to be landed on the sidewalk below. He looked just like her, except lighter, a fair-skinned, raven-haired angel with broad, sensual lips and those lapis eyes.

For a moment Don thought of wheeling around and facing her, imagining the exchange of information and pleasantries. After all, Don's business was booming. But he stopped himself, darkening inside as if a cloud had emerged out of the clear blue. Instead, he stood frozen in place, hoping—and how odd this was again, how ironic—hoping Nissa wouldn't notice him.

The boy pulled at his mother's hand impatiently and succeeded in tugging her away from the window and out of Don's view. He realized that he'd been holding his breath and so exhaled against the glass. For all the items behind it, the window seemed blissfully blank again.

Noting one possibility for Karen, a mauvish knit skirt and top, he pivoted in the opposite direction and proceeded down the avenue. A little whir of cool wind from the ocean caught Don as he crossed to the more open side street. It shimmied up the inside of his pant leg and reminded him, or so Don thought, of the past. . . .

Not for one minute had Nissa been fooled. There was no mistaking him.

It was surprise, not fatigue, that had caused her to loosen her grip on Robin. Her knees had buckled as of old, if just for a moment. Weakening temporarily, she'd let the boy slip for an instant and slide down on her to the ground. Now, she was walking away with her dear baby boy. Robin's pudgy little fingers were entwined in hers, absently toying with the wedding band on her left hand.

Nissa had thought of saying hello. In fact, she might have thought nothing of it had not her eye caught his in the glinting reflection of the window as it stared silently back at her behind him. Don had seen her, she realized, but had not seen her see him. *That* was a familiar metaphor. Besides, he seemed to want to disappear, and she did not want to embarrass him.

Now, dragged gently uptown, Nissa twisted to look over her shoulder. Don was crossing the street, jerkily, slightly stiff legged. The spring was somehow gone from his stride, especially in the left leg.

But God, was he still gorgeous. Still tan. And what a craftsman. Best lover Nissa had ever had.

She found herself humming as she swung her son's arm. "You're so vain," Nissa intoned, "I bet you think this song is about you, don't you? Don't you . . ."

Robin giggled.

• • •

Don remembered when he was a little boy, they had a statue that puzzled him. It was made of wood that had been whitewashed. Mother had placed it on their front porch amidst the flowers contained in this greenhouselike enclosure for the winter.

The figure was of a youth in doublet and hose, bent forward, smiling. It was the sort of smile, as he reflected on it later, that you saw on the lips of Leonardo's women—Mona Lisa or the Madonna and Saint Anne. "He"—but Donnie wasn't quite sure— had long, curly hair and a beardless face. Though he was wearing tights, you couldn't see the bulge of his penis.

Mother said that he was Narcissus and he was looking at himself in a stream. He was going to die and become a flower. . . .

• • •

It's been said that "Don Juan complexes" represent ploys to prove an unsure man's heterosexuality and thus to ward off a still "latent homosexuality."

I don't quite agree with this. It seems too pat. Womanizers do love women, truly, even though they can't stay put for very long. They're too scared, scared to be adult men.

But I do agree that women are very much present in the inner (and past) lives of many men who are homosexual, as I shall show in the next chapter. And like their heterosexual counterparts, these men are forever trying to get away from them, repeatedly "running scared."

4
•••

Gay Men, Grim Women: The Homosexual Controversy

In 1973, before the AIDS epidemic put a damper on sexual experimentation, the American Psychiatric Association declassified homosexuality. No longer seen as pathological by officialdom's mental health experts, "obligatory and/or exclusive sexual relations with other men" now became an "alternative lifestyle."

Rather than expressing the conflictual consequence of seductive mothers wreaking havoc on sons deprived of adequate fathers, as psychoanalysts had asserted (I'll get back to this), according to the new guard, gay men were born to their persuasion. Lacking maybe in male hormones, they were either effeminate or bisexual from the outset. Somehow they had been predisposed by their genes to be aroused by males like themselves. It wasn't their fault, their homosexuality; they weren't "sick." Their sexual preference was only a natural "variant."

Those who sought psychotherapy were simply wanting in gay pride. A selective sample, they had been made miserable by their predetermined lot in life, succumbing to the stigma attaching to their inborn preference for sex with other men. Homosexuality was no longer to be seen as the outcome of damage or turmoil, a problem in and of itself, but rather as a precondition for subsequent suffering. Homosexual men were predestined to be pariahs, fighting themselves in a desperate struggle to fit in. Social prejudice was to blame for a gay man's unhappiness, and not his early history or inner life.

Indeed, these reformers proclaimed, the incidence of homosexuality was far greater than its detractors would have us believe. When it appeared in 1948, the first Kinsey report, *Sexual Behavior in the Human Male,* had already shocked the psychotherapeutic community. For some time, practitioners had viewed homosexuality as a relatively rare aberration. In his survey of 5,300 male respondents, however, Kinsey now averred that 37 percent of his representative sample of white men had had homosexual sex resulting in orgasm at least once from their adolescence to their dotage. Eighteen percent claimed to be predominantly homosexual in fantasy or in sexual practice, while 13 percent had stated that they were exclusively what is now called gay.

What does a biologist know anyhow! So ran the psychoanalytic uproar. How can you tell what people do or feel based on sociological questionnaires rather than in-depth and long-term explorations of their psyches? Much less what they want.

Analysts, they argued, had labored long and hard with patients like these to "straighten" them out, striving to help these men (and sometimes women) fulfill their biological duties, and they believed, hidden ambitions so that they, too, might be fruitful and multiply. Besides, the new ruling seemed an assault on truth, a dangerous denial of the facts, coddling the hapless homosexual with a mental *Good Housekeeping* stamp of approval on his "psychopathology" while actually dooming him to a life of promiscuity, effective sterility, and ultimate isolation.

Homosexuality was not what these guys really wanted underneath it all. At least that's *not* what they started out wishing for. They wanted to be men—heterosexual men like everybody else. . . .

The passions on *both* sides of the homosexual controversy were and still are intense. Homosexual men are no strangers to their own sexual inclinations and dissatisfaction with them. That they should resent having their character impugned along with their sexual orientation—not only by hard hats but by highbrow "shrinks" pretending to care about them—makes sense. The personal reactions and ad hominem proclamations of psychoanalysts, who should know better and who sometimes seem to shun information that doesn't fit with their theorizing about the subject, are another question.

When it comes to sexual orientation—in contrast to, let's say, an obsessive-compulsive disorder or a depression—a good deal more seems to be at stake than "data," something rumbling in the core of everybody's sexual identity. The issue of sexual preferences sets reflex reactions in motion that drive away anything resembling scientific detachment.

It's not my intention in a brief chapter such as this one to enter the fray and come down with my psychologist's gavel, pronouncing a verdict on the homosexual's general emotional health one way or another. Yet no book on men could be complete without attention to sexual activities in which over one-third of the male population may have engaged—at least according to Kinsey's estimate over forty years ago. Besides, when it comes to homosexuality nowadays, men and women can no longer afford not to look behind closed doors.

Maybe it's a matter of definition, reasoned the moderate members of the mental health community. Lots of young men experiment with homosexual relations during their adolescence as a rite of passage into manhood. Look at those notorious Ancient Greek pedophiles for one example. Back in the classical gymnasiums, pubescent boys were required to let older men stick their erect penises between their legs and ejaculate while the youths themselves remained detumescent—like forbearant and demure girls doing an older man's bidding. Any other homosexual act was frowned upon and punished in Athenian society.

Nowadays, there's the frivolity of curious brothers, who become occasional bedmates, group jerks, or the occasional lapse of a teacher or camp counselor with his young charges. Even innocent cliques such as the "dick club" formed by the twelve-year-old bunkmates at one summer camp, dedicated to measuring and comparing their growing organs, might qualify for the designation "homosexual." (See Chapters 2 and 13 for a further description of bisexual temptations and fears in basically heterosexual teenagers.)

Rule out childish things and you still have an infinite number of possibilities. Remember those polymorphous perverse orgies in vogue in the seventies? Or the extreme conditions of prison or a submarine where the only available sex partners happen to share the gender of men in need of genital release and a little human contact? No, the experts rejoin, by homosexual they have in mind, to repeat, exclusive and obligatory relations with members of the same sex—not any port in a storm.

"Exclusive?" you ask. Then what about "bisexual" men?

Once more experts have a ready answer. According to some, "bisexuality" is really a misnomer. Like the compulsive Casanova, men who are *truly* "AC/DC" are simply indiscriminate, enamored more of their own sensations than of anybody else, regardless of gender and anatomical equipment. Even a sheep might meet their criteria for a living piece of flesh to get off with. Why, look at Portnoy, he made it with calves liver, didn't he?

Either this, or men who have sex with both men and women are really struggling to go straight, to deny being what they are. After all, being gay never was easy. First, there was the social stigma. After that, there was AIDS. And there's always been barrenness and without the glue of family ties, the greater than average chance of dying a lonely death.

Disregard the criterion of exclusivity and limit the designation "homosexual" to men who sometime or other *must* have sex with other men, and still there remain any number of variations on this encompassing theme. First of all, what do these men do? Do they mate for life—as heterosexuals are *supposed* to do at any rate? Or do they cruise, invariably driven to have a multiplicity of homosexual partners? Are they uptight or impulsive, inhibited or promiscuous?

And second, once with another man, what does a gay man do then? Or at least *want* to enact in this era of sexually transmitted fatality and mandatory safe sex? Does he mostly enjoy anal sex—being penetrated or penetrating? Fellatio? Mutual masturbation? Etc. Does he do some things at some times and others at others?

And what kind of *person* is "the" homosexual? Is he a wimp—effeminate, soft, narrower in the shoulders than hips? Is he a big, mean, hairy, and muscular S&M type, with cropped hair and mustache that make him more like an SS officer or humanoid Doberman pinscher than your archetypal "fairy" out of the fifties? A sadist or a sissy?

Actually none of the stereotypes fits with all those movie star studs whose hidden persuasion comes as such a shock to their ardent female fans. Nor does it conform with the picture presented by the jocks who've been coming out of their locker room closets of late, all those all-pro "tight ends" hitherto admired and aped by boys aspiring to the models of masculinity they proffer. Men aren't always what they seem.

In fact, the list of possible practices, predilections, and types of homosexual men may be endless. So it's probably safer and truer to speak of "homosexual activities" than of *the* homosexual. Even then the label may be, as scientists and statisticians are wont to say, "overinclusive."

In any event, for women, homosexual practices and the men who engage in them are no longer matters of bemused disinterest without consequences for them. Quite the contrary, with the advent of the HIV epidemic, they touch on issues of life and death, posing a pressing personal threat to anyone, man or woman, who has ever made love to a man.

That men's sex with men can also tell us more about what men want—from other men, from women—is, of course, most important. Perhaps no man fears being infantilized, effeminized, indeed pulverized, by women more than the homosexual. And though he may adopt her role at times in order to take in the masculinity of another as his own, he remains very much a man. A man, that is, with a man's rage and violence and the means, especially nowadays, to exact his revenge. These men, whom the world disparages as unmanly, men such as Dr. Peter Wynn, have much to tell us about their sex as we follow them into the back alleys of deviant desire.

· · ·

It was nearly midnight.

The taxi Peter was riding in hurtled down Broadway, skidding over the asphalt toward his goal. Another time and he would have resented being bounced about, sliding across the vinyl, his neck snapping back and his head being thrown toward the bulletproof Plexiglas and metal mesh dividing him from Sánchez, José, the driver. But just then, he welcomed the speed. For all its yellow dilapidation, the cab seemed a sort of womb on the run, conveying him safely from his uptown apartment through the cold and the dangers of midtown on to this night's nirvana. The quicker he got there, the better.

Peter passed the Metropole, looking just the way it did on Channel J. Its entrance was ceremoniously guarded by a doorman in a green uniform with gaudy gold braids and epaulets. Was Peter fooling himself, he wondered, or was it for real—the facsimile of a big-breasted woman, a mannequin in the window, which he seemed to make out through the dim night and successive glass barriers? A man in a dark coat filed through the entrance and into the musty black tunnel. Its inner goings-on he could only imagine—not that he cared.

Peter's cab turned right before reaching Forty-second Street, with its panoply of movies, peep shows, prostitutes of all persuasions, drug dealers, and undercover cops. It veered right in the Forties, past the unlit theater marquees and after-the-show bars and restaurants, toward Eighth Avenue. There it made an uptown turn, as if heading home again.

It was then, nearing that theater, that Peter's pulse began to race. He was succumbing, giving up boundaries, risking life itself, this Friday night that Karen was away, to know the truth—another flight naked into the night, yet another quest for Eros's Holy Grail. It was sublime, daring, deadly, he also told himself.

José the hack turned to look at him briefly, indifferently he hoped, as Peter shoved his eight dollars into the "movable hole" made for this purpose in the security divider, before hurrying out of the taxi and into the street. Getting home was another matter, of course. He'd have to worry about that later. For all the musculature he'd built up at the gym in the last five years, first at Seth's request and now to keep up with Jim's standards, Peter felt pretty frail still. At twenty-six, looking back on his adolescence, he again realized that not once had he been in a fistfight.

So what. Standing there, now walking, no, almost floating the remaining ten yards to the entrance, he was embarked on a far greater adventure than that encountered by any of those straight jocks whose self-importance had tortured his teenage years. Yes, he was light-headed, as if stoned. And in this altered state, it seemed like an illusion, some legerdemain, when the unseen cashier—again behind safety bars, just like José, and reminding him of confession and puberty—simply received the few more bills that gained Peter access to the inner sanctum.

Just inside, Peter passed a plastic potted palm. Its stiff leaf brushed his cheek as he walked through the yellow vestibule into the cinema itself.

It was entirely silent inside, except for an occasional cough and the vague hum of the projector, familiar from weekend movies at camp and prep school. The image on the screen was a dark-haired young man with chiseled pectorals. He himself was squeezing one of these, now and then licking the tips of his fingers and rubbing the nipple in the middle of the muscle with his saliva. Athlete that he was, Peter figured, still there was no more direct way to get the secretions there.

As he eased into an aisle seat, the camera panned down the protagonist's abdomen to the bulge in his Jockey shorts. Caressing himself all the way, the hero reached under the elastic to grope for his balls. He squeezed and pulled and then, in one fell swoop, swept his briefs away to expose an already substantial cock, but one that, projected on the silver screen in the middle of that midnight black, was larger than life. Peter felt his own penis respond to this one, grow hard as the young man's erection— replete with veins, pulsations, and shimmering glans—filled the flickering tableaux before him.

Now in the dark, he reached down to touch himself, loosening the snap on his jeans, pulling his polo shirt loose, sliding his fingers in, pressing his own abdomen when suddenly he felt a hand on his knee—someone else's. Again a quick reminiscence slipped in—Aunt Bertha cackling over the dirty old man who, mistaking her, "of all people," for a young girl, had reached under her pocketbook at the Springfield Cinerama to grab the varicose veins on her thigh. But this was different.

Peter looked sideways at the silhouette who gracefully, silently, surreptitiously, had joined him. "Let me help you," it whispered, and Peter's flesh yielded to its touch.

"Yes," inaudibly.

The hand massaged his thigh now, its heel pressing into his crotch before unzipping him. It pulled out Peter's "peter"—and he was beside himself, there in the dark, clothed but also naked and revealed.

Now another arm reached over to take Peter's hand and place it in his lap. The stranger's penis was also big and so reassuring, affirming Peter's with its own excitement. Now there were two of them, in tandem, offering themselves to the night, shifting the focus from the images on the screen to what they felt, and felt. They rubbed in silence, as if perfectly attuned to some mutual yet anonymous beat. Nobody was looking, but there were, Peter sensed, bodies and balls like theirs everywhere, in the pews. A dream.

Peter was the first to come, ejaculating into the stranger's hand before his semen could shoot into the unseeing void. His last spasm seemed to coincide with the stranger's first, as he, too, ejaculated, grabbing his own cock now, it and Peter's hand in his, pointing the tip down, so as to spray the back of the seat before them. The stranger groaned a little.

He handed Peter a Kleenex, put himself back in place, and

humbly slipped away into the seats beside them, into the dark again. Wiping himself with the tissue, Peter then put his penis back in his pants and got up to go.

. . .

If sexual politics influences the gathering of statistics when it comes to homosexuality among men (and if, as we've seen, it's difficult to say what homosexuality is anyway), polemics makes determining its causes and consequences an even more elusive matter. Over the years in fact, as their theories have focused on the role of the earliest relationships in shaping the personality, psychoanalysts have changed their minds about the seeds of homosexuality.

It used to be said that the future homosexual was afraid of his tyrannical father. He had turned from women, who were off-limits, to men to appease his punitive father and to ingratiate himself with more powerful men. In this imagery, a gay man is rather like one of those more "juvenile" baboons who avoids being beaten up or cast out by allowing himself to be mounted by the older dominant males.

However, as clinicians listened more attentively to real-life homosexuals rather than "homophobic" heterosexuals struggling with their own "latent" bisexuality, quite another picture emerged. Far from being oppressive and demanding, their fathers appeared to be *absent* from the scene.

Passive themselves, these men's fathers seemed to have been uninvolved in their sons' upbringing. They'd left their boys to their own devices as far as figuring out what a man should be.

Victims of father absence, homosexual men had been smothered by their mothers, psychoanalysts now declared, virtually imbibing their femininity as a result. Overstimulated and underdirected, they found themselves fearing, loathing but also identifying with the woman who had overwhelmed them.

Still, "anatomy is destiny," as Freud remarked when considering a woman's fate, himself paraphrasing Napoleon (whose "anatomy," incidentally, appears to have been none too impressive). Endowed with a penis—however uncertain he might be of its durability—a little boy like this still *wanted* to be the man that he was fated to be.

His homosexuality was now seen as an effort to repair the damage that has been done to his masculinity by symbolically taking in that of another man. The gay man is "father hungry."

Drawn to big strong men, trying to fill up the holes in his body and soul, "sexualizing" his quest for manhood, ultimately driven to incorporate one penis after another, he only aims to have what should have been his. Thus, the formulaic family constellation proposed for the gay man in the making: absent father, omnipresent mother. Or so it then seemed from the histories reported over time in psychotherapy.

The trouble is, this selfsame pattern describes any number of people who don't turn out to be gay. There are lots of other casualties of father absence: underachievers, delinquents, sleepy-headed heterosexuals, normal-enough men, and more. Moreover it's almost impossible to say, when looking at people retrospectively, just what came first—chicken or egg, cart or horse, homosexuality or an alienated father.

Did the father's absence make a gay man out of his son, or conversely, did the boy's unfolding sexual orientation—his unmistakable difference from other boys—drive his father away? Probably in most instances, the estrangement of father and son has evolved as an ever-more mutual alienation, as a vicious cycle in which it becomes increasingly difficult for them to get closer together and to glean anything good and solid from each other.

But even here generalizations break down. There are boys whose first homosexual experiences are of being seduced or even raped by pederastic fathers or other older male relatives, setting them on the path toward future sexual orientation.

Is homosexuality, then, stimulated by frank abuses—perhaps by either of his parents or some other adult close to home? I used to wonder whether this wasn't in fact the case and searched through my gay patients' reminiscences for the telltale signs of homoerotic incest—in vain. And yes, what about the numbers of men nowadays who have owned up to the shame of these violations, many of whom have fought to be straight after all, as often as not succeeding in their efforts?

And back to the question of genes. With the infinite variety of men who engage in homosexual practices, from the most evidently effeminate to the hypermasculine types, how can one begin to identify the hereditary variables?

Alas, the quest to find out what really happened and why may be a misguided enterprise, like mining for fool's gold. What may matter most, psychotherapists have come to realize over the years, is not so much the reality of what took place in the past or the *causes* of a psychological trait or behavior. What counts is what

people feel, what they themselves *believe* about themselves deep
down inside—underneath their defenses. Whatever occurred in
fact, the majority of homosexual men think certain things about
themselves and those close to them and direct their desires accordingly.

For the most part, they do feel their fathers failed them. They
resent both their homophobia and their easier heterosexuality.
They envy the very fact that they had the wherewithal to make
them—to have sex with a woman and procreate. To be a father.
It would have been so much easier had they followed suit, but
they just couldn't. And then again, they wouldn't choose to do so.

And whatever the causes, it's penises not vaginas these gay
men want to be near so desperately. It's male genitals that arouse
them and that they dwell on in their imagination. At best, they're
ambivalent about women, especially their bodies. Yes, they may
at times want to drape women's limbs and dress their hair, even
themselves adopting female mannerisms, affectations of speech
and interests in the process. But when it comes to a "quivering
thigh, and the demesnes that there adjacent lie," as Shakespeare's
Mercutio (a man of questionable sexual drift) remarked, they
avert their gaze. Be it in horror (the fear of "being castrated" just
like her) or relative indifference.

Sometimes, a man like this takes the plunge and has sex with
a woman only to come up from the depths gasping for breath,
groping for an oar to hold on to and pull himself back to his
ship—a penis, that is, and its possessor. Induce or exhort a man
through therapy or persuasion to become heterosexual, and still
he must fight the urge to return to his sexual calling and the
soulmates who share it.

When such a man manages to make love to a woman, often
enough he makes a man of her. Her vagina scares him because it
evokes his early belief that women had penises once but got castrated somehow, and because he sees in her fate a further threat
to his masculinity. Consciously aware of the difference between
the sexes, still he looks for "phallic" women—women who either
act or look like boys with balls or those whom he can mold in his
imagination to fit the bill.

The illusions break down, however, when push comes to shove
in sexual intercourse. Even if he isn't "acting out" his unwanted
desires to be with another man, a man like this fantasizes himself
in the act. More often than not, as his penis disappears into the
dark unknown of a woman's body, he calls up obvious homosexual scenarios to help him prop up his performance.

He may love this woman in his own way—tender, maybe somewhat masochistic, not a little envious, and at times even amorous if haltingly so. But he can't stay with her for very long. She never really has him. She puts him off. His mind and body are elsewhere. With men. Because sex with a man means to be reborn. It's a survival jolt that is always with him.

Like the womanizer (Chapter 3), in fact, the gay man can't stick it out with a woman because he's afraid of losing himself and his balls in her—afraid of *being* her. With a woman, he might never get back to men. Where he belongs and who he is. At all costs.

. . .

Saturday at eleven-thirty A.M., "Patch" (Peter's term of endearment for Karen, his wife) rose, pulled her carryon from the overhead compartment, smoothed her cropped hair, straightened out her gabardine skirt, and made her way up the aisle of the Pan Am Shuttle. She hated being away for any part of a weekend, but the meetings had gone swimmingly. She had shot all the troubles that needed killing. She'd even managed a visit to her parents in Worcester. And Peter, dear soul, would be waiting to pick her up in their Saab 900, skis and all, bags carefully packed and loaded.

Yes, what a dear man, she repeated to herself, he never missed a beat. Two and a half years now, and the marriage still had its effortless quality. No fights. No demands. Neatness and punctuality, and from time to time a poem thrown in for good measure. He wasn't competitive the way some men might be, given her rapid rise at Simpson. Nor did Peter resent her frequent travel, merely welcoming the mileage-accumulation awards this garnered.

"Decent" sex, decent just like Peter himself—not that Patch cared all that much. She hadn't even minded when Peter, unable to go down on her, said she had a funny smell, initiating an extra visit to a puzzled gynecologist. And there were compensations. Unlike Bruce, her boyfriend before him and for a short time Karen's fiancé, Peter seemed to enjoy her being slight and pigeon-breasted. Boyish, he had said, cute and delightfully so, not quite formed. Hence her nickname, Patch.

And now he was waiting for her and going skiing with her. Good sport that he was, Peter had overcome his horror of chair lifts, disgust with the cold, and lack of surefootedness to plummet down the slopes, trailing a wife who had won at least her share of slalom medals in her day at the college where she and her future husband, then merely a friend, had first met. Catholic Youth had united them then, before the pair, each separately, had let their faith lapse.

Isn't it interesting, Karen further reflected as she strode toward the down escalator—coincidence, fate, timing? Just like "kissing cousins," they'd waited. There'd been Bruce in the meantime. And then she and Peter had gotten together at last. Petey and his Patch.

"Safe sex," Peter was muttering to himself as he examined his hand, trying to reassure himself. It was dark under the overhang at the airport's curbside waiting area even on a bright weekend morning. So he'd turned on the map light the better to see himself.

Like one of Caesar's "dumb mouths," a paper cut stared back at this Antony. Had any of Our Mystery Guest's bodily fluids seeped in between the cracks of Peter's permeable derma? Had he, for all his trepidation, become another HIV positive to be added to the list of the damned, and damning?

He'd called Jim, whom he'd met two years earlier on the first of his visits to Eros (last night's was perhaps the fifth), but he had not had the heart to ask him. Peter hadn't wanted to tell him about this daisy chain of betrayal, make his sweet lover fret because of his own hypochondria.

In a doctor yet! A no-nonsense "orthopod."

Yes, he loved Jim, whom he called his "mastress," understood his jealousy and so had taken a Dalmane instead. But the aftermath of these nocturnal emissions left him still in doubt.

The opening of the door stabbed through the veil of worry.

"Peter, didn't you see me?"

No, truly, he was preoccupied. "Sorry."

"Never mind." And in she bounced, kissing him on the cheek as she chucked her raincoat, one-suiter, and attaché case into the backseat. "Let's toot."

Peter pecked back. But what would they do that night? He teased:

"Peter pecked a Patch of pickled peppers."

Could he possibly find a reason to use a condom? Twelve hours later, and Sweet Patch had given him a quick but moist kiss on the cheek and then rolled over, drifting into sleep. Peter had then made a quick call to Jim from the kitchenette. Now, free to be with himself, he sat by the window in the couple's suite at the inn, surveying beyond the frost and icicles the brittle blanket of white on the bare branches of the trees and the star-speckled midnight sky. He felt relieved but, he concluded, lonely.

Karen had her period and hadn't wanted to make love after all, for which Peter was thankful. Jim hadn't suspected anything either. The softly sinking tone of his voice over the phone had felt gentle and reassuring as it always did. "Bye, Pete," it had concluded before the click, caressing him with the thought that people did love him.

But how come, Peter thought, he couldn't bring it all together? The pretty girl in the bed, the brown-eyed lover with his extraordinary physique and genuine solicitousness—how come he could feel no passion for either of them anymore? His intimates, his wife and the secret sharer—instead of desire, their presences evoked only remorse and, he noted, resentment. It was deeper than Peter liked to admit. He felt trapped by them and hated them. He felt guilty because of this and because, even when he didn't succumb to real temptation, still Peter sinned in his heart every minute of the day.

"Shit," he said into the darkness, sober now that his life had returned to "normal." Last night's fix would last him a month. He was nowhere near as compulsive about sex as Seth had been, whose anonymous excesses had finally infected him and two years after the ordeal had started, killed him last August. Seth had set upon this path a couple of years after initiating his college friend into the mysteries of gay love. And again, selfishly and ruefully, Peter was nonetheless grateful. But that stranger—why, he could've . . . Pete shuddered to think what that man, any man, might have done in the dark and what could have become of him.

So far he'd been lucky. Instinctively self-preserving, he had failed to relent, to give in to others' requests or to the depth of his own desires. In fact, Peter reminded himself, he stood more of a chance of getting sick from a patient, from a pinprick on the front line of duty. But how long could he forbear and hold out?

Nor had his worlds collided. There were attendings and other residents in his program, Peter knew, who were not what they pretended. Some definitely gay, others suspect. (Like that Sapperstein in urology—he was sure she was butch!) Yet he had encountered none of his colleagues in his midnight comings and goings. Not so far.

The clock clicked as it showed twelve. Peter got up from his solitude, lifted the comforter, and slid into bed behind the curve of his Patch's sleeping back. Seen from that angle, she could have been anything—boy, girl, anything. After a final glance at the skis and poles propped against the wall, the boot bags and parkas, he closed his eyes and waited for sleep.

He'd always known he was gay, Peter reiterated to himself. At fourteen he had once masturbated with the peculiar fantasy of ejaculating into a life-size woman doll. He'd dated. But the sexual part turned him off.

Peter had even thought of becoming a priest, thinking it was the flesh, sex in general, which put him off. Not so. He'd always been drawn to men though he didn't want to be—to images of their torsos, buttocks, rods, and balls. While other guys looked at the stats in *Sports Illustrated*, Pete found his attention riveted by the bods.

Not that his father would even have noticed, he reminded himself, beginning the long litany of familiar laments. Why, he never showed him how to throw a football or even ride a bike. He was always out, golfing with the boys, or fucking some bimbo! Etc. Etc. Ugh, what difference does it make now anyway! Peter exclaimed to himself sotto voce, having bored himself, and blew his nose.

Alone in the bed beside Patch, Peter called up pictures from the night before, trying to reverse the morning-after blues with little jolts of eroticism. In the flickering rays from the projector's light, through which the film's images had made their way invisibly to the screen, he had caught sight, he thought, of the stranger's face—lined, he realized now—and his hair, salt-and-pepper. Jeez, the guy was old. Remembering their parallel sex play, their transient and tandem entwining of body parts, Peter reached his hand down to touch himself. Resting it on his crotch, he slowly fell asleep.

• • •

And what about the dialogue again and the ways in which women collude with men's misuse of them? What about the women with whom the gay man tries to "get it on"? What do they get out of it?

A man's secret sex life may not be so obvious. But then again, whether or not they conform with stereotypic preconceptions, homosexual men do reveal the telltale signs of their more or less hidden persuasions. They may act like "regular guys" much of the time—except when it comes to sex.

Gay men, as I've said, tend to be either indifferent to heterosexual sex or openly turned off by women's bodies, and especially by the ways in which these respond when aroused. Vaginas and vaginal secretions usually repel them. (It is a matter of degree, of course. Heterosexuals can also be ambivalent early on about women's vulvas—their odors, aura, etc. Yet, if a man is fundamentally heterosexual, his urge to enter her will overcome the vestiges of castration anxiety evoked by a woman's "penisless" anatomy.) Whatever the conflicts that are activated, the bottom line is that gay men tend to shun sex with women. When they do it, they may try to get it over with fast. They may seem passive, finicky. Blocked.

If she's tuned in to what is taking place in the act of sex, a woman will pick up on the "vibes" her partner gives off. The trouble is, many women are not in fact attuned to the ins and outs much less the nuances of the heterosexual encounter. Skittish themselves, they may also be *disassociated*, "spacey." They may be vague about who is doing what to whom much less about what they or their partners are experiencing.

Women have their own conflicts about men and sex to contend with, and because of their problems, some women may welcome a lover who isn't quite there, whose masculinity and libido are lacking, blunted, even suspect. Some such women find men like these less threatening than what they see as their boorish, aggressive, slam-bam-thank-you-ma'am counterparts. Consciously or unconsciously, they may have sought men who aren't so male or obviously sexually so. Until the last decade at least, their husband's or boyfriend's homosexuality might even have come as a relief from the "insensitivity" and "bludgeoning demands" other men seem to have made on them.

Sometimes without ever knowing it, women like these may enjoy taking charge. They like wearing those proverbial pants in the relationship, being the "ballsier" of the two.

There are periods in their lives, especially in their adulthood, when a variety of women tend to surround themselves with non-heterosexual men. They can snuggle, giggle, and even flirt with these guys without any real "threat" of going "too far." Not prepared for sex as yet, younger women may rehearse for the real act with men who seem safer because they're disinclined to go all the way. Later on, homosexual men, who often share women's interests in fashion, design, and the more sensuous and finer things in life, may still serve as undemanding companions for women who, more comfortable now with their sexuality, have also become more used to "real" men.

Their more superficial gentleness and their aesthetics may make homosexuals appear to be more apt soulmates than their rough-and-ready counterparts. What such women may not see so clearly is the hostility toward them when it comes to their sexual needs and anatomy. A smoldering misogyny is sometimes concealed by its apparent opposite. The gay man may be fascinated with the trappings of femininity, but not its essence.

Moreover, were she to acknowledge her conflicts about men and sex, a woman would have to call into question her own sexual "adequacy." So she tends to repress her ambivalence, paying her own lip service to normal heterosexuality but choosing partners who share her desire for her as a woman. Hers is also a compromise, one that helps to keep her from knowing the truths of her heart, and his. Such a woman ends up colluding with her man's deceptions, aiding and abetting his duplicities and the secret sharers of his body and soul.

• • •

Whussh. Crunch. Whussh and crunch. Karen glided and carved her way down the north face with a speed that propelled her well past the other experts, streaking beyond them, leaving them like flies on a window screen. She remembered the feel of the slapping of the gates and flags, as if whipping her for her prowess, as she had won that last qualifying heat nearly five years earlier.

Bruce had been waiting at the bottom of the mountain. He had made a great show of applauding her time. But that night he had virtually raped her, skewering her from behind as if she were a thing or a dog to be fucked into submission, after all.

As always, Karen had gotten up and brushed herself off, going on to take second place the next day before telling him it was over between them. Besides, by then Peter had reappeared in her life.

She was flying to him, through him, Karen imagined, as she pictured Peter waiting for her just inside the main lodge. A fleeting look at her watch as she continued her descent told her that ski school would be twenty minutes over by the time she concluded her run. He'd have a hot chocolate in hand, maybe a nice funny story or two about his and his classmates' misadventures, and certainly some apt compliments on her grace. How slender she was in her one-piece.

Without warning, surges of adrenaline kicked in to dislocate her reverie. Karen had been suddenly and uncharacteristically upended, catapulted into the air by some abrupt impact on her and by her momentum. A blur of white and the broken patterns of colorless trees filled her purview, replacing the pictures in her mind's eye. Gravity slammed her rudely into the snow. Something solid had thudded into her downhill ski, she reckoned as she lay supine like an incongruous cockroach on a hillside.

And Karen was right—she didn't make simple mistakes. Twisting, she caught sight of a black tube, some kind of cable probably, protruding through the granular snow like the coils of an insidious snake.

"What is that goddamned thing doing there!" she said out loud. Well, never mind. She'd be a little late, that's all, a little wet, too.

About to right herself, Karen pressed into the snow with the palm of her right hand only to be confronted with a stabbing pain. She pulled off her glove and discovered that her thumb was not where it should be.

Okay, it wasn't the first time. And Peter could fix that. It was his job.

Grabbing both poles in one hand, Karen slipped into her bindings, noted the site of the treachery, and proceeded down the mountain, slowly and cautiously this time. Peter's picture had faded further into the background. Karen didn't want to complicate matters by being responsible for any further damage to herself. She was thinking of lawsuits. What Karen still didn't see, of course, were the hidden and even greater dangers closer to home.

• • •

The heterosexual community's hostility toward gay men and women and their persecution of them—Oscar Wilde comes quickly to mind—are familiar to us all. The very existence of homosexuality seems to subvert the sexual order. Not only does it call into question the masculinity of the heterosexual; it also threatens to undermine the inevitable interdependence and uneasy alliance of male and female, the tense truce the two sexes have arrived at in order to "use" each other for the purpose of love and procreation.

But for their part, homosexuals also fear and hate heterosexuals. Years of persecution have left them bridling, at times thirsting for revenge. They begrudge heterosexual men their ability to perform with and enjoy women and to complete themselves with them. Women, in their turn, figure not only as the mothers who may have manipulated them with premature seductions—tantalizing at first but ultimately humiliating—but also as rivals for the hearts of men. Real live women are, after all, more of what men,

men like their fathers, want than any male pretender could hope
to be for all his affectations. And so the gay man despises not only
the individuals who loathe him but these precincts from which he
has been excluded.

And fate.

Just as they were gaining a measure of acceptance, of coex-
istence, AIDS—what was called the gay plague until it made
more and more inroads through drug abuse into the inner city—
came crashing down as an ironic and hideous reminder to homosexual men that theirs was the "sick" lifestyle after all. Forced out
of collective action and into silence, intimidated and exiled from
normal life once again, left without a leg to stand on, sexual
pariahs, not a few of these men found the fires of old hates being
rekindled. Once more, many asked themselves, why should we be
made to suffer for an act of nature? Why should the straight world
have it easier—always?

A time bomb is ticking away, and the "safety" of men like
these, whatever their conscious good intentions, is an illusion.
They are, as I've emphasized, men, too—endowed therefore with
the aggression that seems to go along with being male and asserting a man's prerogatives. However docile and compliant some of
them may seem on the surface, when it comes to matters of the
heart, and of sex, homosexual men are not "pussies" or push-
overs. They are certainly no more benign than their heterosexual
brothers.

Like all men, these men can exploit their potential for violence
to reassert their sexual identity. For the gay as well as the straight
man, being male can mean causing harm.

The new curse on them has also provided the gay man with a
new weapon. It's one he may or may not use, consciously or
unconsciously, on a "partner," that is, one who stands in for the
mother who led him on and who personifies the society that has
cast him out.

Beware then. As one patient who came to me put it—a man
who had struggled to do what the experts had told him, namely go
straight, but whose sexual appetites and compulsions proved
stronger than his power of will, a man who had married a wife and
fathered a baby, a sexually active homosexual man, who had been
declared HIV positive—as he aptly said: "Now I have a gun
between my legs."

• • •

It was another year before Peter told Karen the truth, ten months after the chief resident in orthopedics had cut away her cast to expose a perfectly mended thumb. His more frequent midnight strolls, the times he didn't answer the phone while she was away and other lapses—all these had already roused her suspicions.

So did all the silent phone calls—the brief voiceless intervals before the concluding clicks during which Karen discerned a slight expulsion or inhalation of air, telling her someone was on the other end, disappointed by the sound of her voice. Karen had now and then thought about Peter's having an affair, though he hardly seemed to have enough libido left over for another woman. What she couldn't know was that Peter had also broken off contact with Jim, his erstwhile lover.

When Peter told Karen he was gay, and no longer chose to live a lie, it fell into place. No, she didn't want to admit that she had fallen for a homosexual, raising, as this revelation did, all her old doubts about her femininity. And she was angry at the betrayals and deceptions. Still the news came as a relief. There was time to pick herself up yet again and dust off the debris. And she wondered, had she ever been in love with him anyway?

She'd get herself some professional help. Her sister-in-law's brother Chuck had referred her to a *woman* therapist. She might even find a new man—older, more fatherly, maybe. Like the gorgeous Cummings guy whose deal she was helping to put together.

And yes, Peter reassured her, she was safe—protected, clean, out of harm's way. So far he'd tried nothing truly dangerous. He'd even had himself tested for the virus just in case, with negative results.

It's just that he could offer no guarantees for the future. Even if he continued in his contortions, there might be lapses—and he dared not take responsibility for jeopardizing the goodwill and physical health of an innocent and nonconsenting adult. He'd thought, too, about giving up a specialty that involved surgical procedures—with the specter of that fateful slip of the scalpel or needle and the commingling of body fluids that had best be kept apart. He just couldn't trust himself anymore, Peter added, and he would rather die than have others trust him.

He did love her, she noted, in his muted and, yes, nonsexual way. As always, Peter was a "decent man."

He'd had a dream the night before, he went on, that night he finally moved out. In it he'd walked in the darkness toward an electrified fence that, in his associations to it, reminded him of a burning cross. Envisioning himself in the scene, feeling his way into it, he'd found himself more afraid of being alone than of searing, aching death that seemed imminent. He was struck by the fact that in the dream nobody had followed or preceded him in his dreadful journey. Peter was on death row. Condemned. It had been a rarity—a nightmare with a cast of one.

Having said this much, and having promised to clarify their living and financial arrangements, Peter rose from the couch in the living room that he and Patch had begun to put together perhaps three or so years earlier. Glancing at their picture on the end table—from yet another ski vacation—he walked to the front door, opened it, and eased it shut behind him. Separated by its metal structure, as by all the less tangible barriers and gulfs between them, he and Patch were now on their own.

· · ·

Vive la différence? In fact, even for most men and women this sentiment proves only half-true. Threatened by women, all men would at times like to do without their "better half." Homosexual wishes and feelings are one expression of the negative side of a universal ambivalence, and of a longing cast in sexual terms to be intimate with members of the same sex. Since a male's development is not a linear process, no man ends up completely "straight."

All men, in fact, have had doubts from time to time about being "queer," particularly in their adolescence. In other males all find the idealized and desirable embodiment of themselves as well as the father whose body was forbidden to them on so many counts. The prospect of sex with a person of the same gender can also hold out the promise of crossing over the boundaries of gender—in a man's case of playing with the tabooed feminine aspects of his sensuality. Homosexual wishes are natural, healthy components in all of us.

Still this can be very scary. Having such passing fantasies means being homosexual to most men. And this, in turn, means not being men. Out of fear, in what has been called something of a "homosexual panic," heterosexual men reject the inevitable "bisexuality" in their constitution—and by extension, in others. Often they retreat into a caricature of masculinity and a hostile "homophobia." If such wishes are to be expected, so, too, are the anxieties and defensive postures they mobilize.

Others, who may have consciously flirted with affectionate

and even sensual feelings for their fellow males, ultimately discard their homosexual desires. They do so before they discover that however much they may also resent it at times, the differences between men and women are exactly what they crave. They may resent a woman's ability to provide what a man lacks—breast, vagina, womb, along with the sensibilities and attributes that seem to go along with a person's sexual anatomy. They may envy her ability to make babies. They may begrudge a woman her ability to arouse, satisfy, and control them as no one else can. They might like to live without her. But they can't. Besides, these men find that the best way to enjoy being womanly is to do so vicariously, empathizing with a woman's body and emotions as if they were their own. Only in her presence do they find completion, calm, fulfillment. Being a caricature of her doesn't do the trick.

One patient of mine, a heterosexual young man struggling like so many people with his fears of rivalry with other men and curiosity about homosexuality, said that sometimes he thought that it might be better to spend his life not with a woman, whom he felt to be more irrational and emotional by nature, but with another man like himself. Were it not for AIDS, he would have tried his luck and at least experimented with sex with other men. But then he thought, "The hairy chest, the penis and balls—why, I already have these. How boring! It's something else I want."

This "something else" frightened him, however, moving him to retreat from sex with his wife. Unable to penetrate her much of the time, he preferred to pleasure himself instead, masturbating to the tune of thinly disguised "homoerotic" fantasies. But this brings us to the subject of the next chapter: the persistent sex failures that can compromise the love lives of even the most loving men.

5

Whiter Shades of Pale: The Sex Failures

Understanding the sexual failures that can compromise the erotic and thus emotional lives of so many men requires that we turn our attention not only to men's "libido," sexual identity, and capacities for intimacy but also to the activities in which these emotional qualities and characteristics find concrete expression. Before we can appreciate the anxieties that can inhibit it, we must scrutinize the sex itself. And sex, real sex, is a subject about which most people are reticent, including the practitioners whose job it is to hear and talk about it.

Kinsey, whose work I mentioned in the previous chapter, was the first investigator who asked people to describe actual sex. Nor did the biologist and his collaborators confine their questions to fantasies, childhood imaginings, and so on—the sort of things psychoanalysts had been inquiring after for the fifty years before the survey came out. Rather it was real-life *sex* practices in adulthood that concerned them.

Not satisfied with secondhand descriptions, twenty years after Kinsey's report appeared, St. Louis researchers and sometime spouses William Masters and Virginia Johnson instructed their

Missouri subjects: "Show me!" First it was prostitutes who were studied. But in time staff members, medical students, and other more respectable subjects—312 men and 382 women—were selected from over 2,500 volunteers.

One by one, and two by two, they marched into Masters and Johnson's lab, readily stripped, let themselves and their organs be weighed and measured, and had at it in one way or another. Under objective and inquisitive eyes, these cooperative people were examined macro- and microscopically as they masturbated, had intercourse, and engaged in a variety of erotic acts in order to demystify the subject and get at the truth about *The Human Sexual Response*.

And a number of misconceptions did, indeed, fall by the way-side as a result of these direct observations and the book that appeared in the late sixties. For instance, rather than a sharp distinction between the two, the researchers found that vaginal and clitoral orgasms exist in a continuum. Direct stimulation of the latter organ often proves to be a precondition for climax. No clitoral contact—or no clitoris for that matter (Chapter 13 discusses such tribal rituals)—no pleasure!

So there was no such thing—to quote Woody Allen's *Manhattan*—as the *wrong* kind of orgasm. Many women were thus spared at last all the demeaning labels—"abnormal," "inadequate"—inflicted on them by psychoanalysts, even by women clinicians such as Helene Deutsch. (See Chapters 1 and 3.)

And men—they found comfort, too. Their age-old worries about penis size were dismissed as well. If you were small before you got excited, Masters and Johnson found, tumescence proved to be the great equalizer. The larger a man's phallus when flaccid, the less it expanded in erection. Men with smaller equipment in an unaroused state could enjoy the power of being turned on to double the length and width of their genitals. In their first tome, Masters and Johnson seemed almost reluctant to discuss penis size at all, ponderously reiterating just how hard it was to get an accurate measurement of the organ at the height of its tumescence. And as if deferring to their male readers' "castration anxieties," later sex guides also tended to omit such statistics altogether, pretending to take for granted those proverbial "six inches" and underplaying all the individual differences.

And when men and women came together in intercourse, the length of a man's penis proved immaterial as far as the mechanics of climax were concerned. Only the outer third of the vagina had sufficient nerve endings to respond to stimulation anyway. So width was more crucial than length. Besides, since it was the clitoris that proved most sensitive, the dimensions of a penis had little to do with the technique of setting a female orgasm in motion.

In this vein, the standard missionary position, with a man in the "superior" stance, often proved least satisfying. Women did best on top, researchers found, often also requiring more rotating and grinding than thrusting along with a good deal of manual and/or oral stimulation. Once again, then, the power of the penis to penetrate didn't seem all that vital.

So much for your cocks, the modern-day sexologists seemed to proclaim repeatedly, toppling men's "phallocentric" views of sex. Women had long been less fixated on their genitals per se, enjoying the surfaces of whole bodies and the people wrapped in them. Now men were to follow suit and expand their sensuality.

Sex. Sex. Sex! By the seventies and early eighties, the media now trumpeted everybody's right to a good time in bed. *The Joy of Sex, The Sensuous Woman,* and *How to Make Love to a Man* rivaled Julia Child's *Mastering the Art of French Cooking* for places on the best-seller lists of how-to and self-help publications. By the eighties, Dr. Ruth, that incongruous minimaven on sensuality, made her way through the talk shows of radio and TV to the movies and even a short-lived sitcom of her own. Women's magazines now dealt with the topic in every issue gracing the newstand and the supermarket checkout lines.

RELAX, as the incandescent letters on those T-shirts in vogue a few years ago proclaim. "Don't worry, be happy!" advised the experts. And you men—take your mind off your cocks, and oppositional organs that they can be, unbidden, they'll do your bidding.

After all, a man who has to be a sex machine—as some try in fact to be—has problems now and then. And sometimes these are matters of opinion—like that of one couple who complained that the husband suffered from premature ejaculation, coming before his wife had had a chance to climax. Upon inquiry, it turned out that he would finally let himself reach orgasm after thirty, sometimes forty-five minutes of driving away to no effect.

For some men, however, sexual difficulties have become unmistakable and habitual. They are matters of course—personal norms and not exceptions to the rule. When a man is incapable of getting or keeping an erection; when he always or mostly ejaculates before giving a woman a chance to hold on to his penis for any reasonable if variable length of time; and/or when he doesn't feel physical pleasure, we can speak of at least a temporary sexual dysfunction. And when he has either suffered these "sex failures" for his whole life or at least, for a long time, either with every woman or with his primary partner (wife or girlfriend), then we can speak of persistent sex problems.

So, in the wake of the Kinsey studies and the new sexual environment, there grew up a whole new field of intervention—sex therapy. Spearheaded by Masters and Johnson and Helen Singer Kaplan, practitioners now began to treat sex not as an idea but as a behavior. They aimed to modify it where it didn't work by employing sex surrogates early on and then discarding this practice to rely on a couple's homework and talking cures instead.

In fact, the behavioral strategies advocated by the proponents of sex therapy have had some uncommonly quick and good results. Perhaps without understanding much beyond the physiology involved, nonetheless these behavioralists have given people permission to have sex, dwell on it, and discuss it openly. In the process they've gotten their patients—the men especially—to *experience* the sex act. In this state of receptivity and self-reflection, feeling fully, they can begin to treat themselves as truly sexual, or better, *sensual* beings—sometimes for the first time in their lives.

Busy as he had been, Congressman George Whitford from Georgia hadn't been able to do so. That is, not until Dr. Hyman Bassin got him to take a different view of his body.

   • • •

"Have you tried incest?" Dr. Bassin could feel his forehead reddening. "Er, I mean, incense."

Even shrinks made Freudian slips, he told himself in a vain effort at self-reassurance. But oh, boy, this was a bit too much! A congressman yet!

Besides, the guy had been referred by Uncle Milton, "The Great Uro Dr. Hurst." So it was the last referral he would want to mess up.

Had Dr. Hy Bassin been just a little less self-conscious at that moment, attuned to the two patients sitting across the desk from him, then he might have registered the two sets of no's that were barely discernible in the static of his mortification with himself. He would have realized that his faux pas had either passed unheard by George Whitford, U.S. House of Representatives, and his wife, Barbara, in a slip of their own, or had simply drifted by, graciously unacknowledged by them. The "incest," having been uttered, Hy would have understood, had never happened, falling on deliberately deaf ears.

His head swimming, Hy stared back at the two uncomprehending faces before him. The first thing he'd noticed about George was how powerful and anemic he seemed at the same time. A little ruddy now, creased and puffed with age, he had one of those D.C. bull necks, testimony to his weight-lifting days as a star fullback at Duke. His blond hair, whose boyhood hues had simply eased into gray, was slightly thinned and combed straight back to expose an expanse of brow, also basically pale but ever so slightly flushed. Light blue eyes gazed back from behind George's McNamara-style wire-frame glasses.

To Hy, born in Brooklyn thirty-eight years earlier, the fifty-four-year-old George Whitford was the quintessence of WASP. So was his wife. Did he call her Babs, Hy wondered, with her tiny neat face and likewise peppered but also flaxen hair pulled back in a sensible bun? She exuded Lord & Taylor, Hermès, Gucci, and a youthful indulgence now and then in the second-floor offerings of Ann Taylor. The kind of woman who used to be a "Peck and Peck Dame," in the words of Uncle Miltie.

Look-alikes—tall, refined, once enviable. But unlike Hy, who a generation ago would have felt inferior to them, people like the Whitfords couldn't use their physical assets, mobilize their resources, he went on in his head. All the TDs in the world hadn't helped George do what Hy did at least every other night.

So Hy thought, musing on until he realized that he'd been privately recovering his composure at the expense of his patients, by way of prejudice and meanspiritedness. Why, he reminded himself, he'd been reluctant to shake the hand of the great legislator (whose work and "balls" in the House he'd so long admired). He'd been afraid to reveal his own inadequacy by extending a moist palm.

Compassion was Hyman's business, and he had no business forgetting that his patients were his patients. George had a right to have a problem, and it was his job to help him. In this humbled and reflective frame of mind, Dr. Bassin then wondered why he had said the dreaded I-word, and why the Whitfords hadn't heard it.

"No," Barbara finally responded, punctuating the silence.

"Well, sometimes it helps, uh, establish a mood, takes one

away from stress and concern, makes one relax, takes you away from thoughts about a performance of any kind . . ." He couldn't end his sentence.

"Like *Scheherazade?*" Barbara inquired, instinctively helping Hy escape his awkwardness.

"Exactly."

It was an odd and maybe telling comment.

Still, Hy was grateful for her unflagging decorum as he stared ahead and beyond the people before him. As Barbara's smile lingered on her lips, he again wondered at George's inability to—

"But you see," Mrs. Whitford interjected, cutting the pause short and glancing tentatively at her husband in an unspoken bid for permission to continue, "you see, Dr. Bassin, George hasn't been able to have, er, sustain an erection for over four years now."

She rested her hand gently on his without any effort to hide her affection. The Great WASP, the Lord High Legislator, returned her smile of comfort. A tear, unmistakable as such, had sprouted from the corner of his left eye and was wending its way down the congressman's cheek. It ran over his chin and onto that formidable neck, where its progress was finally halted by George's shirt collar.

There had been no effort to hide, and none at restraint. In this office at least, if the Representative's dick didn't stay stiff, then neither did his lip. So much for stereotypes, Hy again told himself. And rolling up his mental shirtsleeves, he went to work.

. . .

Probably all men have suffered from either impotence or premature ejaculation at one time or another. Alcohol, an occasional binge or a chronic indulgence, along with other abuses and perhaps necessary drugs and medications, may have, as the Bard put it, "provoked the desire" but "taken away the ability." So may have stresses, preoccupations, and disappointments left over from the job together with illnesses, losses, depressions, and momentary angers at the person who is also the object of one's lust.

A man may come too quickly when it's his very first time, when it's the first time with a new and exciting lover, or simply, when it's the first time in a very long time. Nor are his orgasms alike. Some take place as convulsive explosions, propelling a man's seed a goodly distance into the recesses of his lover. Others emerge as little trickles, ending the world of pleasure "not with a bang but a whimper." Occasionally a man may suffer from retarded ejaculation, remaining hard and thrusting away, giving his partner pleasure but never finding any consummation of his own.

And whatever actually happens to his body, there's a subjective element at play. No two ejaculations feel the same—however much many men would like to pretend that they are not as vulnerable to the capriciousness of emotion as are women, for whom different orgasms are commonplace. In fact, under certain conditions, some men may expel their semen without sensation, simply ejaculating without the valleys and peaks of a climax. Orgasm, the neurological response, and ejaculation, the physiological one, are not the same.

An odd thing, isn't it, with all those nerve endings and with God's gift to man before them, with the greatest of pleasures there to be had, just waiting to be claimed, free for the asking, and still so many men persist in depriving themselves of all this voluptuousness? Why would a "body" *want* to act like that?

The sexologists like to explain sexual inhibitions mostly in terms of men's anxiety about performing. Men are afraid they can't handle the situation, that they'll never rise to the occasion. Too nervous to stay hard or hold on, they become shrinking violets of the male variety. In time, such men create self-fulfilling prophecies. They become like baseball pitchers who self-consciously aim the ball and tense up, losing their natural rhythm and missing the strike zone, after all. Take their minds off their performance, and their penis, and they'll find themselves doing just fine.

Rationalized in this way, the tactics the sex experts have devised have another impact, it seems to me. In deemphasizing the work involved, the activity in sex, these techniques further compel men to tolerate and indeed dwell on their *sensuality*. Not only does the authority of the therapist give them permission to be sybaritic, he or she *demands* that the patient play the hedonist. Being sexual has for many men been confused with being Marlboro Man— powerful and aggressive. Sensual pleasure has been unconsciously equated with sissy stuff, effeminate and babyish.

Consider the tried-and-true method for dealing with impotence. Lie around, the sex therapist enjoins his patients, enjoy your bodies—exploring the tingling eroticism and tender comforts of stroking and being stroked just about everywhere. Everywhere that is, except there. There's much more to sex than genital prowess. Don't focus on the power of your penis and your erections.

In fact, even though you may under these unpressured con-

ditions get the erection you've been looking for, refrain from coming. Yes, eventually you may let your genital organ enter the fray
and have some fun, as well. After all, it does have a right to a life,
too. But still, hold back your expressions of excitement for several
such encounters. Restrain yourself until at last you can no longer
fail to satisfy your urges and move on to what Masters and
Johnson dubbed the phase of "ejaculatory inevitability." Feel before you leap.

Exercises like these allow men "not to be men" for a while.
They create interludes during which men can immerse themselves
in the tactile sensations, the eroticism of the skin, the whole-body
pleasures women are used to. Scared of women, afraid that being
physically close to them will make men like them, that they will be
unmanned in the very act of sex, sexually inhibited males thus
begin to learn what it feels like to be otherwise. It's almost as if
they'd stopped having a penis for a little while, in the process of
permitting themselves to be pleasured, to get where they have
given.

Being passive in being made love to is not what a woman is all
about sexually, of course. But to the extent that a *man* believes
this, caricaturing a woman as a passive and/or merely receptive
sex object, he becomes desensitized to his deepest dread. Men,
he's thought, are supposed to "get horny" but not "feel sexy"—
not really. They're not supposed to give up control and be done to.
But now he can do all this, do nothing, just be—forgetting the
"job" at hand—and still reemerge as a man, balls and all.

Scared of being caressed, squeezed, and aroused, men are also
guilty about being made love to. At some level, lying there naked,
being touched and feeling stimulated all the while by a woman
who is his peer harkens back to his earliest sensual encounters
with his mother. Yes, when he made that slip of the tongue, Hy
was on the mark, after all.

Nursed, wiped, bathed, dried, every nook and cranny of his
body inspected and tended to, as a little boy he got involuntary
erections, which came to nought. Either these were simply ignored, or he was reprimanded for them. Overstimulated as a boy,
he found himself increasingly anxious about the *incestuous* implications of his penis's getting hard in his mother's presence. Not
that he knows all this of course—the sexually inhibited man just
finds himself going dead.

The sex therapist instructs the impotent man to be a pre-
adolescent and rather androgynous child again. Asking him to stay

still and toy with being "feminine," he or she also commands the male patient to be a "mama's boy." In this way—and remember how much the therapist becomes invested with authority—he or she simultaneously addresses two of his patient's competing needs. At the same time that they reveal to him their origins in the sensuousness of his childhood relationship with his mother, the therapist's instructions echo his guilt over getting aroused under such charged circumstances. In his *behavior*, rather than in his words and recollections, the dysfunctional male can thereby partly relive and re-solve his incestuous conflicts. All along he's been unconsciously attacking himself for these wishes by denying himself the gratifications to which he as an adult is entitled. To some extent, the therapist, in directing him *not* to consummate his desires, relieves him of the burden for self-punishment and deprivation by temporarily depriving him and punishing him from the outside.

A therapy session like this is rather like a confessional: sin is inescapable, so do some penance and you can get on with your life. Give up something desired for the duration, and the resurrection will come. You'll get that erection and ejaculate properly after all.

Perhaps nowhere is the punishment provided clearer than in the most effective tactic devised to deal with premature ejaculation. Just as a man is on the verge of coming, his partner (sometimes the patient himself) is instructed to squeeze the penis right below the glans—firmly and unequivocally. With this the urge to expel semen is halted while simultaneously the man's hard-on is maintained, permitting him to continue with intercourse steadily but less urgently.

In part, the patient's diminished erotic frenzy is due to the physiology involved—to the impact of the "squeeze technique" on blood flow and nervous excitation. Psychologically, however, there's also a clear message here: "Don't come, you naughty boy!" At one level, his partner admonishes the prudish child in the man, who believes that all sexual satisfaction is inherently "bad."

Yet at another and more mature level, the message is that, indeed, it *is* too soon. For me. Confused by their conflicts, dysfunctional men are unable to tune in to their own bodies much less their partners' needs and feelings. When it comes to sex, it seems people, even people who should know better, can find themselves utterly at sea. And thus a colleague of mine, teaching the human sexuality course at one of the country's preeminent medical schools, found that his students—among the top nurses, residents, and attending physicians in the nation—simply forgot what he'd taught them from one lecture to the next. Conversant with the intricacies of cell biology and with every bone in the human body, nonetheless when it came to sex, they simply couldn't remember what went where and with what and what they and everything did. As one resident, a woman this time, put it after reviewing the controversy about vaginal and clitoral orgasms, "Somehow, I just can't put my finger on it."

Neither could George.

• • •

He'd been married to his beloved Barbara for over thirty years and had fathered their two children with her but had yet to find her clitoris. Now, his wife had had her inhibitions at the outset of their life together and had called "touching like that . . . dirty." Maybe Southern WASPS, and ex-magnolia-queens in particular, weren't supposed to do that sort of thing.

But Barbara's strictures eased over time. Feeling more womanly, she wanted more, and still George couldn't handle it. He had to admit to himself and to all three of them, now that Dr. Bassin had entered the scene of their sex life, that, in his kids' lingo, he was "pretty uptight and spaced-out."

The odd thing was, George was certainly no stranger to female genitalia—human, animal, and he tried to add with a chuckle, "otherwise." He'd been the principal caretaker of the family farm beginning at eleven (three years after his father had abandoned the family). So he was conversant with the breeding of horses, dogs, cattle, chickens, and other of the farm's more haphazard denizens. Nor had George's mother been any too modest about her body. Well, there was hardly much room for privacy there in that ramshackle house—"and she, uh, never even tried to cover herself up . . . even after Dad left."

There was the communal kitchen tub whose tepid and increasingly murky water she typically shared with the two boys in descending order of age. And once or twice, at night and after she'd caught the glow from the bourbon that was Betty Sue's sole solace, she'd gone skinny-dipping with her sons, George and Timmy.

George recalled trying not to see and not to look when this first Mrs. Whitford took off her clothes, exposing the dark and misty outlines of her private parts. A couple of years into his individual treatment, he would later recall the time she bent over and his gaze fled in horror from the sight of what looked like a wound, a gash between her legs.

The sight was scarier for him than for other kids, he later understood, because of everything else that was going on. But all he'd been aware of then and now was how much her uninhibited behavior inhibited him.

Timmy. He'd always been a problem—the proverbial younger-brother syndrome. George's escalating successes seemed to leave the younger Whitford repeatedly and then chronically dispirited. Moreover, without a father around, Tim had nobody to turn to or to take him in hand, try as George might to fill in the gaps.

George had berated himself for his inconsistency in acting as his brother's keeper. He seemed always to be looking over his shoulder from the end zones of life as the pudgy and floppy little guy failed to get off the bleachers of the local football field. While George proceeded from four-letter man to Duke and football fame to Rhodes Scholar to law review to state legislature to the U.S. House of Representatives to the chairmanship of three committees and now to the prospect of a vice-presidential candidacy or cabinet post (the Senate seats were still locked in)—and from courtship to marriage to fatherhood to grandparenthood—Timmy Boy lagged more and more behind, sinking deeper into the morass. "Jus' like a pig in shit," he'd been fond of saying on nights when that same bourbon that did in their mother and father had swelled his eyes and slurred his speech into an unintelligible whine.

First Tim had turned not only to the sauce but also from girls to boys—yeah, real little ones—and thereby earned his first stint behind bars. More followed when Timmy tried to buoy up the sinking resources he'd gotten from George but then squandered them on a variety of schemes and self-indulgences with more of the same—embezzlements, scams, and other maneuvers that carried him beyond decency and into the arms of the law.

Four and a half years before George and Barbara consulted Milton Hurst and then Hy Bassin, Timmy Whitford, aged forty-seven and weighing 239 pounds, had expired. Gallbladder and liver, bloated and inflamed as the wages of sin, had been implicated as the causes of his passing. But to his older brother, as to the few remaining relatives of theirs scattered about, it seemed that Timmy simple rolled over at last and died.

A little arithmetic along with common sense served to date

George's absolute impotence from the period of mourning follow-ing his younger brother's death. And indeed, consciously if irra-tionally, he had felt guilty.

But it was George's father, Hank Whitford, who had in reality given his superstar son the hardest time. That is, on those few occasions when he saw him following that unceremonious leave-taking in the wee hours of the morning when six- and eight-year-old boys were still abed. He was another "damned drunk." Once Hank had shown up in the locker room after the last regular-season game of George's junior year at Duke. He was blotto—loud and obnoxious—but had managed to talk his way through the guards, ostensibly to "congratulate the great kid who was the first fruit of my loins."

Barbara was waiting outside, George remembered. And so the minute he heard from behind him that slobbering, preverbal, guttural farting sound of his father's voice (etched in his memory of childhood nights despite the infrequency of their later encoun-ters), he had frozen in fear. This scene was bad enough. But suppose the old bum then revealed himself to Barbara when George had yet to tell her about him—unable as he had been to divulge his sordid origins to her.

"Oooo, you little fucker," Hank snarled. "You did it, didn't you. Broke a record! An' now you're gonna take that little blondie hanging outside the door and sock it up her pussy before she knows what fer."

How did he know!

Hank's breath, hot and smelling of golden bourbon and yel-low belches, had caught George's neck from behind. George felt a surge of fear, greater by far this time than any trepidation he had had that day as he had danced about Auburn's massive linemen. The bruises and gashes where the ground and the cleats had caught him stopped hurting now, replaced by the pain of his father's presence and the ache of remembrance. Before George could turn, he felt a hand, clawlike, reaching, it seemed, for one awful moment, up his rear.

Obscenities and towel snappings are commonplaces of the showers. But in this instance, everyone in the place seemed to sink into stunned embarrassment and gape at the confrontation taking place between father and son.

George had just undressed. His pads and uniform a grimy heap of sweaty rubber and cloth at his feet, his body stained with dirt, blood, and sweat, he had been standing there in only his cup.

And now his father was yanking at one of the jock's straps, leaning back against it as he pulled. When at last he let it go, the elastic snapped back into place, spanking his big son's backside and making a cracking sound that seemed to reverberate off the metal locker doors and offend the ears of each of his hitherto thankful and admiring teammates.

Ol' Hank Whitford, suddenly deprived of his ballast, had himself fallen back and down, crashing into the benches and onto the floor. Cackling throughout, he didn't notice at first that the pint bottle secreted in his raincoat pocket had been smashed as a result of the impact. Booze bled out of him and down his pants.

"Get out, you bastard," George had wanted to hiss. Instead, he reached under his father's armpit and hoisted him to his feet with one sweep of an arm.

"Too much for the ol' man—what'll Mom say," George said. And for further effect, he deliberately turned to his silenced audience and grinned, working up a laugh from the pit of his stomach until his teammates followed suit—blocking, once more running public and private interference for the star they at least had grown to love.

That was the night he told Barbara his story. She would have heard about the commotion, he reckoned, so he might as well get it over with.

In fact, Barbara offered to "comfort" him, nestling into her boyfriend's neck with that cool, calm sweetness of hers. George had turned down the offer, sticking by his resolve to wait out the year and a half till they were married.

Anyhow, George had never been free with his body, as jocks were supposed to be. Instead of breaking training to make the rounds of the bars, mostly George hung back. Or he took walks with the girl who by the end of sophomore year won his heart. He went to church.

Once his friend Mackie had taken him to the local cathouse. After much work on both their parts, George and his bed partner—a big-breasted Cajun with a muffled, honking voice—managed to get it on. And in. But when his penis plunged into her vagina, George felt nothing.

Even when he came, he couldn't feel a thing.

• • •

In addition to everything else, men fail sexually, failing their partners in the process, because they're angry at women. They have felt tempted by them, teased, betrayed, seduced, and abandoned, smothered and let down their whole lives from boyhood on by the female sex.

It's inevitable to be frustrated in these ways even by the best of mothers, who stimulate a boy's desires simply by tending to his physical needs and by being there. In some instances, however, this sort of tantalizing crosses the boundary into the realm of deliberate cruelty.

When a man gets a woman into bed, the opportunity's there not only to tender his love but to exact his revenge. Unconsciously, a sexually inhibited man like this often wants to skewer his adult lover because of injuries long past and forgotten but *transferred* onto their relationship as if it were yesterday. Yes, they'll give it a try, still choosing women over other men, unlike their homosexual counterparts. But when it comes to sexual union, they'll retaliate by teasing them—as they once felt cockteased—and then letting them down.

But rather than become a sadist, rapist, or sexual aggressor of any kind, the sexually dysfunctional man becomes *passive aggressive* instead. His dysfunction represents an unconscious effort to reconcile his vindictiveness with his guilt. His physiology expresses his conflicting feelings for him by stubbornly not doing what it's supposed to.

He doesn't realize any of this, of course. When it comes to sex, bodies—penises in particular—seem to have lives of their own. They can readily tune them out as if "they," their minds, didn't live there. Their anatomy and physiology tell men what they want even while they keep them from getting it.

● ● ●

A generation and a half later, George lay there, naked and on his side, facing the woman who had borne his two grown children, just as Dr. Bassin had instructed them to do. The first time they tried this, maybe three weeks earlier, George had felt like his baby granddaughter, what with his "slight pot an' all" reminding him of a little child's distended abdomen.

Then, too, after all these years toughing it out, he realized that he, like her, had so much to learn. So it made complete sense that he didn't quite know what was happening with his penis. It followed that he couldn't handle the sensations, purely physical but also so much more. More, well, emotional. He felt he was waking up.

He used to envy his younger cousin Lilly, who came to stay with him a few years before he left for college. She always knew what she wanted, and nothing stopped her.

Why, she even had the nerve back then, oh, a dozen years after he'd left, to up and marry a black man. A guy named Robinson. He was the younger brother of a black football player, Robinson again, who, people said, would've given George a run for his money if they'd played in the same high school league. That wouldn't have happened in those days, of course.

Well, anyway, this other Robinson gave Lil two kids before he died in that car wreck. After that, Lil moved up North first and then on to Europe. He'd heard she was married again and living back in the States. But they'd pretty much lost touch.

Why was it, "they" always seemed to be named Robinson? George was muttering into his head as he lay there—"free associating," a shrink would call it. Why, even the new head of the Mailman Center, where Barbara was on the board, was named Robinson. They couldn't all be members of the same family, now could they?

George caught himself. The vestiges of racism, never so deep in him anyway, embarrassed him. He saw how people used it— poor white trash like himself—to inflate themselves.

This sort of thing made him feel guilty. It was a guilt—genuine within another sphere of responsibility—that was more outside, somehow more real than the irrational self-oppression that haunted his sexuality. Yet here as there, for all his self-determination and willpower, he found himself a plaything of forces coming into him that he didn't understand. Now here he was again trying to wake up—with his body, as he had decades ago in his politics.

George'd been ashamed at first but had gotten used to it, even enjoyed all this child's play—just lying there, feeling. Among Congressman Whitford's assets had always been his willingness to listen and learn. Outside of sex, he could always take a lot in.

And now he stared at his sweet Barbara, nude like him save for her pearl choker and wedding band.

While others on the Hill played the field, covering up their tracks the morning after, George had remained chaste and true. Once, on a Far East tour in Kyoto, he'd thought of joining his neighbor and fellow representative Burt Wilcox on an escapade at some so-called bathhouse. But when he got to the door, he turned back without a moment's hesitation, stopped in his tracks by two thoughts.

First, he wouldn't enjoy it even if he did manage to make it. Secondly, he couldn't bring himself to betray the woman who had simply saved his soul. Period.

Unusual, he mused, for a pol with his power. Or was the reverse the case—was it his strength that was so unanticipated?

Smiling her demure smile, Barbara rose to a kneeling position. She reached over George for Jergen's lotion on the night table, brushing over him with her body and its scent before returning to her haunches. Until this point, at least, George still felt that he had a mashed, maybe a half-baked, potato between his legs. But now her smell seemed to breathe a certain life into him.

"Ssssh," she whispered, and gently pushed against her husband's massive shoulder. He obeyed, rolling onto his back, wondering just for a moment whether it was his turn or Burt's to usher at church the next morning, nine hours later.

They had been forbidden to turn off any lights or close any eyes. So George stared up at Barbara as she squirted the contents remaining in the bottle onto her hands. She looked the way she had when at twenty-two she had tended to their daughter, Ellen, and now to her granddaughter.

George tried to banish incongruous or extraneous thoughts as she then began to apply the cream to his body, beginning innocently with that bull neck and forty-six-inch chest and moving down his abdomen across the hips that were beginning to grow ever so slightly arthritic, running over the great fire-hydrant quads to the knees crisscrossed with surgical scars and up again. Inward she went this time but assiduously avoided the lion that had slept so long.

One of her rings, the diamond maybe, which he had scrimped to buy her for their engagement long ago, danced across the seemingly empty bag of George's scrotum. He could feel a little stirring now, the head of the penis inching or, better, millimetering, its way to peek out of the foreskin. But just as soon as he began to feel aroused, another scene, some flashing tableau, a strobe from a poor white boyhood forgotten, took him from the room and from Barbara's touch.

He was in that kitchen tub, and Mother was reaching down to wash him. He could smell her now, the damp strands of her hair, the pungent odor of the soapy water drying on her skin. As she bent over, her son, maybe four—or was he older, seven?—could see her robe open to expose a breast, the nipple still engorged, dripping he now imagined with the milk on which Tim, at two, was still fed. She had reached down his then little body, slipping her hand and the washcloth across his dick almost as if to say that it didn't exist. Catching hold of something hard—yes, his prick— she had squeezed and moved on with a laugh.

Was he imagining all this? George wondered as he and his body, in unison now, shuddered and shrank. Had it happened? Or was it Tim, Timmy being fondled, not himself? Had he been the onlooker merely?

Now his thoughts ran to the besotted brother of their adult years, to the boys he had fondled, to the ugly spectacle of his indecent fate, one that George had escaped by just leaving a little bit of himself behind. Thank God for Aunt Alma and Uncle Bob and for the "something else" they had offered him. Thank God for Lil. Thank God for Barbara. Thank God for himself.

George felt a little push on his lower abdomen. He had closed his eyes, he realized, and as she'd been instructed, Barbara was applying pressure with the heel of her hand. Brought back from his reverie by her touch, George opened his gaze and stared up into her face. Yes, it was she—constant as always, there as before.

Reaching up, he took her head in his grasp, framing her face with those huge hands that held so many footballs, returning the caress and the contact. Imperceptibly, he began to stir again, though they both knew the resurrection, or the second coming— and would this were a pun—would not occur this night. They'd have to wait.

• • •

No, the backdrop for impotence is not always so dramatic as in George's case. Nor could he have attained such superstardom without brighter moments in his childhood—without those special gifts that set him apart and brought more uncomplicated joy into his life. There were also those relatives, teachers, coaches, who, responding to the promise that a boy such as Timmy failed to hold out, to George's undeniable golden-boy glow, who offered themselves to him as his models for more. And so he found and made his own fathers. Greedily, resourcefully, he devoured their moral and human goodness to fashion something for and of himself and to focus his aggression—thereby sealing his fate as a great man in the making.

It's just that George also bears the scars of his ascent out of ugliness. He carries the legacy of indecency and envy, the fear and guilt, the sequestered hatred of a man who was forced to leave behind a history of weakness. In men like this, strong for reasons no psychologist can quite explain even after the fact, isolated symptoms rather than his whole soul—problems in sensation and behavior rather than a compromise of character—betray the faults that lie beneath the surface.

Such men can and should modify their *behavior* in what is a hard-fought battle with unwanted and unknown parts of themselves. However, the psychoanalysts are right, and they can't really make these changes their *own* unless they also know who they are.

The trouble is, often they buy in to the Victorian myths about virgin-mother wives, to deny their mother's "whorish" sexuality. They reverse the reality of their childhoods. Believing sex and penises to be bad, instruments of male violence, they can conclude that their women don't want them. They can forget that their wives have erotic needs—which can't be denied.

• • •

It had been George's turn to usher after all. Or so he learned from Burt Wilcox in the back of Saint Bart's that sunny Sunday morning in March. Shaking his friend's hand, and exchanging broad smiles with him, George walked Barbara and him down the aisle and into one of the center pews of the still almost empty sanctuary. Burt and Barbara were both on the board of the Miami Mailman Center. George pivoted and departed, leaving his neighbor and his wife to sidle in and then chat with each other while he made his way to the back again to greet the congregation as they entered the chapel.

Burt had just returned from his annual stint of permit fishing and bonefishing in the Keys. His own strong hands—not a former footballer's mitts but the sinewy talons of an Ivy League baseball pitcher—were still dark and slightly parched from the reflected rays of the coral flats. He had rested both on his knees as he stared unwaveringly straight ahead, and at nothing in particular.

If one—Dr. Bassin maybe—had been studying him carefully, then perhaps this onlooker might have noted the slight twitch in the corner of an eyelid, the ever-so-slight start with which Wilcox registered the unseen stimulus.

Barbara's hand on his.

It had made its way in private across the slight span between the two of them to rest briefly but knowingly—she hesitated to think "reassuringly"—on top of the paw of her pleasure. She hated herself for even this memento of betrayal. But she'd needed that hand, which had known her so well, and which had so soon offered her what George could not.

It had given her what she had never had before. Not once in all the thirty-two years of marriage had she betrayed George until a late-winter evening almost exactly a year ago. A putative board meeting that never did happen, the roads between their houses covered with the remnants of the day's snow, had enabled that first night of simple abandon.

And then they'd done that site visit in Miami, and there'd been a second time—that deliciously sultry afternoon at Hawk's Cay. Well, she had been Bacall for a day! In toto, two half-days of joy, the joy of sex. It was "fine," she told herself.

She did not love him as she did George, whom she'd seen grow from boy to man, who had impregnated her, who had nursed her, as she had him, through the hard times of a long life. But yes, she had had to have him, this other man with the whispering hands. And even there—feeling desire and with God as her witness—Barbara felt no guilt. Merely this: the need to hide, to keep this part of herself from her husband, to spare him what he had secretly always feared.

• • •

It was time, Dr. Bassin told them the Tuesday following that Saturday night and Sunday morning, time for a change. He'd gone as far as he could working with them in "couples therapy." They were making progress, but they could do what they had to do on their own. Now George needed treatment, his own "individual" and in depth.

There were "secrets"—secrets he kept even from himself. So he was referring him on to Dr. Putnam, Valerie Putnam, psychoanalyst.

"Okay, all right with you?"

"Yes," George, never a docile man, agreed, "but Barbara needs someone, too."

• • •

Yes, wives can stray, too, and from marriages that have a lot going for them. Perhaps it is the frequency of infidelities that moved one psychoanalyst to borrow from Freud's famous book and refer to the adulterous affair as the "psychopathology of everyday family life." Women tend to "do it" when their husbands haven't been sensuous or even feminine enough in their lovemaking. Men wander for somewhat different reasons. But this takes us to the subject of our next chapter.

What Men Don't Want, II

Love Sickness

To have and to hold . . . For better or worse . . . Till death do us part.

So run our oaths of betrothal and our hopes for the future.

Men, decent ones at least, enter the covenant of marriage expecting to honor that contract and looking forward to a long life of togetherness. Yet often enough mounting resentments and dis-affections drive husbands into half-wanted love affairs. Nearly three-fourths of married men stray, according to the most recent estimates, with errant wives not far behind.

And if you think about it, all marriages are doomed to end unhappily. Either that inevitable death we owe nature lays claim to one of the partners, leaving in its wake for the survivor the voids of loss, loneliness, and mere memory; or more unexpectedly and precipitously, the bond may be stretched to the breaking point by an ambivalence that undoes those illusions of unwavering love with which most marriages begin. Unanticipated maybe, nonetheless divorce will bring to a close the marriages of at least 50 percent of today's newlyweds.

Both these circumstances, adultery and divorce, further serve to expose the vulnerabilities and hostilities beneath the surface lives of so-called normal family men. They are indeed instances of what Sigmund Freud once called the "psychopathology of everyday life" in contrast to the more extreme neurotic suffering described in the previous chapters. They tell us about ordinary men's needs of women and of their simultaneous desperation to wriggle free from women's hold on them and of the impulsive violence and emotional chaos that can emerge once those ties that bind have been severed forever. Finally, they reveal how easily the frightened little boy comes out of hiding once the trappings of adulthood have fallen away.

6
...

The Tryst Twist: An Affair to Forget

At least half of the husbands surveyed by Kinsey and others report having strayed at least once during the course of their married life, in contrast to a minority of married women.

Well, the truth is, nobody knows for sure. Whereas the statistics forty years ago had 50 percent of husbands admitting to adultery in contrast to 26 percent of the wives polled, more recent surveys have the figures growing—up to 72 percent with the gap narrowing between the sexes. Some, such as Shere Hite, believe that about as many wives have affairs as husbands, though her critics have faulted her methodology (her selection of subjects and use of questionnaires) and argued that even now many fewer women are unfaithful than men.

In all events, it becomes obvious that even married men who don't fit the criteria for womanizing (Chapter 3) have their lapses. In fact, both spouses may turn elsewhere for what they lost in the way of passion for each other. Usually they do so with guilt, with no intention of ending what they do have, and sometimes with the tacit intention to make the marriage work by salving their wounds and quelling otherwise unmanageable angers.

Maybe people live too long nowadays—too long together. Romance, the Bard along with Professor Freud reminded us, tends to be short-lived. It is one of those "quick bright things come to confusion" . . . or "fire and powder which as they kiss consume." Ambivalence is inevitable, and the stresses of making a life together can erode affection and convert love into its all-too-ready opposites: hate and indifference.

While both sexes are at risk, wives and husbands succumb to infidelity for somewhat different reasons. If she's not playing out some illicit erotic scenario, a woman forsakes her conjugal bed for a love's trysting because she's searching for an intimacy that seems to have vanished from it. In a certain sense, using sex as one vehicle for a communion, a wife like this is looking for the sort of companionship she has found with her women friends, and her mother before them. Her lover represents the promise of such a soulmate—a womanly sensibility and sensuousness in a man's body. If she's heterosexual, this may seem to be the only way to get both.

And, oh yes, she's getting her revenge.

With unfaithful men, it's only slightly different. They, too, are after more than sexual conquest. They're also looking for emotional satisfactions that are no longer to be found with their wives and whose waning finds a metaphor in an increasingly lackluster sex life. With errant husbands as well as wives, it's less a matter of impulse than of need.

Like women, men wish to be admired by the opposite sex, though, unlike them, it's not so much their appearance they want applauded as their performance. Other men won't do. For one thing, men tend to compete with one another, putting down the other guy's achievements and posturing. For another, their gender doesn't mesh with these grown-up boys' most pressing needs, imperatives left over from childhood.

So married men have to look to their wives for recognition and approval, to carry on the pleasurable "mirroring" that their mothers once provided. They're still like little kids in this sense, constantly demanding that their "mommies" look at them as they ride seesaws, slide down slides, and otherwise show off. A woman's admiration helps define them as separate beings—as men with penises. Since she is so deeply identified with her son—who embodies, among other things, all her vicarious tomboyish yearnings—a "good enough mother" can be fairly tireless in tendering what psychoanalysts call "narcissistic supplies." But a wife's husband didn't come from her body. He isn't her baby.

Quite the contrary, she often feels she must struggle to separate herself from her man and establish her own life. She resists identifying with him—especially these days. She resents being eclipsed by him, and so a husband's displays begin to wear thin. All those obligatory dinners with bosses, and the endless shoptalk—and this even when a woman has a professional life of her own—come to grate on her over the years.

Men, in their turn, may have grown tired of perusing and praising a wife's figure and the clothes she acquires to adorn it—usually at his expense. Slowly and insidiously, she begins to retaliate for his indifference to *her* needs to show off. She may shop with a vengeance. And she often exaggerates her inattentiveness to make a point: "If you're bored with me, you don't matter to me anymore either."

And so it was that indifference came to descend on the household of the Knights, becoming inescapable once the children had gone their own ways.

• • •

Antonia Knight—Toni to her American friends—turned away from Andrew Knight just as he addressed her.

"What's the matter with you!"

"I'm busy," she said.

All Andrew could see of his wife as she spoke was the studied tangle of highlighted and permed hair. Her back to him, she slammed the dishwasher door shut, smacking the lever with the heel of her hand—trying to be indifferent.

Inside its claustrum, Andy heard glass crunching—a wine goblet, a cheap one, its stem and base evidently jutting too high for its own good. Thud, crunch. That was Toni. That was what the glorious and elegant Antonia had become to him since their first dreamy night together twenty-five years earlier.

"I'll walk the dog," he told his wife's shoulder blade.

"Yeah, you do that. You just do that. You always pick just the right moment."

Toni released the lever and opened the door to inspect the damage as this time Andrew turned from her to leave.

"Ambassador . . . Bassie," Andrew called out as he exited the kitchen.

The Shar-Pei bounded toward him, all folds and jowls. Clicking on the extending leash and grabbing a Baggie from the front hall table, Andrew headed out the front door.

He was thinking of Sherman in Tom Wolf's *Bonfire*, of Philip Roth cum Philip Roth in *Deceptions*, of Martin Landau in Woody Allen's *Crimes and Misdemeanors*. He was thinking of all the duplicitous, cruel, and comic adulterers who had ever been. And now Andy—good old familial, faithful, high-minded Andrew—now he was one of them.

And that was why, in search of Ma Bell, he'd headed not into the backyard of his Cambridge home but along the four additional blocks to Mt. Auburn Street, where suburb became city again.

As, ten minutes later, he pondered the excrement snaking out of Bassie's ass onto the concrete, Andy tried to ease his guilt. Antonia, he reminded himself, had only herself to blame—the antipathy, the envy, the unrelenting undertone of undermining. "Un," that should be Toni's nickname, he spat into his bitter inner lament. She *un*did everything he did. Was it his fault that Toni couldn't find her "autonomy"—or some such bullshit?

Maybe he shouldn't take it personally, Andy thought. Maybe she just hated men. Look what a hard time Toni had given old Chuck Watson on the house!

But oh, was she beautiful. Still. Nobody could hold a candle to her. Not even Nell, who frankly adored him.

Almost defiantly he reached with his plastic-covered claw to scoop up Ambassador's shit and then, reversing the membrane, dumped it into an anonymous neighbor's trash basket. He reached into his pocket and pulled out a quarter, dropping it into the slot of the pay phone. He dialed. Andrew almost resented the act, angry as he was that he needed this "other woman" to make up for what was missing, to remind himself that he was still a man. Now he felt bound to her, too. Another touchstone of guilt.

It was her voice, Nell who answered. So he would need no practiced ruse. Like: "Hi, is Dr. Buggerstein there? This is Mr. Snot. . . . No? Oh, sorry, wrong number, maybe. . . . Three nine three, six oh three two? Oh, two, three, okay."

Andrew couldn't quite figure out why he'd gotten so scatological all of a sudden. Is that what a love affair does for you? It didn't make sense.

"Hi, hi, hi, my sweet Nell, Nellie Nell," he whispered over the Harvard Square traffic and into the receiver, the metal so cold it almost stuck to his chin as he spoke. "I've been aching for you."

"Yes, my darling, so am I. I'm thinking of everything—everything I can do to make you happy—no, make you fly above this 'mortal state.' " She giggled and added, "Oh, yes, I have a surprise for you." Giggle.

"Tomorrow then, my love."

"*Demain.*"

"*Domani.*"

"*Mañana!* Oh, my wonderful Andy, tomorrow!"

His errands accomplished, Andrew trudged home.

Shutting the front door behind him, he unclipped Ambassador's leash. The dog bounded forward.

"Bassie!" Toni was calling from the bedroom. Drooling all the while, Bassie tore down corridors, up steps and over landings, past the empty rooms of the kids now in college, into their bedroom, and finally onto its owners' bed and into its mistress's welcoming embrace.

Andrew slumped into one of the chairs in the front hall, imagining his wife's kissing every crease in the brute's complaisant face, suffering his great rasping tongue in response. Andrew sat alone in the semidarkness and turned his thoughts to tomorrow. Adrian Walsh was out of town.

• • •

Over time, mutual indifference and a quiet but chronic disparagement find their way into the conjugal bedroom. Rejecting her husband's overtures and making fewer of her own, a wife begins to undermine his performance as her lover. In so many words, she tells him, "You're not much of a man to me anymore." A wife like Toni finds it harder and harder to hide her growing disgust along with her lack of sexual arousal. To assert herself she puts her man down and denies him in his hours of need.

A man, too, longs to forget the workaday world and its pressures without being made to feel inadequate. And what better way for an adult to be suckled and succored than in bed, just as a little boy—scared and unsure of his ability to perform—runs into his mommy's lap. Here, with his woman, a man can lose himself in the sex and in the pillow talk, the languorous hour or so after intercourse when lovers converse in low tones, close by each other, warmed by the shared heat of their bodies.

It's no surprise, then, that a woman learns that much of her power, including her capacity to hurt, resides in her control over her womanly resources. If she's angry at her husband for the accumulating slights of everyday life, she will be moved to withhold from him—not only out of fatigue, as she often pretends—but also as a passive way of being aggressive toward him. The more he wants, the less she has for him. The more he asks of her, the more she simply dismisses him.

Opening and closing—here's where her strength lies, a woman has learned. In these ways, she can win or deny love. She can show a man just how much he wants her and has always wanted her. By denying herself to him, she can reveal just how much they are as one and how rent he is without her.

Spurned and shut out by the very woman whom he once loved so dearly and to whom he's devoted his life, a man finds himself increasingly enraged. Here he's sacrificed his freedoms and toiled for her and the children, and "look," he says to himself, "what do I get for it? Nothing."

Men then turn to other women to siphon off their mounting resentment toward their wives and thereby short-circuit potential explosions that might destroy their uneasy alliance. Less frustrated and less lonely, the discreet adulterer can weather the volatile recriminations and undercurrents of indifference with greater equanimity.

Consequently, such mental strains don't necessarily end in divorce. Indeed, the vast majority of men are so dependent on their wives that they will cling to them even in the worst of marriages until they find an alternative. Men don't leave one woman without another waiting in the wings. (As I shall go into further detail about in the next chapter on divorce.)

In this era of AIDS and other sexually transmitted diseases, one would think men would demur from committing adultery because of real-life threats to health, hearth, and home. Yet, as I've suggested elsewhere (Chapters 3, 4, and 14), rarely have we been free of such risks. And men have always erred.

In fact, dangers like these or, more likely, the chance of being caught, add spice to forbidden fruit. Sex that's too easy, too routine, "safe sex," can become boring—although this boredom is usually a cover for more intense underlying ambivalences that have intensified over time.

According to certain poets and philosophers, romantic love requires obstacles in its path to reach its highest pitch. And in a marriage, no one (nobody real, at any rate) stands in the spouse's way. Tradition thus has it that first love, unrequited love, and adultery best fulfill passion's requirements. Divorced from family economics, these circumstances are said to foster a love that is, ironically, more pure and true.

An affair may revive the glow of passionate infatuation prevailing during courtship, before husband and wife were known quantities. There was danger, then, too, in the young lovers' defiance of their parental taboos, in the precipitousness of exposing themselves each to the other, in the thrill of mutual discovery. And adultery can reawaken an eroticism that has long lain dormant. And this vibrancy attests to the fact that a man, now a lover again, has remained a sexual being—young and alive.

More practically the current research indicates that people do indeed need their passion to prosper—emotionally and physically. Pheromones and the scent of sex, which betray a woman's arousal, keep men interested in her. And the mere thought of sex in both men and women stimulates neuropeptides, which, in turn, promote the production of T-cells, which in their turn are the bedrock of the immune system. In other words, feeling sexy helps keep males alive. Where the feeling has emptied out of the marriage, because of the predictable nature of the relationship or because of conflict, a man may be moved to look elsewhere for essential "libidinal refueling."

And this, alas, was what Andrew seemed to need.

• • •

"Come in," Nell's voice whispered through the intercom as she buzzed open the front door to the Walshs' Beacon Hill brownstone. "I'm upstairs in the bedroom."

Andrew entered and began his ascent up the two flights of stairs. At the top, on the landing, Nell's bedroom door had been left ajar. He pushed it open.

Nell stood before him, radiant, expectant with desire. Her "surprise" was a little silk lace teddy through which most of her erotic parts could be glimpsed. Her erect nipples pushed against the lace in the bodice. The bottom was scalloped in such a way as to expose an inviting curve of thigh and cheek.

Twelve years younger than he, she still looked like a girl, a virgin even, a maid to be broken of her free will, to be taken. Everything about her seemed aquiver, goose bumps and all, as, naked as a child bride, she rushed into Andrew's arms, still swathed in winter wool, and planted her lips on his. She reached through the layered bulk of aging Harris tweeds and Shetlands—to grope for the zipper of his fly.

Responding to her passion, Andrew pushed her away to look at her face. Her eyelids were heavy, she was sucking on her lower lip. Not so elegant as Antonia maybe, but wholesome in her erotic single-mindedness, even in her adultery. And she was—at this moment at least—his.

He felt large and friendly—her protector, her guide. And he answered her touch with a search of his own, reaching down to cup her crotch in his hand. And she was wet. The secretions of her yearning seeped through the satin and told him of her love—or was it just desire?

He pulled up on the teddy gently and firmly, driving the seams of the crotch between Nell's labia, lifting her, teasing her just a little, adding to the interval before they would consummate their desire—or was it need?—for each other, savoring just how much she wanted him. Nell groaned and buried her head in the nape of his neck. She winced slightly, and Andrew let her sink back a little and began to undo her teddy as her questing fingers also found their goal.

She was still awash and afire with anticipation. But, he thought, as he unsnapped that final snap, one day she, too, would dry up. One day he would reach down and there would be nothing there. How it would happen, and just why, he didn't know. But one day, Nell, too, would turn cold and dry.

• • •

Once again, family dynamics and biology only begin to tell the story. Here, too, a deeper analysis is called for to figure out what men *want* out of adultery. Love affairs, the psychiatrist Otto Kernberg has suggested, can serve to stabilize a precarious marriage—and this for a variety of psychological reasons.

For the psychoanalyst, breaking any taboo harks symbolically back to breaching the barrier against incest and the Oedipus complex. In a marriage, having been the objects of a desire that starts out as unhallowed, spouses find their roles in this drama reversed over time. No longer sex objects, no longer forbidden fruit, they have become embodiments of obligation and reincarnations of parents who said no to their child's unacceptable sexual wishes.

In other words, not only wives but also husbands develop "father transferences" to their partners. In his wife a man sees the father who served as the model for his conscience and by whom he felt oppressed. Responsibility constrains him but also erodes his desire. And he resents this—and her. With a love affair, the adulterer defies this dulling sense of duty just as he did years ago when he first fell in love.

Most love stories are short stories. Endless, uninterrupted love seems almost an impossibility—even in fiction. Romantic passion seems to require obstacles in its path. And where barriers don't actually separate the lovers, they will tend to insert their own psychological blocks and inhibitions.

Like compulsive womanizers, the occasional adulterer, a man generally more comfortable with sustained intimacy, may also have felt a need to shore up his sense of self. Until he strays, he may have done so by progressively muting his libido, by numbing himself. It's enough to live with a woman day in and day out, he may reason unbeknownst to himself, without becoming obsessed and possessed by her as well.

An affair may then serve to demonstrate to him that his wife is not the be-all and end-all after all, and that there are women and worlds apart from her. Infidelity may be exploited by some men just to create distance and options of another sort—to free themselves up. Proving that there are alternatives to his wife, adultery may permit a man to return home with passions that no longer threaten his autonomy and manhood. For some, betrayal thus makes a man's heart grow freer and fonder. It may rekindle his attraction for his wife not only as someone toward whom he owes his loyalty, a father figure, but as a *woman* to whom he remains drawn.

Or at times a man may "try out" another lover just to show himself that his wife is the "better" woman in the end, "for better or for worse." When he comes back to her having established this, he finds her more desirable, more beautiful, smarter and kinder underneath the crust of irritability built up between them over time. More so than any other woman, he discovers, and more than she seemed to him before he wandered. No longer feeling bound to her, he can want her again.

So any affair may enhance a husband's love for his wife. That is, if a man's guilt over his duplicity toward both the women now in his life isn't overpowering. And guilt it is, along with the fear of loss, that gives the potential adulterer pause.

An adulterous liaison often takes place in an internal climate of moral dislocation. It's something of a cliché, but many men start extramarital affairs after the death of their father, when they have no external authority to whom they must answer even if only in the privacy of their own minds. But apart from such figures in reality, there are still consciences to be contended with—the edicts, injunctions, and ideals within ourselves.

"Thou shalt not covet thy neighbor's wife," said the Lord to Moses, and he to his errant flock, not, "Thou shalt not betray *thy* wife." Many modern men are still bound by this sort of prohibition, with its roots in the universal incest taboo, and by their terror of defying the authority of God, father, community, and the harsh "superego." It's fear rather than concern that lies at the heart of their self-restraint. Commit adultery, they imagine, and in punishment, your marriage and family will be taken from you— almost magically. It's superstition, pure and simple, that stops them in their tracks.

For others, however, whose consciences are more developed, independent of the specter of pure retaliation, their guilt feelings have more to do with people and their care for them than with punishment. Such men, like women in fact, believe that their bodies, including their penises, "belong" to their wives. To offer themselves to another and to pleasure her so intimately is to violate and perhaps permanently *adulterate* the trust between marriage partners. Even where the affair escapes detection, the deception is such as to erode a couple's tender and more openhearted intimacy.

For such men, monogamy is not a rule dictated from on high but a safeguard against mistrust, a contract to which both parties have agreed in order to draw a boundary around themselves and thus ensure their freedom within it. For such men, the felt loss that is threatened in committing adultery, and that is brought on once the deed is done, can be devastating. Life after betrayal is never quite the same—whatever its limitations may have been in the first place.

The more the merrier? Hardly. Adultery leaves a man alone and in more ways than he had anticipated.

• • •

Two hours later and Andrew was dressing again, beginning the laborious process of layering up. Glancing at the photos of Nell's daughters—Maud, seven, and Diana, ten—whom he'd never met, he felt pangs of longing for the days when he and Antonia had tended a family and were filled with hope. Nervously now, feeling rushed, he slipped on his socks, followed by boxer shorts, which camouflaged the genitals he'd taken pains to scrub clean, effacing the evidence of this Sunday tryst.

So Andrew's mind had moved elsewhere. Still Nell's affection remained unbridled. Wrapped in her terry robe, she slipped yet another piece of homemade shortbread into her lover's gaping mouth.

"Got to go, got to go, you know. Can't tarry. Not even for you."

Why the anglicized affectation, he wondered, with Nell of all people? Oh, never mind, he told himself, and he slipped his hand under her robe and over her breast, squeezing it for the last time. And once more she melted, drawing toward him, probing an ear with her tongue—like a little she bear, he mused, searching for honey. He could feel her damp hair caressing his neck again. A last snuggle—a shot of warmth. One for the road.

"Whoops, I'll get my smell all over you."

And in recompense for the leaving, she finished by dressing him herself, soup to nuts, concluding by patting his fanny underneath all the tweed as she closed her front door behind him.

"See you tomorrow—*domani.*"

Yes, they would. But in a meeting this time, hiding their personal relationship—the publisher and the most talented of his young senior editors. Tomorrow . . .

Nell watched the door close in front of her. A pause and a little woosh, and the big mahogany slab thudded into place with the definiteness of its mass. Andrew was gone and on his way.

It was six P.M. on Sunday night. Kidless, husbandless, and now left loverless, Nell was alone. Walking back upstairs, she ran her hands over her pelvis, just about where her ovaries should be, through the rough terry to reassure herself that it had been worth it—the two hours for a whole weekend.

Plunking herself down on the rumpled bed, she reached for the phone absently. A photograph of Adrian, tennis trophy in hand, tumbled off the end table onto the carpet. Rebounding off its thick and cushioned pile, it almost bounced back to her. Nell retrieved it, put it back in place, next to one of the two of them and the girls, and dialed.

"Rok Rizard," came the doubly muffled greeting over the receiver.

"How about some lizard Szechuan style," she'd wanted to say, but ordered Chef Wu's Wonderful Scallops, pot stickers, and eggplant with garlic instead. Clicking on the TV, Nell waited for the Wizard to deliver.

• • •

As a result of his history of marital unhappiness, the sense of loss and of sadness and the nagging worries, a man brings a whole lot of emotional baggage with him on his journey into an extramarital affair. His conflicts tend to be fairly raw, and the other woman, a lover like Nell, gets much more than she bargained for.

It takes time, of course, for ambiguity to cast its shadow over the new relationship. In the beginning of an affair at least, lovers try to exclude from their bower their human limitations, liabilities, and petty preoccupations. A wife may have to wait her turn in the bathroom while her husband does his business as he reads the paper. But it's a rare mistress who ever hears her lover passing gas or sits with him while he does his taxes.

In fact, to some extent, the adulterers try to maintain themselves as two-dimensional figures. They enact their roles as pure, erotic, and emotional beings without the sort of human complications that make real-life relationships so arduous. Lovers play out a fantasy of "blind" love as it should always be. And having so used their imaginations, they become their own audience, willingly suspending disbelief.

Being idealized isn't easy, however. Soon enough what psychoanalysts call those "transferences" from the past and "projections" from within oneself begin to bring this secret honeymoon to a close. Not only must a lover fill in for a wife's failings. She herself becomes the target of the hostility these have generated. In what may be called his "uxorial transference," the wandering husband sees his wife in his mistress and sometimes treats her accordingly. His lover—who, for the time being at least, cherishes him without stint—becomes the recipient of insensitivities that her behavior has yet to justify: abrupt departures, unmade phone calls, and more. The "homebreaker" becomes the victim.

And however much he berates himself as the agent of his indiscretions, the adulterer views his mistress as the temptress who threatens the well-being of the family that he's worked so hard to create and sustain. Irrationally, he resents her, or more precisely, his growing longing for her. Guilt is hard to bear, and so he rankles at the remorse their relationship evokes in him. He tries to spread the blame.

Then, too, there's reality to be dealt with. The other woman is not only his lover but an individual with ties outside their liaison, her own conflicts, and her own "transferences." Recognizing this, he begins to feel both morally beholden to her and increasingly angry at the demands her presence now makes of him, even where these are only implicit. He becomes more and more ambivalent, torn not only by two sets of opposing desires but by competing obligations.

The husband in an affair begins to experience this new relationship as a marriage on the side. Unless their time together is
clearly circumscribed and the terms and conditions of the sexual
friendship established and agreed upon, soon enough a mistress
becomes another wife, and adultery a variation on the age-old
practice of polygamy. A husband starts out trying to escape en-
trapment, but he gradually finds himself feeling overwhelmed
again. By women. Women, women—everywhere he turns!

But perhaps worst of all, and this adulterer is mostly unaware
of at the time, is that his mistress in fact owes him nothing. There
are no ties here, no vows, no shared history, no glue of reciprocity
and economic interdependence, no children binding them together. Where she herself is married, a mistress's obligations, legal
and otherwise, reside elsewhere.

She can lie to him. She can leave him at any moment. And
there is no court of appeal. Risking all, he may end up with
nothing.

So the bubble's bound to burst. Yet when it does, the felt
calamity also comes as a relief.

And what about the "other woman"? The wife, that is?

• • •

Toni Knight perused herself in the cheval mirror. They'd bought
it a week ago—a perfect addition to the bedroom. A heap of suits,
skirts, tops, obscured the bed, and still she wasn't satisfied. Well,
hell, she thought to herself, it was only six-fifteen, and they weren't
due at the Roths' until seven-thirty, and Andy wasn't here, and so
he'd have no right to hound her about being on time.

Time, what did it matter—where was she going anyway?

Okay, this one will do, she decided, selecting the Gigli jersey
dress, and then she (too) slouched on a disheveled bed. Not because of any sex, of course, but because of Toni's solitary trials
and errors in adorning herself. She foresaw the entry to come in
the next ten to twenty minutes, the dull greetings that seemed to
sink into the gut of each utterer, hollow and uninviting.

Twenty-five years earlier, they had met their first day at Ran-
dom House as readers. The young woman "freshly emigrated
from Cambridge, England, was supporting [her] poesy habit by
tending to other people's prose." The Princeton summa cum
laude, conceding his "lack of fictive fancy," had decided to parlay
his love of reading it into a "potentially lucrative and established
career." The two tyros were made for each other and so almost

immediately and for several years after that, fell into passionate love with each other.

Look, Andrew had told himself and her, look at his brilliant cousin Roger Cummings. Chaired professor that he was, he was always broke. He would have done much better in sectors outside the university. Not that one had to go so far as to follow in his brother Don's crass footsteps—"but an academic's lot?"

The further reference was clear, but Toni ignored it. Instead, for a while at least, she let herself enjoy the ripening fruits of Andrew's effort—his money.

Marriage. A son and daughter. A move to Cambridge, Massachusetts. No more jobs. A slim volume of poetry published by Advantage Press—just to avoid the "taint of nepotism." A *Kirkus* review, and one in *The Phoenix*. A couple of magazine acceptances. Nothing else. Nothing. All Andrew.

Toni pictured him opening the door. Bundled. Another success. A whir of them. Andrew, that was his middle name, too. Andrew Andrew, Andrew, Andrew, Andrew, Andrew.

No, this was not the Great Mentor, she went on to herself. Despite being a mover and shaker of literary fashion and finances, her husband remained after all these years no match for the rumpled old man, her dear dad, widowed now and puttering about the house he still managed in Brighton. The old Oxford don had turned the Sussex English Department into a late-sixties powerhouse and could now enjoy the ease of retirement.

His wife, Anna, scooped up from the pastures of Trenton, when Duncan had spent a year at Princeton's Institute for Advanced Study, had been no match for his wit and learning. Becoming what she always was—a placid Jersey "gal"—his wife had yielded her place in Duncan's heart to the first of their two daughters, Antonia. He'd taught her just about everything he knew about literature, which was considerable, and life, only negligible.

When Anna died of breast cancer on the eve of her oldest child's thirteenth birthday, father and daughter became even more bound to each other. She'd heard that when they're widowed young, fathers turn to daughters to fill in. Widowers don't do well by and large—though, with her, her father did. As she understood it years later in psychotherapy with her venerable Boston headshrinker, she'd simply had to get away, coming to America to escape this "impossible situation" and to find, as they say, "a suitable Oedipal substitute."

For years it had worked all right, though it didn't help that

where they should dovetail, husband and father had been at loggerheads—"the antique, ambling anachronism" going toe-to-toe
on each of their Christmas vacations with the "brash neo-patrician
from the New World for whom books are business." It had taken
Duncan a decade to succumb to such name-calling, whereas Andrew had spewed forth his elegant epithets early on, after their
very first meeting in fact. He'd sensed in the puckish old man an
elusive but formidable rival.

Thank God oceans divided the continents on which these two
men ruled—or ruled her, though she hated to admit it. But when
the children had gone, and their grandfather had begun to fade,
she'd visited him more. The tensions had grown with her ab-
sences. And then an invisible wall inserted itself between husband
and wife, each of whom, having banged up against it often enough,
bounced and spun off into their own distances.

Toni saw Bassie's ear twitch and his eyes open expectantly
even before she heard the front door open and shut.

"Hi, hon. Home. Are you ready?"

Already. The dog sprang to its feet and pattered forth to greet
his master. Toni turned back to her clothes.

"Uh-huh."

Another dull thud for a response. Yes, she was sure of it.
Andrew was having an affair.

• • •

Antonia's matter-of-fact reaction to her response is perhaps not
typical of the betrayed wife. Even where a wife has tacitly encour-
aged, condoned, or simply tolerated what she infers or knows for
sure to be her husband's infidelity, she usually reacts with jealousy and outrage. Like her husband, she has committed body and
soul to him and expects him to repay her trust in kind.

When a man has an affair, their intimacy is ruptured. For her
as for him. He's endangered her. Not only has he punctured the
membrane encapsulating them and their sexual exchanges, he's
lied to her. Never more can he be trusted. It will never, never be
the same between them. An affair expels a married couple from
the naked innocence of Eden into the disillusioned remainder of
their lives.

And most painful of all, with all their shared and complicated
residues from the past, an unfaithful husband has introduced a
real-life rival into a wife's life. She's already had the specter of her
mother, her daughter or daughters, and a mother-in-law to con-

tend with in vying for a man's loyalty and affection. Now a genuine, hard-core interloper has entered a scene with real-life sex. In actuality or in her imagination, this homebreaker may be younger, slimmer, prettier, less used—the sort of "girl" who from childhood and adolescence on always seemed to edge her out in competitions of one sort or another, but mainly for men.

Yes, the hurt is unbearable.

The rules of the game, the monogamy ensuring trust and the freedom to be oneself, change with an extramarital affair. If she is not so unsure of herself as to subject herself to almost anything from a man, the deceived wife will be moved to battle back.

Divorce—but why concede victory? An affair of her own perhaps? After all, she's still a woman. But does she want to lower herself the way "they" have done? Or a fight to the death—a full frontal assault on the pretender and challenger before she can undo the marriage? Yes, that's it . . . maybe.

Or, well, denial—that's the most common response. Simply pretend you don't feel anything if you know anything. Or let it all slide by you—like the thousand betrayals of the heart that have preceded and led up to this one of the body. Let it go like everything else. Deal with it later. Out of sight, out of mind, out of existence!

Ice them out.

Indeed a man in the middle of an affair, a man like Andrew Knight, the betrayer, can find himself betrayed, hurt, or rejected by both of his women. Too much to handle, it seems—too much for one man.

Poor Andrew.

• • •

"Friends."

The hackneyed but still dreaded euphemism had been uttered at last. Six months, then eight, then a year plus—it had had to come sometime. Andrew had been expecting the end from the start.

Over the three months following the Wok Wizard delivery on that chilly Sunday night, he'd noticed Nellie's disengagement from him. She called less frequently now, answering his messages after extended intervals. It was she who said when it was time to get up and go, she who concluded their two afternoons together with a "Well, let's get going, honey." . . . Honey!

Andy had wanted to chalk all this up to some autonomy stuff

once again. Her calling the shots. Fair enough. But there'd been
that faraway look in Nell's eyes, as if her sights were set on something else, something farther away than him. He hadn't pried. It
wasn't in their "contract." And truly, he hadn't wanted to.

What he hadn't reckoned on was a job, work. Nell was moving
on, she told him, on and up the ladder—surprise of surprises.
He'd been shunted aside not by family ties but by work ambition.
Pure and simple. Or was it?

"Drew has been interviewing me for the past two months.
Obviously, I couldn't tell you."

"Obviously." Andrew felt light-headed.

"Actually, Ray Slavin has been approaching me for some time
now to move over. They've offered me a division."

" 'Approaching.' " Andrew could feel his jugular and temple
throbbing in tandem.

Slavin, the little wimp. In conservative Boston, he'd made no
bones about being "bi," and still he kept on coming. The flashy
wunderkind was making bucks for Drew nobody at Howard and
Bell could've imagined possible three years ago. The little fairy
brat had been breathing down Andrew's neck for two of those
years, and now he, of all people, had nabbed Nell.

"Anyway, Andy—Andy? *Andy!*—it would be too complicated
to go on. I'm ambivalent, of course, but that's the way I want it.
We can't have a sexual relationship anymore."

"But—"

"That's the way I want it. It has to be." And she set the cup
down and rose from her chair.

Getting up, Andrew felt his knees wobble. His cheek felt
numb, just like the time his jaw had been broken by a lacrosse
stick at Laurenceville, as it received Nellie's final peck before she
showed him out. Out of her life. For the last time. No more
tomorrows. *No mas mañanas.* She closed the door behind him.

• • •

They were sitting across from each other at Boston's fashionable
Biba's on this, the occasion of their twenty-fifth anniversary. The
second bottle of Clos du Val merlot had been emptied, and Andrew at least felt warmed almost to his groin as he toyed with the
remains of Sisteron lamb Cajun-style on his oversize plate. For the
first time in a year maybe, Antonia was smiling and, it seemed, at
him.

"There's something I have to tell you—" he'd begun, only to

find his sentence cut short and his jaw hanging open. Open-mouthed, he heard instead his wife's announcement.

"Well, there's something *I* have to tell *you* first." For a change! she thought to herself.

"I've sold my book."

Book? What book? he asked himself incoherently.

As if anticipating him, Antonia went on. She looked radiant.

"You know that novel I started on the Cape, oh, ten years ago? Well, I've been working on it again for two years now—yes, on the sly. I got an agent—Susie Bowles—but kept it all under wraps. And two days ago Drew made me an offer."

"Drew," Andrew gasped, aspirating enough of the '83 down his windpipe and nasal passages to make the back of his brain burn.

"Yes, honey, I know they're your competitors, but they are a great house. Full of new blood. Women interested in women's lit. Very exciting."

"Who's your . . . " Andrew began, his voice a high rasp.

But did he want to know? Her "editor." Did he? Women—Antonia'd said "women"—so it couldn't be Slavin the Slime. But it could be—and his heart stopped in his throat. He couldn't go on.

Pausing ever so slightly, Toni now turned her attentions back to him—without hesitancy, free now, again, in her giving of herself. And she was still glowing. A sudden star.

"And sweetheart, what was your news?"

No, he couldn't.

"Sorry," he said in spurts. "It went down the wrong way. Be right back. Ugh. That's *so* wonderful."

And scrambling to his feet, he whisked himself down the stairs to the men's room. Spitting into the sink, he imagined Toni upstairs, still luminous. No, never, he'd never tell her. Something about a second honeymoon (or a third)—that was it. He'd take her away. Away from it all.

• • •

That's the thing about an affair. It ends up controlling a man from start to finish, without his knowing it. Oppressed in his marriage, he initiates his other relationship to regain the comfort and power that make him feel like a man. In the process, of course, he does a lot of maneuvering and manipulation of the people he cares about. If he's a decent guy, the guilt over using, deceiving, and positioning them to his advantage then begins to take over, driving other feelings away.

What an adulterer can forget is that these other players are dynamic characters, too, not just cardboard figures in the tableaux he's made—however reluctantly. They really can't be controlled, no matter how compliant or acquiescent they may seem for a while. They will choose what they will. Once there are actors acting in it, the playwright finds, the drama is no longer his alone. The women involved may end up surprising him and throwing him for a loss (in more senses that one).

Yearning for greater passion and intimacy, men initiate affairs in an attempt to feel more, have more, experience more, be more. But often if not always, they end up with less.

And in general, men don't like too many surprises. They don't like being out of control—as the next chapter on lovesickness will show.

7

...

Men Who Love Too Much: Divorcing and Being Divorced

It used to be that a woman, who had been in the home for so much of her adult life, dared not end a marriage. However unsatisfied she might be with him, a wife found herself bound to the husband who had met her survival needs for the better part of her adult life.

But the women's movement has changed all that. More and more women are divorcing their husbands in midlife. In fact, according to expert Judith Wallerstein, 35 percent of the breakups are initiated by discontented wives, and Hite and others have pointed to even higher percentages. Economically liberated, more integrated as members of the work force, women are leaving their men to fulfill themselves and, yes, to punish husbands for count-less old hurts. Empty nests no longer mean merely an emotional vacuum but also the promise of personal freedom and self-vindication.

As a result of broad economic changes, then, men now find themselves becoming not only the agents but also the recipients of midlife crises. The sexual revolution has threatened a husband's automatic ability to dominate his wife through money and to count on her being there for him, no matter what. At home as on the work front, men's greater preoccupation with their careers and their myths of masculinity are being assailed.

And it seems, all sorts of men can be divorced. Not only are the "bad guys"—the loose cannons, martinets, and ne'er-do-wells—being cast out for their sins. Having misunderstood all that is expected of them, the "good Joes" are also at risk. The men who love too much and forget themselves are in jeopardy—any man is who doesn't listen.

Whatever the warning signals, not only is a wife's decision to leave her husband unwanted by most husbands, it amazes them. All along a man has tended to listen little and hear even less, blinding himself to events that don't fit in with his game plan and discounting all those telltale murmurs that he's no longer the center of her affections. Since most men simply can't accept being out of control, being told they are being divorced is a trauma they're helpless to forestall or "process." In fact, men are generally more vulnerable to the shock of divorce than are women.

Unanticipated as it is, a divorce can become an emotional catastrophe because it resonates with some of the worst imaginings of a man's childhood: abandonment and loss, punishment and retribution, a cruel blow to his manhood. The collapse of a marriage is symbolically a cheap shot that effectively devastates and, temporarily at least, "castrates" him.

Left reeling, like a teenager who's lost his girlfriend to another guy—only more so—the divorced man finds himself becoming angry and rebellious. And this regressive defiance, his "me first" and "fuck you" response to his undoing, not only comes to target the wife who deserted him. He also turns on the children with whom she is associated—kids, ironically, who may be teenagers themselves.

Divorce makes for a confrontation not only with a grown man's hidden feelings of vulnerability but with his unwanted violence toward those who are truly vulnerable and continue to depend on him. He can amaze himself, in fact, with the extent and ingenuity of his cruelty, the reservoirs of which, he can't help sensing, must have been there in himself all along. There's a violent edge even to his despair and those thoughts of suicide. Who would then take care of the children, pay their tuition, summer camp, the doctors' bills, who will promise protection and assume authority—once he's down and out or gone altogether?

Being divorced calls upon men's fears of emasculation and effeminization and the promiscuous aggression that are legacies of his having been a boy. Even the most mild and mature of men are at risk—men like Marvin, the CPA from Long Island.

• • •

On August 9, 1988, Marvin Landsman walked into the surf. It was four-forty A.M. in East Hampton, and it was his intention to kill himself.

He propelled his 215-pound bulk into the ocean, feeling rather than seeing the froth on the crests of the waves. He should have suffered the chill of the water but found himself numbed instead from inside—by an uncharacteristic fifth of Johnnie Walker Black Label, forty milligrams of Valium, and even at fifty-six years, two joints of marijuana left over from his college-age kids' last visit home.

"Slightly ridiculous," he sputtered to himself as he paddled on. "Highly undignified in a man my age"—he tried to giggle through his tears—"but so's the horrible situation."

Marvin had bought his house in the Amagansett dunes fifteen years earlier, the year *Jaws* came out: "Moby Dicky." Just now Marvin likened himself to the girl in the movie's opening sequence—"Chrissy, was that her name?" He saw her naked legs dangling in the overlit water and heard the ominous chords announcing that the great white was on the prowl. He visualized his own legs, pudgy and swathed in the folds of his capacious Brooks Brothers boxer shorts. He remembered the desperate clanging of the bell in the buoy to which she vainly clung. "It hurts," she'd moaned.

Yes, it did.

In the book, the first victim hadn't been an innocent, he dimly recalled, but rather a somewhat older woman having an affair. He thought about his wife, Ethel. His wife.

Though his toes shuddered, Marvin swam on. A hundred yards from shore, Marvin Landsman paused, treading water. Now he remembered another film—Dom DeLuise in the Burt Reynolds movie about suicide, *The End*. Like the character's Polish father, he was sweating. Yes, sweating in the middle of the icy currents.

It was then the ache hit, seizing his chest and piercing his gut. He tasted the salt water and felt cold all of a sudden. Marvin was alone and didn't want to be. He was instantly afraid.

He didn't want to die. He didn't want to be divorced, that was for sure. But also Marvin didn't want to die. His loneliness was inescapable any which way.

Digging with his pumping feet into the unfathomed sea beneath him, he changed course, pointing his body homeward, lurching toward the shore. "Don't panic," he breathed to himself as he began to kick forward in earnest. "And for godsake, don't get a cramp."

The beacons provided by the lit windows here and there in beach houses—those "summer cottages" he could never himself have afforded—invited him to live and warned him of death. The splotches of light grew bigger, rewarding Marvin's efforts to reverse himself. In fact, he found himself riding the benevolence of an incoming tide—later he would wonder how, against it, he'd managed to get out so far so fast.

Marvin pushed on, more imperiled by the increasingly forbidding specter of drowning. Ten minutes later, and one of those giant breakers on which he, Ethel, and the children used to body surf (so long ago it seemed) slammed him nose first into the sand. His underwear having filled with pebbles, reminding him of his first seashore days as a little boy, Marvin heaved and staggered his way to his feet. He stood erect, only to teeter backward for a moment, backward toward the jaws of the sea.

Righting himself, he found that he still remained in a most ignominious of positions. It was five forty-five and the sun had begun to sneak over the horizon, illumining the beach and, on it, Marvin himself. And his clothes were nowhere to be seen. While they had been kind enough to carry him back in, to shore, to life, the tidal currents had swept him down the beach.

Sober now, he began to trot for cover, jogging the sands in search of pants, shirt, and Top-Siders. His great walrus belly trembling with each heavy footfall, Marvin comforted himself with the contention of experts on the subject, namely that people in the throes of divorce do "crazy things." Thank God for the Living and Science sections of the *Times;* thank God for the Sunday magazine.

· · ·

It's become a familiar story by now. Eleven months earlier, Ethel Stein Landsman had asked her husband for a divorce.

The second of their two kids was a year into college, the rest of their education already paid for by ripening zero-coupon bonds long ago secured by the foresight of her accountant husband. She herself had started working during their junior high school years, when they'd begun to require less of her. Ten years later, she'd parlayed what had started as an avocation into her own booming residential real estate business in Huntington, Long Island. In fact, her commissions rivaled her husband's draw and bonuses at the firm whose New York office he headed.

"Who would have thought?" she and Marv marveled. Well, maybe success just ran in her family.

Besides, having delegated much of the work to salespersons in her employ, Ethel had joined a health club, which, together with occasional visits to the "fat-farm spas" of California, had peeled twenty pounds from her form. No liposuction, no breast implants or reductions, maybe some UV tanning—the beautiful new body was Ethel's own doing. Marvin "kvelled with pride" as he admired the wife who at midlife had come to look better even than the eighteen-year-old Brooklyn girl he'd married a generation ago.

But then she pulls the divorce business: "I care about you, Marv, and I know we'll always be friends. But we've never been close, and I've gone through my whole life not knowing who I am on my own. Now's the time. I'm independent. The kids are gone. You've got time to find somebody you deserve." Bull.

It turns out Ethel has already rented an apartment—after all, that was her business—and plans to move out that night. So she goes. And there he is, thirty-two years later and fourteen hours most of those days, alone. Alone in a no-longer-mortgaged house. Alone with the beach house, college funds, Keoghs. Fat, bald, gray, and alone—his great puffy eyes bursting with wet grief and dry fatigue.

And then she hits him with another zinger. Yes, he did it—accepting, nonintrusive Marv did it. He went through Ethel's things, even through the phone bills of the house and her office. And there, sure enough, there it was, again and again: 203-967-4332. Fuck you, William Schneiderson, Stamford, Connecticut.

Yes, she admits, yes, Ethel's been having an affair. "Didn't you, sweetheart, with Cynthia Roth eight years ago? Don't deny."

Yeah, I slipped. But for four months. Not two and one-half fucking years! And I didn't leave you for her either. She was just some lonely divorcée—whoops!—who needed me. And you were working all the time, and I was middle-aged. And I didn't leave you.

Marv had tried to lay it on her deprivation as a kid—the degradation. But he'd long made up for her Coney Island girlhood, so he couldn't really.

But what difference did all the bickering and blaming and explaining make? Ethel had made up her mind. Nothing held her anymore. Her feelings had changed. And he couldn't control them.

So Marvin was left alone. He tried visiting Darryl and Naomi in their colleges. He started with a therapist. Once he even picked up a woman at the Windows on the World national firm party and went to bed with her with a condom on. But mostly he sat in the den of his eleven-room Long Island house and ate.

Beer washed down the mounds of cold pizza and chocolate chip cookies, topped off with Dalmane and the B&B to help them along so that the fat man could sleep through the night. Droopy eyed, body sagging in his overstuffed chair, Marv sat and stared across the room and out the window. With his bloated gaze he held on to all the things he and his wife had bought together, trying to assess what they had become and what had become of them.

No, he hadn't been perfect. Ethel was right—there had been Cyndy. When he was tired, he lost his temper pretty readily. When they ate late, he'd farted in bed. But this—jeez, what was left?

Years ago Marv had wanted to become a genuine mathematician teaching someplace or just a statistician maybe. But he had felt obligated to build and buy instead. So he'd worked himself to the point of self-anesthesia, still loving the effort because of the people it served. And now this.

. . .

There are as many kinds of divorces and reasons for them as there are individuals and individual relationships. Divorces can come at any time along the way, whether two years into a marriage destined to fail from the start or two or more decades down the line, when the couple has made itself into a family and then become a couple again. So to generalize about men or women in the process may be a disservice to the variety of people involved. Yet, from my experience with men in the midst of a divorce as well as that of other clinicians who specialize in this particular area, certain trends assert themselves as unmistakable. And as distinctly male.

Like a marriage, a divorce is not an event but a process. Just as there's a prehistory and an aftermath to the wedding ceremony, so, too, the severing of the nuptial bond does not begin or end with the signing of the legal documents declaring one's marital vows null and void. And men tend to participate in this stream of events, setting some in motion and reacting to others, in striking and revealing ways.

Usually—though not always—the fracture of a marriage is the culmination of years of discord. Dissatisfaction, alienation, deception, and tempestuousness at one time or another have accumulated to erode the love, intimacy, and trust of the couple. (See also Chapters 1 and 6.)

Husbands and wives have developed expectations of each other, many of these negative, based not only on their early lives with their parents and siblings but on their past experiences together. "Spouse transferences," I've called these. And in their context the mere hint of an old hurt is greeted with the bitterness and terror of wounds that have never healed. The mysterious phone call, the charge on the shared credit card, the lateness yet again, the night of sexual apathy, become ominous reminders of all the betrayals and simple letdowns that have ever been between them. In a climate of such essential distrust and despair, it becomes ever more impossible to change. The only way out is "out."

You would think, then, that both "partners" would agree on the desirability of divorce. Not so. In fact, Judith Wallerstein discovered to her amazement that of all the couples she studied, only one had come to the decision jointly. Well, maybe that's not so surprising, she concluded, given the fact that divorce itself is the quintessential expression of chronic disagreement. What is striking, especially for the men involved, is the extent of a spouse's ability to deny both the disaffection leading up to a divorce and the dissolution of the partnership in which this culminates. Often husbands are thrown utterly for a loss when the failure of their marriage becomes undeniable.

Without his acknowledging it and despite the shared pretense that he's the lord of the castle, a man's wife has come to fill in for the mother of his earliest years on earth. In infancy, the man-to-be was "his majesty the baby," in Freud's turn of phrase. Or he feels he should have been. (See Chapters 3, 6, and 10.) And so this son brings to his marriage and his wife the sense of unending entitlement that went along with the "primary narcissism" of this unequaled status. As one psychiatrist put it off the record, "What men want [out of women] is a mother they can fuck!"

This first paradise was destined to be lost because of the demands of a younger sibling, the claims of the father before him, or women's work outside the home. And these displacements only add an almost moralistic conviction to the demands a man con-

tinues to make of "his woman" later on in life. It is she now who
must make good for all past slights on the part of his parents, for
the whole cold, hard world. It is inconceivable that a wife should
do otherwise—much less abandon him.

All this is unconscious in most adult men, of course—sane-
minded as they like to see themselves being. But when the super-
structure of a marriage falters and then tumbles, the wreckage
exposes a husband's childish incredulity, his excess of basic trust,
the unflagging naïveté a man has brought to his relationship and
his infantile neediness. Especially nowadays when likely as not it
is the wife who does the leaving. The abandoned husband is
rather like a little puppy, who, doted on, can't believe his mistress
is going on without him.

The painful consequences of "paternal deprivation" and "father hunger" in children of divorce have been well documented.
(And I've discussed these already in Chapters 4 and 5.) But what
about all those men living alone? What about their feelings of
deprivation, their hungers?

Whereas most ex-wives affirmed the decision to divorce ten
years down the line in Wallerstein's study, and this regardless of
whose choice it had been to terminate the marriage, only one-half
of the men interviewed thought it had been a good idea to break
up. The older the man at the time of divorce, the worse his feelings
about the breakup and his consequent life circumstances and prospects. And this, even when it was his decision to leave in the first
place.

Successful second marriages can make all the difference for
many men. And about 80 percent of divorced men remarry. Unfortunately, most of these romances on the rebound also fail—
particularly when the initial divorce occurs later on in a person's
life.

Men may be better off financially and more solaced and sta-
bilized by success in work than their exes. But otherwise their
isolation is excruciating. Their houses and apartments seem still
and silent, without the din and hum of the children who used to
live there. And men's friendships with other men usually lack the
physical and emotional intimacies shared by most women.

Whatever the financial gains, then, these prove to be poor
compensation for the human losses involved. Indeed, a divorce
reveals just how much a husband has taken for granted and just
how vulnerable and needy he really is.

Maybe this is why every man who actively sought a divorce in the Wallerstein study had another woman waiting in the wings. Every one! Whether he would end up staying with her or not.

These findings may seem to fit at first with the traditional picture of a divorce. In the throes of some midlife crisis, the husband in this scenario gets tired of his older and "used-up" wife. Taken by some younger and fresher "tootsie," he flies the coop in search of good sex and renewed horizons.

But there's another possible explanation to be found even when the cliché holds true. It's not that he simply wants another woman but that he can't be without her. Needful soul that a man is, he simply can't be alone—not for very long at least. Either he's unwilling to leave without having first found a "substitute" to fill in for his wife; or, if she kicks him out, he finds someone to fill in for her as soon as he can. Even when he thinks that he is proving his masculinity by "making it" with another woman, a divorcing man is also betraying his childlike dependency on the opposite sex.

And what about how wives feel once the divorce takes place? More in touch with such feelings and false expectations all along, most wives have known better what to expect. They've done the lion's share of the latter-day mothering. Moreover, to the extent that their husbands tend to represent "father" and to the degree that fathers always love "conditionally," leaving a daughter feeling forever on trial, women have counted on less from the very start of marriage. For all their superficial demands, they know a man's sights are pointed elsewhere—toward the world, work, other women, his ideals, himself—and have felt they can't quite win him altogether anyway. When the relationship actually crumbles, a woman will often see this as a vindication of misgivings she'd had since it began. For a woman, a divorce, whoever initiates it, it tells her that the marriage was simply a mistake. So she just picks herself up and prepares to do what's necessary. And having "identified" with her mother, she's got her with her, in her wherever she is. She can take comfort in herself.

In contrast, for a man the breakup—particularly when it is instigated by the wife—undermines what the existentialist philosophers have called his "ontological security," his raison d'être, the very basis of his existence. Losing his wife and mother, his family, and his identity within it, a husband, father, and provider also loses the better part of himself. Yes, as I noted earlier, divorce symbolically "castrates" a man—at least temporarily. Being divorced feels like a "low blow"—at times quite concretely so.

Especially to dedicated family men like Marvin. Having long ago sacrificed their youth and the exercise of their special gifts to spend the hours and suffer the anxiety necessary to make money for a family, having put their wives and then their children first, they are then forced to wonder whether they've been rejected because this very grind has made them so boring and undesirable. What a terrible irony, they grumble.

That these men's sex lives have also dwindled in the process only adds to the bitter conviction that they gave up their manhood long ago and look where it got them. When his ex happens to take a lover and later acquires a new husband, a man's wounds are laced with salt. No matter what the circumstances of their previous relationship, a rejected husband comes to see himself as the consummate loser, the chump par excellence.

The onslaught leaves most men reeling, and regressed. Men in what Wallerstein and others have called the "acute phase" or the "divorce crisis" go backward in adult psychological time. Afraid of retreating all the way into infancy, they act like the kids they were before their marriage—like teenagers, tentative suitors, or insecure young studs. Stung to the core of their manhood, they may find themselves masturbating with a frequency unknown in their adult years. "Does the thing still work right?" they wonder at the same time that they comfort themselves with sensations other than pain and emptiness.

Such men are utterly unused to being without a woman. So when their grieving is done or momentarily suspended, they try to renew themselves by tracking and conquering "girls" with an adolescent's urgency and ineffectuality. The prospect of sexual freedom is called up to offset the specter of rejection as a man, yet it calls into question their adequacy. Their first steps out are tentative and they fall back on themselves.

"I haven't done this in years," these guys also tell themselves—dated, courted, seduced, and successfully penetrated a strange woman. So, having "forgotten" their bodies until now, when they are not abusing them with alcohol and other intoxicants, divorced men start attending to their appearance with a meticulousness hitherto observable only in their insecure adolescent children. Fussing over what to wear, dieting themselves back into sex appeal, they are not only seeking the fountain of youth.

These men are also immersing themselves in their own being to protect themselves from the danger of loss that now seems to come with caring about other people (see Chapter 3). They are solacing themselves with themselves. No longer able to control their estranged wives, they're trying to take control of everything, including sex and pleasure, which in the past they'd given over to another—to a woman, to somebody you can't live with or without.

Then, too, in acting like their wives, whose feminine vanity they've come to resent, they've made her part of themselves. They've kept her with them as their own. "When you can't be with the one you love[d]," not only "love the one you're with"—another woman, for instance—but "love yourself."

This strategy doesn't work, however, because a divorced husband is overwhelmed by feelings of failure and self-hatred. Unable to vent his recriminations on the wife who has left him and isn't there, he identifies with her and comes to loathe himself instead. Identified with her "badness," he becomes depressed, punctuating his melancholy with sporadic and futile outbursts of anger.

Unpleasant in its own right, his rage may still be easier to take than the feelings of emptiness or the inwardness of the "burning funk" that result when hatred is turned back upon oneself. Kids can't really mourn, psychologists have found, often acting out aggressively in order to ward off the restless and relentless emptiness of loss. And it's much the same with adult men during a separation. Regressed as they are, it can be easier for them to act mean toward other people than to feel bad by and about themselves.

"And it's not as if she died either!" bemoans a Marvin. She chose to leave him. And somewhere out there she still exists—if not for him. The spurned husband cries, "Who did this to me? Who!" And he sharpens and informs his confusion with anger and subsequent recourse to fantasy. Since he's lived so much of his life with her, and left so much with her, he's hard put to vent all of his fury on the wife who was once his helpmate and better half. To do so is to call into question his earlier choices and judgment as an adult. And so a man like this looks for other enemies—unseen tyrants, subversive rivals, elusive or not.

His mother-in-law. Her therapist or counselor. A lover. The lawyer. The children.

The children?

Yes, the children. They become the divorced man's unexpected emotional adversaries. Giving up the children may be the supreme amputation. Now, deprived of their mother, he is most likely robbed of them, too—both of their presence and their affectionate admiration. It's as if, having given birth to them and then grudgingly having relinquished them to a father's guidance, their mother is sucking her babies back up again, reiterating that, born of her, they are still hers after all. When another man happens to enter the scene, co-opting the kids' filial loyalties, acting *in loco parentis*, and becoming privy to their daily routine, the further competition with the stepfather salts the wounds even more. Severed from the divorced father, the children can also become the enemy.

• • •

Six months after he'd plopped and plodded the three miles down the beach to his bungalow, Marvin was having lunch with his son, Darryl, in Ithaca, New York, at the town's only sushi bar.

"What's twelve inches and white?" Marvin said, chuckling.

The boy, still tanned from his winter ski trip, smiled faintly. It was an old joke.

"Nothing."

Marvin guffawed into the silence, met only with the son's perfunctory "Ha, ha." Not finding himself funny, either, he aborted his laughter. His family had always teased him about his timing, and he'd stopped telling jokes to them years ago. But now things were different.

Six months, and thirty-six pounds he'd lost. Pretty damned good, he mused to himself as he stared sideways at the lean mien of his son—with his black, curly hair and almost equally dark eyes. Darryl the prelaw tennis player, a college senior now, whose every match and debate he'd canceled clients to go see in the boy's high school days. Oh, not so long ago.

He'd given it all to him, Marv mused, and the little shit couldn't even laugh at the old man's jokes. Besides, he wanted to ask him about Ethel, who'd joined the boy and his buddy Paul Mandell in Aspen with the still-new flame from Stamford— "Schnei the schnake"—and he knew he couldn't. He'd be embarrassed. Darryl wouldn't answer, and he'd feel even more humiliated.

So he ended up shaking hands with his son, saying good-bye, and driving home.

• • •

"Ex-fathers" see in children of a first and failed marriage unwanted reminders of fruitless efforts and of hopes and ambitions gone awry. And in so many words or not they can tell them so. At times they can convey to their sons and daughters the sense that, like the marriage, they would be better off dead. At the very least, having been the apple of a father's eye, the kids should now fade into the background while he retreats into his private blues and then tries to begin again, burning off the old and planting anew. And in fact, in the Wallerstein study of middle-class families, only 10 percent of the children of the divorced lived with their fathers or in joint-custody arrangements.

It's become something of a truism by now that divorced couples continue to wage war with each other through the children. Family courts and counselors of all stripes have come to expect the protracted battles over custody, visitation, and child support. In these deliberations it soon becomes apparent that the parents' goals have less to do with the best interests of the child, or practical self-interest for that matter, than with getting back at each other, inflicting the greatest possible pain.

Bailiffs and marshals are familiar with the fact that the financial support decreed at the end of these courtroom campaigns rarely comes when it's supposed to. The majority of divorced fathers remain obliviously and wantonly in arrears. Only 45 percent of the 4 million women to whom it is owed receive the full child support (not alimony) due for their children. Nor are the ex-wives blameless in all this, with their insistent and sometimes unreasonable demands and their accumulating false accusations. According to divorce attorney Eleanor Alter, mothers and fathers continue to use their children as pawns in their legalistic quest for vengeance toward the partner who betrayed them.

But there's more here than meets the eye of the family court judge—more to a father's response to his children once his marriage and his pride in it have been shattered. As Wallerstein and her collaborator Kelly remarked a decade ago, the relationship between father and child after a divorce can't be predicted on the basis of what took place before it.

Sometimes, of course, relief from a bad marriage takes the tension out of the relationships between parents and children. Under less strain, some fathers can do a better job with kids, whom they've come to enjoy more. Occasionally, deprived of their wives, they may realize what they've been missing all along and take the kids less for granted. And they may turn to them for mutual understanding and reciprocal care and for an affirmation that they've done something right.

But these are not typical turns of events. Far more common is the tendency of divorced men to invest their energies elsewhere, disengaging from a family that is no longer really theirs. Their presence has become either negligible or negative in their children's lives, lives over which these men no longer have much control. The children's loyalty to them, if not necessarily their love, can no longer be counted on. To the extent that we in this culture still count on our offspring to comfort and to protect us in our old age, men in this position fear that all they have given has come to nought. Feeling misused and left by the wayside, they up the ante of abandonment. The kids still have their mother, they tell themselves, and in having her, they have what he does not. So why should they also have him, thinks the provider who feels exploited and embittered. He retaliates, revolting against his morality, against his paternal duties.

The fact is that all along men have felt competitive with their children, sons especially—as I will suggest in considering abusive as well as normal-enough fathers (Chapter 15). From pregnancy and birth on, they've had to share their wife with the kids. All along they've denied themselves and their freedoms to make room for the kids. In an intact family, a man's anger at having been intruded on, replaced, superseded, and surpassed is offset by the primacy of the couple's mature sexual relationship and by the pleasures of active fatherhood. However, when family ties are torn, so are the restraints that rein in a man's more impulsive expressions of "filicidal impulses"—his urges to hurt sons and daughters. Since they no longer "honor [their] father and mother," he is less constrained by the commandment not to "kill."

In this circumstance as elsewhere, men reveal their abiding tendency to exploit their aggression toward other men—their sons, their own paternity, the ghosts of the father they've identified with—to deal with their complex feelings toward the women in their lives, including those who are no longer there. By being tough, indifferent, fighting mad, simply selfish, the divorced father is proving he's whole, male, able therefore to survive on his own after all. "Don't get sad," he trumpets, "get mad!"

Most divorced men don't become filicidal, of course, but they do neglect and abuse their children in remarkable ways. I've already underscored their tendency to forget them—how they don't see and don't pay for them. Beyond these sins of omission, fathers in divorce expose their sons and daughters to the rawness of their frustration and to their sudden self-importance.

Try as they might to restrain themselves, most divorced fathers can't refrain from maligning the child's mother, of course. In the process they call into question a son's or daughter's very origins, making emotional foundlings out of them. Often enough, they expose children to their new sex lives, to grown-up "sexpots" the kids still can't have, whetting their appetites while demonstrating their own prowess as sexual men. And when these desirable bachelors remarry and have more children, many make a show of lavishing more love on a child's successors—on stepsisters or half brothers. After all, this wife has yet to do him in.

Vulnerable as they are, buffeted by these unwanted feelings, men can prove to be remarkably resilient. In rediscovering his virility, a divorced man can also reassert the wisdom gained over the years and organized as an enduring paternal authority. In other words, men of all ages can fall in love again, have fun again, and further expand their boundaries by taking in the experience of a new person. Even an "old schlepper," as Marvin was wont to call himself—even he can.

• • •

"It turned out to be the best possible thing that could have happened," said Marvin earnestly and happily to Tony O'Brien, his client and confidant of twenty-five years, after catching his reflection in the revolving door of the Soleful Seafood House. He couldn't help admiring the Armani tie and jacket with shoulder pads and lazily sloping lapels. Lily had taken him to buy this, his first Italian-designer outfit, and Marvin, not a little awkward still, couldn't help savoring the effect.

It was another year later, and Marv had just returned from Pritikin in L.A., where he'd dropped four more pounds from the thirty-six already lost and lowered his cholesterol to 197. He'd wanted to preach to Tony about the virtues of his conversion to health consciousness. Tony, face ruddy from J&B, pack-a-day Tony was still fat and still married.

"The best thing." Marv's words seemed to echo into the vestibule beyond the door. How many times had he heard other poor saps—his dentist, his broker, even his brother-in-law, Big Stu Stein himself—rationalize away the whole morass once they'd stopped bemoaning their fate. Sometimes, he reflected, his whole inane life seemed like a walking cliché or as Rabbi Hurst had mused, "a bad Jewish joke." Still, trouble was, Marv added to himself as he cradled Tony's elbow, it was true.

The scent of Joy (the perfume that is) only added to his

conviction and conviviality. It had swept upon him from behind, wafting with it the tickling texture, the henna strands of Lil's hair. Behind him, Marv heard the whoosh of the revolving door.

Lil announced herself to him, all forty-six and a half years of her, with a hickey to the nape of the neck and pinch to the tush that in the veil of darkness was just enough beyond decency. Inhaling for a moment, he introduced the two intimates, each from a different life.

"I'm so glad to meet you, Tony. Marv's told me so-o much about you," she said, the hint of a Southern drawl adding a lilt to Lil's words of greeting.

Another cliché, but true, too, its genuineness set in relief by the further fact that he, Tony, had known nothing about Lily. Nobody had.

It builds character, Marvin thought, chuckling to himself, and other things. So they, the goyim, might have said. Again it was true, too true. It had been a crisis and in more senses than one, he'd risen to the occasion. Ha! So there! Ethel's leaving had led him, old affable Marv, to rediscover his sexuality. They'd been married for three decades before that, during which Marvin had strayed only once—and what a deal she'd made of that one—and before which he'd had only a few bumbling, fumbling late-adolescence experiments. He'd "known" Ethel his whole life— and only her.

Sex with her had become routine and monotonous when he thought about it, their inhibitions structured into repetition and perfunctoriness. Over the years, they'd come to forget what she had refused to do and simply did what she did do without a whole lot of questioning. It was much the same with their emotional intimacies—Marv and Ethel had stopped wondering what they didn't or couldn't talk about.

And then Lily walked into his life and brought something different. It almost doesn't matter how they met, but it was at the Roslyn Health Club. And she'd spread worlds before him, by opening up her body totally, and to him. He was tempted to tell Tony, but he wouldn't. As "Sweet Georgia Lil" herself might have intoned, "A gentleman never tells." He'd tried everything with her—everything. Things he had thought about, things he hadn't. For the first time in years, he felt excited, accepted.

Lily, an ex-actress, worked as a paralegal. Before that she'd had a stint in Paris working for the *International Herald Tribune* and doing some dancing. She was widowed and then divorced—with two teenage kids from her first marriage. There was a daughter who liked him and a boy who was obnoxious to his mother's new "boy" friend ("boy," yet!). The kids were, to put it decorously, of mixed race. ("Schwarzes," his mama would've said more bluntly.)

Maybe she *was* after his money. He'd discovered how much of a catch he'd been, even fat and fifty-plus, how every unattached woman had seemed to come out of the woodwork in hot pursuit of a new "eligible." Maybe Darryl, that relentless critic of his pop without honor—maybe he was right. Maybe Lil was a gold digger, and it wouldn't last. . . .

• • •

"But so what?" Marvin snorted another half year later as he popped a gherkin and some salmon mousse into his mouth at the wedding reception—his wedding. Darryl just wouldn't let go of it. A Columbia law student now, in *his* Armani suit, his hand on his fiancée's svelte waist—even then and there he was staring his father down with those unblinking black eyes of his.

Marvin suppressed all sorts of unsavory thoughts about his son's relationship with Maud. She looked pretty pinched and frigid to him, he thought, this little "shiksa"— But then he reminded himself, "You love this kid, remember!" before any other improprieties became conscious. That Darryl had said, "Maud is worried, too," only salted the wounds after the boy had picked at his father's scabs. Read between the lines: "Bimbo." Marv let that pass as well.

"You know, Son [a form of address he'd never heard himself use before], you never know how much time you have—alone together—none of us does." He was reiterating Harrison Ford's words of epilogue in *Blade Runner*. It was Lil's favorite film, a genuine profound sleeper, and she'd rented it for them two nights before. Darryl's friend Jeremy, who happened to be Rabbi Hurst's nephew, had also said how he loved this flick. So maybe his son would get the reference.

Marv swigged a little more Perrier-Jouët and stared back at the boy. He loved him. Darryl was twenty-three, he was financing the kid's education and rent, and he would pay for their honeymoon. So, why should he stop himself? He was entitled to say what he wanted, what he thought. He had rights! Besides, Marvin once again believed what he'd said. Nothing need be forever. He could love and lose. And the loving phase was wonderful. Darryl didn't know this yet, whatever he thought he knew, and how could he?

Swallowing his canapé, Marv reached out and gently patted the boy where his cheek met his neck, just below the ear. He let his hand rest there for a moment. Darryl felt to him the way he had when he was five years old, and his father, having opened the door to the onrushing youngster, hugged him after a long day apart: Warm, smooth, untouched by worry. Darryl couldn't help smiling back. Marv gave a parting squeeze and walked over to Lil. Loving this woman, Marvin found himself gentled once more.

. . .

Men like Marvin learn they can cope with what at first looms as the end of their life. Sometimes they emerge from the ordeal of a divorce with profit. Especially when it comes to sex, they can find out what they've really wanted all along but were afraid to ask for.

Marvin, for example, learned that being a "schlepper" doesn't pay off. He'd allowed the years of toil to take its toll on him—beating down his body, authority, and virility. Martyring himself to the people he loved, he'd made himself undesirable to them. Being "respectable" had culminated in their losing respect for him.

Reflecting on what had happened, Marvin came to see that it was no wonder Ethel had gotten tired of him. No, he hadn't been a philanderer or a flake. But he hadn't taken himself seriously enough. He had forgotten that, like men, women need to find their lovers compelling. And Marvin had long lost anything like his sex appeal. Deafened by his irrational guilt, deferring to his duties, he hadn't understood what his wife felt, wanted, and needed. He'd been selfish in suffering, selfish after all.

Masochism, again. Women don't have a premium on it. Indeed, from the very first Freud was thinking about men, his male patients and their problems, when he talked about *"feminine* masochism." Many men caricature women as passive victims and identify with them in this guise, unconsciously expressing their femininity by unmanning themselves.

"*Moral* masochism," clinicians would say as well, in Marvin's case. Being beaten is not his thing. Nor is he simply "womanly." Instead, a man like this seeks to punish himself by denying himself—by ceding his rights to beauty, freedom, sensuality, fun. Guilty about any wish of his own, especially any aggressive impulse, he compromises his masculinity and authority. Fading into the background, he relies on others, his son for instance, to express his ambitions and desires for him. He sits on himself because he doesn't want to alienate, lose, or hurt people. And ironically it is this that has made him eminently divorcible. Having deprived others of himself, he enables them to give him up.

Even self-sacrifice can be self-serving.

• • •

With half the marriages undertaken now ending prematurely, divorce is a possibility all of us must reckon with. Even where it doesn't occur, its specter has begun to give most men pause. All those threats hurled in the throes of anger can no longer be dismissed as idle manipulations. They are real. Hardly a man hasn't had some close friend or relative where the worst has happened. Whether or not they crack, most marriages have their serious flaws. These shift, rumble, and sometimes screech with the burdens and stresses that come when a working couple tries to maintain the family.

These are hard times. And Marvin's right, nothing is forever.

As with the specter of nuclear war, so with divorce: thinking about the unthinkable may move men to improve on the status quo. For all the compensations people make, there are no true winners when a family disintegrates. And there is plenty of hardship that didn't have to be.

Realizing that he is far from invulnerable, a man can take steps to take nothing for granted. To tune in, that is, to those needs and desires—his partner's and his own—that might otherwise be dismissed as selfish or irrelevant. If two people are to weather the forces of hate and indifference mobilized when they get close to each other, the bond between them needs to be continually nourished with love. It is a love, moreover, that is mindful of who the individuals are—oneself included—in the collective saga of their evolving family.

When he reflects back on it then, even when he has done what seems to be his best and even when it wasn't *his* idea to break up, a disenfranchised husband must take his share of responsibility for the ultimate failure of a marriage. A divorce may feel like simple bad luck, but it doesn't quite fit with the other misfortunes that can cast their shadow over a man's life. Indeed, for these calamities a man, just because he is a man, may assume a blame far out of proportion to any reality—as we shall see in the next series of chapters.

What Men
Don't Want, III

Bad Luck

If most young men and women were apprised from the start of
what awaits them, they might choose not to undertake a journey
that ends only in death. Indeed, even this mortality of ours isn't
so bad because it is both inevitable and unknowable. It's the
setbacks along the way that are wrenching. Sigmund Freud referred to these as "common unhappiness" in contrast to the "neurotic suffering" we bring on ourselves, the sort of psychological
symptoms and problems that were explored in the previous section.

In fact, cultural dislocations and the ecological imbalances
brought on by our technology have upset our more pat generalizations about what we can take for granted in the course of a life.
No single person can expect to suffer all the calamities of adulthood: failures at work, disabled children, untimely illness and
loss. Yet the odds are that at least one or another of these misfortunes will cast a shadow on most lives.

Such "stressors" leave their stamp on these lives—the sense of something sudden, evil, and unjust, something over which we have no control, something that changes us forever. We can't accept just how capricious and cruel fate can be, and so we try to understand it as we do everything that happens to us.

Growing up, children invent and repeatedly tell themselves a variety of stories about themselves and their experiences. Like primitive people, they concoct myths to explain the causes of things. And into these scenarios or "personal narratives," the developing individual fits most of the events that befall him.

An "omnipotence of thought" characterizes childish reasoning. A baby bawls, and this activity itself makes its mother appear. Somewhat later on in childhood, children endow parents with a control over the physical world—blaming them when things don't work the way they want. As one four-year-old put it to his father, "Daddy, please, please make the sun come up!" Such thinking is "magical" and "wishful."

As our abilities to conceptualize real cause and effect ripen with age, we consciously reject the superstitions of childhood. Grown-ups strive to figure out how things work, to prove their inferences and to act accordingly. Deep down, however, in the realm of "unconscious fantasy," we hold ourselves accountable for events in reality. Repressed from awareness, the child's logic will out. In its perspective, we are never creatures of circumstance but rather mystical masters of the universe. For all that befalls us, good and bad, we take a profound responsibility.

So when things go wrong in a man's life, the little boy inside him feels he deserves it. Each external stress is matched by an internal one. Incursions on our well-being are interpreted as statements about our inherent self-worth, as demonstrations of inadequacy or culpability. Their emphasis on performance, feelings of fragility, excesses of conscience, and proneness to rage make men particularly vulnerable to outrageous fortune. Men's masculine pride is wounded by misadventure, disappointment, and human limitation.

Tradition has it that women are the dreamers, awaiting their fairy-tale prince. In fact, they tend to take life as it unfolds more in stride. From Eve on, women have been told their lot in life is to suffer. They may hurt, but they expect to. Suffering doesn't mean they're not women enough for the world. If you think about it, that old fairy tale should have been about the prince and the pea, for it's men who take these blows most personally. They view them as affronts to their honor and are moved to fight back in order not to feel the brunt of such assaults. Indeed, undermining his habitual defenses, life crises often reveal the true man, the perennial boy, in all his naked frailty.

The challenges of adult life resonate with a man's fears of being helpless and needy—qualities that he's projected onto women and that he therefore equates with being infantile and effeminate. Because these crises make him wonder whether he's enough of a man, they also rouse the anger and hostility in a way that may make him feel more of a man yet also leave him apprehensive that he might have been too much of one. Too aggressive, too competitive, too much on top—his temerity inviting the wrath of the gods.

In this section, then, I'll look at ordeals of men who don't get what they want. I have selected some—not all, obviously—of the major trials and emotional problems met with during the course of an adult man's life. Though sometimes men may have unwittingly contributed in one way or another to their demise, when they come, a job loss, illness, a "defective" son descend, it seems, from outside and on high as harsh judgments of nature and God. While many of these adult disasters are excruciating in their own right, they take on added weight because of what they revive from the past still alive within. Ironically, it's in accepting these feelings of childish helplessness that a man can find the resources to pull himself back from the brink—often, in fact, with sort of an existential profit.

8
• • •

Fired

In the late sixties, urged on by self-styled gurus such as Timothy Leary, kids dropped out in droves, extending what Erikson called psychosocial moratoriums (see Chapter 13) into noncareer tracks. When their experiment had run its rudderless course, this generation and the one that followed in its wake got straight again, and with a vengeance. Everywhere the quality of life came to be defined by professional success and the making of money.

To be free, women now had to participate in the economic process (see Chapter 7). Those who didn't were now frowned upon by their sisterhood as throwbacks or turncoats. Men simply reiterated what they'd always been told and had only forgotten for a decade or so. Men are men at work.

Within most socioeconomic groups, it's simply expected that a man will perform and make a living—a good one. To do otherwise is not, as it used to be at least for his female counterparts, an option. As Steve Martin put it (rather chauvinistically) in *Parenthood:* "Women have wishes. Men have responsibilities."

Even where schoolwork may not have figured prominently in a man's list of boyhood priorities, when it comes to adulthood, the pressure's on. And it mounts. Pretty soon, there's no escape, and often no fun. And so a man's twenties, the age of all the cowboy heroes of his boyhood, of Prince Galahad, Tarzan, and Buck Rogers—well, these beginning years are not what he had anticipated.

All work—no play—is the order of the day. The *things* he acquires, like Paul Mandell's toys, may be fun, but their owner has hardly any *time* to spare for them.

· · ·

Paul Mandell watched over the garage attendant as he backed up the 300E into its commuter parking space. It wasn't flashy like Darryl Landsman's Porsche. But, oh, what a lustrous black beauty, with pearl leather seats, antilock brakes, and an air bag for safety's sake. When the kids came, they'd be well taken care of. He ought to get that dimple in the left door fixed, though.

Paul fingered the wedding band, thinking of Judy, whom he'd dropped off three blocks earlier at her office at Gordon, Stone. He loved every inch of her—the long, California-girl blond hair tied up in buns Monday to Friday, her WASPy, lanky torso, and her neat but spongy breasts, even the Calvin Klein business suit with the slit skirts. Number three in her MBA class at Columbia, too—just behind Karen. The genuine article. A great couple they made.

Unlike him, actually, Paul's wife had done it the straight way, with credentials in place as she rose up the hierarchy. Not so, Paul. He'd been handpicked out of his graduating class at SUNY Purchase four years earlier by Amos Stein. "Uncle Amie," he called him, this elder cousin thrice removed, like everybody else ignoring the fact that the diminutive was also feminine and hardly fit Stein's balls-of-brass persona. It was Stein who had taught Paul the ins and outs of the trading desk. And now the kid from Queens was raking in nearly a half a mil at Lewis and Simson, surviving successive Black Mondays, to boot.

Amie liked his stock traders young. Most were under thirty—go-getters still, young guys yet to burn out. Hardly seasoned salesmen, Amie's boys worked fast.

Actually, Paul was a little edgy. He had been slipping lately, maybe as a result of being stressed out by his father's illness. Amie wanted to see him, he'd said yesterday, first thing in the A.M. Things hadn't been all that great at L&S for '90, and it might just be he'd be getting a cut in compensation. Not that May was bonus time yet—not for months. Just a "warning period"—like the rest of the long year. The new mortgage and car payments might make for a strain if this happened. But he'd just deal with it when he had to.

Paul emerged from the concrete underground and made his way through the crush and street noises to Number 43 down the block. Even at this hour, long before the market's opening, the crowds and the hectic pace were remarkable. He hadn't been paying attention, he figured, because he found himself caught for a moment with one of the secretaries in the revolving door. Propelled by the crowds, it caught him sharply, slamming his pinky nail into the cylinder wall.

The tip had turned an ugly blue by the time he reached the twenty-sixth floor, and he imagined the nail would be coming off in a day or so. Thinking about his Sunday doubles at the East Hampton Club, Paul ran the water from the cooler over it before making his way to his glass-enclosed cubicle and then on to Amos's office. He didn't get out to the beach all that often, leaving his new house vacant much of the time, and didn't want to miss this rare opportunity for some R&R.

"Work," Amie began after he'd let go of Paul's hand. "We Americans are always working. . . . Nearly a quarter of the work force, including blue-collar laborers, puts in fifty hours per week, and this excludes the seventy-plus types like me, and, uh, you. And leisure time: from a healthy twenty-six hours weekly in 1973 when I started out here to a mere sixteen now—again excepting workaholics like me and uh, you, too, Paul, right? We could all use a little more R and R—idleness, quality time, heh?"

Amos Stein was always spouting odds and ends from the *New York Times* Week in Review as if they were his own—info that he had long been processing like ideas he'd put together himself. Like Paul, he didn't have the time or inclination to read the paper cover to cover during their frenetic weeks on the Street and at posh restaurants with clients. But he didn't quite admit it. Maybe he was trying to keep up with his well-read big brother, Stu.

This little white plagiarizing was standard stuff from Stein, and Paul didn't give it a thought. It was the "right's," the "heh's," and then the talk of "idleness," of all things, that began to unnerve him. Moreover, Amos asked questions only when he was angry, jabbing at his adversary with rhetorical quips. And Paul had never heard him mention the word *leisure* and didn't know what to make of it. No, "know" wasn't quite right; Paul had an inkling of what Amos was getting at and didn't like it.

"Sit down, Paul. I haven't seen you in quite a while—have I?"

The change of pitch at the end of Amos's last sentence caught Paul off-balance, just as he was settling into the chair in front of the desk. So he sat down abruptly and awkwardly, scraping the feet of the chair against the bare floor and banging his knees against the desk before him when he landed. Amos's coffee cup teetered in response, and Paul reached out to steady it before the black contents could stain any of the computer sheets laid out underneath. To his embarrassment Paul noticed that his fingers had begun to tremble, like an old lady's. That his fingernail was badly bruised and pulsing with pain now only added to the atmosphere of frailty and damage closing in to define him.

"Thanks." Stein smiled from the safe confines of his kneehole. He paused, then continued, "Paul, I'm just going to get down to it. You're a smart young guy, and you've done great. Until just about ten weeks ago, I mean. But Paul, baby, you've been slipping."

"I, uh—"

"Just let me continue." And now Stein raised his hand like a traffic cop giving a stop sign. "Last week you missed the opening for the third time in a month. The week before you lost eight hundred and fifty grand on the Metcalf trade—"

"I was just following the instruction. I never concur—"

"You'll let me finish, right?"

That was it, Paul realized, Amie meant business now. Having tossed out some pleasantries in the way of hors d'oeuvres, he was now getting down to the main meal, which, Paul saw, would mean some pretty bitter pills. When push came to shove, Amie cared about himself first and foremost, about his trading block's performance, about *his* compensation. Being nice to people meant motivating them so he could use them. It was the productivity, not the person, that counted.

Paul had always sort of known this, though he'd enjoyed the conceit of having a surrogate uncle around—especially since his dad got sick. Anyway, it hadn't mattered since the kid had always produced until now. And basically, he still felt he did—or could, would.

"It doesn't the fuck matter what you're told to trade and who for. If you gotta do it, then you hedge, remember? Basic Trading 101."

Another question.

"You're distracted anyhow, Paul. And that's not possible for you here. You've got to stay right on top of your screen and make your best calls. Period. And being late—heh, that just won't wash. Okay?"

A pause indicated that Paul now had permission to talk. He was nervous, knowing he had to watch his step. He'd seen what had happened to Fischer just two weeks ago. When somebody was used up, Amie chucked him without a second thought. Besides this, Paul was angry because he felt betrayed. Because Amos was his father's cousin.

"Uh—um. Amie, Amos—you know what's going on with my dad. Um, I mean, Judy's been talking with Stella [Stella Stein] about what's been going on with him." He was repeating himself, he noted, piling embarrassment upon embarrassment. "Jason and Jhana just have flaked out on us, and Mom can't cope at all, you know. It was just unavoidable, I mean, I couldn't be here."

Paul's father was dying of prostatic cancer. He lived out in Roslyn with his sixty-five-year-old wife, who had always been a hypochondriac and pretty flaky, too, but who now had a diagnosis of what looked like early-stage Alzheimer's. Paul's younger brother and sister lived in Manhattan where school and dating occupied their interests. And so they couldn't help out. Nor were they inclined to do so, resenting Jake Mandell's frank favoritism toward his firstborn son. And so it fell on this older brother, on Paul, to handle the myriad emergencies befalling the old man. Judy helped a whole lot, but still Jake was *his* father. Stu Stein, Amos's generous older brother, and Marv Landsman—also just a cousin, and by law—assisted financially as best they could. But the day-to-day stuff was pretty much his to deal with.

The cure had been almost as bad as the disease. Jake's allergic reaction to the chemotherapy, then his kidney failure and then pneumonia (because his white cells had been killed off) had forced Paul and Judy to get him rushed to the hospital on the mornings Amie was talking about.

Judy had been confiding in Amie's wife, Stella, about the ordeals, and so he should know what's been going down, Paul figured. "And besides, at least bit, Amie should know how lonely all this is for me," he muttered into his head. Despite his better judgment, Paul felt Stein should be more fatherly to him. He still had the good sense not to impart these private complaints, of course, knowing full well how little Stein liked to be made to feel guilty. Indeed, his motto might have run, "Don't get guilty. Get mad."

Having listened, Amie prepared to bring their brief meeting to a close. "Look, Mandy [Paul's nickname at times—the use of it easing the tension just then], I'm going to give you an analogy. Imagine that dick surgeon cutting away around your father's *cojones*. Like, imagine the patient's all ready to be laid out for the knife. Well, suppose *he* gets a call his father's just up and died."

She, not *he*, Paul couldn't help thinking to himself. Dr. Sapperstein was a *she*.

"Do you want him not to show up or maybe lose and slip up? Paul, we're dealing with bigger balls and not-so-funny money here—people's jobs, people's bucks are at stake. No more excuses. No more mistakes. The only deals to be made are the ones you're trading for. You get my meaning?"

Indeed, there was no mistaking it. Walking light-headedly down the hall to his office, the only thing Paul could feel was the pain in his finger.

• • •

Work now dominates the lives of most men and women. The average American household has been shrinking since the affluent and sexist fifties, now containing only two-plus individuals (as I have noted in Chapter 2). Simply translated, this means that in addition to there being more single parents, more and more couples are living together without children and the family life that goes along with them. Values have changed along with the realities. The work opportunities generated by feminist consciousness-raising in concert with economic exigencies have conspired to alter the expectations and lifestyles of many middle-class Americans.

Time and money, money and the time to earn it, have taken people out of the house, cutting into the myth of a homelife. The action's elsewhere.

Everybody works, and hard. They can't afford not to. But it takes its toll.

In 1988, nearly 25 million American families were supported by two or more wage earners, a dramatically larger proportion than figures for the 1970s, when most of these men and women were coming of age. And not only this, but according to estimates like Amie's, everybody's toiling harder and longer, leaving little time for "idleness."

The overall effects of these trends have been a reorientation of what might be called an adult man's primary affiliations and attachments. His proverbial "priorities." You would think, wouldn't you, that the women's movement and the debunking of stereotypical sex roles would have moved more men to reconsider these values? Men should have become softer and more sensitive, shouldn't they, sharing with their wives domestic work loads, such as childcare and housework, and placing a greater emphasis on the tender virtues of family than on tough-minded career advancement?

But it's not necessarily so. And here, too, an understanding of the complexities of what men really want helps explain why they continue to place such a premium on their careers. In so doing, secretly vulnerable souls that they are, they're only meeting their hidden needs.

Since the home has less to offer—because there's less of it and because, even when they're there, people's minds are elsewhere— men have come to seek from their jobs the sort of comforts and satisfactions once asked of a wife and family. There's been a de-centering, and the workplace has begun to supplant the nuclear family in men's affections.

And there's reality. Everything's more expensive.

In our culture now, great stock is placed on money, achievement, and the aggression necessary to earn it, with a whole host of other longings submerged beneath the surface: for instance, the search for parental approval as a form of love, a quest that is often disguised as the drive for success. But however unacknowledged they may be, indeed exactly *because* they pass unheeded, these childlike needs emerge every now and then—often in insidious and sometimes undermining ways, in the wrong place and at the wrong time. In the guise of ambition, and at work.

The problem is that at work it doesn't work both ways. Not really. The ties that bind aren't reciprocated there, not really. Many if not most bosses "love" their employees only to the extent that they can use them. It's like a father's conditional love—the conditions having multiplied exponentially.

Men just starting out, guys in their twenties and early thirties, such as Paul, may find themselves at risk in particular ways. They expect so much. Later on they'll have gotten used to the realpolitik of professional life, taking it all less personally and playing the game themselves. Earlier, during their apprenticeship years in whatever form these take, they still have their parents to return to for a sounding board, advice, a pat on the back—for the simple reassurance that they can go home again. Despite their apparent drive and bravado, they can still think of themselves as kids, just rehearsing for the moments of truth to come later.

People age at different points in their lives. But typically, at the very juncture when their children begin to make it on their own and for real, illness and incapacity begin to lay claim to the resources and availability of the older generation. Old age makes parents more takers than givers, more needful of grown children than able to be there for them. A father's loss of power and function is felt as a profound personal void by his sons.

The beginning of a career is thus a scary and lonely time for most men, especially nowadays when their wives find themselves subject to similar pressures. There's nobody to turn to, they discover when they stop to catch their breath, nobody who really has the time or inclination to listen to their doubts and anxieties, nobody to back them up financially anymore should they fail. On the work front in fact, such admissions of weakness can be unwelcome or counterproductive.

The transition into "middle adulthood," as Daniel Levinson and other students of adult life have called the postapprenticeship years, is a time fraught with inner conflict. It is a period when men find themselves confronted, on the one hand, with fathers on the decline, and on the other, with all-too-forceful bosses, men (or women) at the height of their powers, standing midway between the generations. Getting contradictory messages from these two sets of authorities, they are constantly shifting emotional gears.

They find themselves irrationally angry at their parents because they no longer run interference for them, and just as unreasonably, guilty because they are surpassing and superseding them at last. The Oedipus complex, again—but with some further twists.

The fathers who once controlled them or stood in their way are acting like children now. Regressed, they want to look up to their sons, to depend on them. And they want to let go. Or rather, they want to hang on—to rely on their sons. The way it was in the days of the extended family and still is in some cultures.

At the same time, orphaned because of these role reversals, a young man finds himself uncertain about just how far to go with his bosses—just how much initiative to take. Be tough, aggressive, they tell him, but not too tough—or at least with me. Don't cross me, they say. Do it, and do it well, but do what I tell you. And for godsake, never tell *me* what to do. Don't hassle me!

When, he wonders, will these authority figures, onto whom he has "transferred" ambivalences from his evolving relationship with his father—when will they get fed up? When will they let him be his own man, as he's supposed to be already? When will he be on top? When will it all let up? And what *does* he want, anyway?

Tensions like these can mount under the impact of certain typical stresses outside the professional arena—for instance, the terminal illness of a parent or the end of a long-term relationship with a wife or lover. Beleaguered and needy, a man in such a predicament can't stop to think. Harried as he is, pushed at times to the breaking point, he often falls prey to the internal pressures of his unconscious conflicts about his male aggression, which only makes matters worse.

Under such circumstances it becomes all too easy for him to lose his bearings and get himself fired. Indeed, not a few such young men at this point act to bring down on themselves an outcome, a frank failure, that on the surface at least they dread more than anything else in the world.

And it may be quite a little straw—an oversight, a slight error in judgment, an accident—that breaks his employer's and his own back.

● ● ●

By Wednesday, Paul's nail had dropped off. He hadn't had time to get to the doctor's office to have the thing properly tended to. But following the nurse's instructions over the phone, before catching her plane to L.A., Judy had cleaned and disinfected the finger, swathing it in bandages. Dr. Ganglioni had called in a prescription of codeine that softened the pain.

The analgesic had had the further effect of making Paul high, soothing his emotional aches as well. So transported was he when he got up on Thursday that he almost forgot his Monday-morning warning from Amie. A profitable week so far—and some home-work had helped as well, combining with the drug to ease his anxiety. A good thing, too, since Judy was gone for two days on business and wouldn't be home for him until tomorrow night. Though they couldn't hang out much—no time—still he needed her.

The hell with tennis on Sunday, Paul told himself as he exited the cleaners, suits in hand, and shimmied between the bumpers to his double-parked car. He'd do some more catching up and make love to Judy instead! He was actually in a damned good mood again.

Da-da-da-da! The remote signaled. His "Kit" responded, and in a trice he was in. Flipping his suits into the backseat, his body compensating for this backward extension, Paul accidentally stepped, not once, but twice on the accelerator. At just about the very same instant, that is, that he automatically inserted and turned his key in the ignition. The starter sputtered, the dash lights flashed, and yes he should have known it, the car failed to start.

Paul had committed a cardinal no-no with his posh fuel-injected Mercedes. He'd pumped it. By stepping on the gas, and so emphatically, he'd flooded the engine. There was no helping it or him now. Offended, its spark plugs swamped, the vehicle simply refused to give way.

Paul opened the door, got out, got in, got out again, in and out—all rather like a chicken, he reflected later, with its head either cut off or about to be. He glanced at his watch, discovering that he had only twenty-five minutes to make the opening. Under other circumstances it would easily have been enough, but here he was on First Avenue in Manhattan, at this special cleaners—damn it, and not his good old staple shop in Montclair—double-parked. Double-parked, when the single-parked cars were rumbling and grumbling their way out of already-illegal zones. Double jeopardy.

Dazedly, he pulled cards from his ostrich wallet, many of which tumbled to the pavement. He retrieved most from the ground and managed to ferret out the one from the Triple A. This in hand, repeating the numbers to himself as if they were a mantra, Paul raced down the block to the pay phone—shit, he should have had the modular installed after all—and got his call through soon enough. But no, they couldn't make it for forty-five minutes, which no doubt translated into three or four times that, he now calculated in his panic.

Well, damn it, he'd just leave the car there, leave the key, for all it was worth, with La Plage ("Fancy Pants") Cleaners, getting a cab to work, if he could flag one, taxiing safely "home," he hoped. So raced Paul's thoughts as he jogged back down the sidewalk, sending excruciating jolts of hot blood into his no-longer-numbed little finger. Interposed between him and the Black Beauty, however, was a blue-and-white car with a revolving red beacon on its roof, suitably attended, Paul also saw, by the men in blue—a man and one short, plump woman, to be precise. Cops.

"Move it."

"I can't," Paul answered imploringly as he tried a smile out for size on Officer Janine Hernandez. "It's flooded."

"You know you're not supposed to double-park—"

"But only for an instant."

"No such thing as an instant."

"Look, Officer, I got an emergency. I've got to make it down to my office in, oh no, fifteen, uh, ten minutes."

"What for?" Officer Hernandez asked with uncharacteristic interest.

"The opening."

"The opening?" She hadn't a clue.

"The market. The stock market's opening."

"That's an emergency?"

"Yes." Paul tried out the charm that until now had always stood the test. But the affable salesmanship had been swept away by his urgent helplessness. He grinned at the bulbous-hipped officer—like a disingenuous boy whose teenage voice still cracked. Oh, he'd appeal to the maternal instinct to be found somewhere underneath the badge. "My job's on the line."

Janine Hernandez paused to study this citizen and, Paul realized, her latest potential collar. She took him in—took it all in—the stalled Mercedes. The Cerruti suit. Oh, hell, even the Rolex. And she smiled—not that she'd even had to bother to make up her mind. It was cut-'n'-dried.

"I'm sorry, sir, this is very busy here. I don't have to forgive you your double-parking, but I will." Pause—the "good cop."

"But sir, you'll just have to remain with your vehicle until the tow truck comes. Okay?"

"Okay."

That was it. And Paul simply sank to the ground. He just sat down on First Avenue.

He couldn't even get up to call Amos. The lights on her squad car flashing and flickering, Officer Hernandez had wandered out onto the avenue to redirect traffic around Paul and his disabled vehicle. Ten feet away, every now and then she glanced back at the stalled stock trader and sent him a compassionate nod, which also held him in place. . . .

Friday came, and what it brought was, of course, not unexpected. Amie called Paul into his office first thing and fired him. Or to put it more precisely and fairly, he told his cousin to look elsewhere for employment. And where Fischer had been asked to clear out his desk then and there—his infractions had been greater, after all—and wait for his two months' severance in the mail, Paul was allowed to stick around for a while. He'd have his desk for up to two months, no bonus but salary for this period. A closet lame duck. Nobody would know. He'd even get another two months' pay after he'd left for real. Pretty generous, huh?

What surprised Paul was his reaction. He didn't feel a thing at first. He figured he'd been numbed by the blow. But beyond this, and it disconcerted him, he felt relieved. The trauma had come, the worst was over—or so he felt at first—and he could relax.

Just be. Like dying.

He'd have some time for himself to cool out and reflect on where he was going. He'd spend more time with his dad. Judy was working. It wasn't so bad. Life on the Street was tough now so he needn't take it personally, what with those thousands in his very dilemma. Yeah, a cast of thousands milling about, knocking on locked doors, having cut short their auto leases and sold their second houses before the banks could foreclose on them.

Oh, hell. Money wasn't everything. And he'd make it anyhow.

What Paul couldn't do was look at Amie. The minute Amos Stein smiled after the fateful announcement, giving a quick squeeze to Paul's forearm and telling him he had an "okay future if you can get your nerves under control," Paul averted his gaze. He looked down, anyway, anywhere but at him, avoiding eye contact then and there and for the two months to follow.

Amie had become a blur before him. Paul felt a surge of pain in his pinky and of rage in his heart. The relief gave way, not yet replaced by anxiety for his situation nor by anything like despair. It was hatred that erupted in him, hatred for the man who had betrayed his trust in a time of need, who had undone him and half seemed to enjoy it, and at whom, fearing for his future, he dared not get openly indignant.

"Thanks, Amie." And Paul, having extended his maimed hand and looking down, turned to leave.

He would have called her. But Judy wasn't home, he remembered. Yes, she was out of town, working.

• • •

When a man's let go, sacked, terminated—such feelings of relief don't last long. Partly rooted in his unconscious wish to be punished for outdoing and outlasting his old man, and partly deriving from his denial of what's happened to him and what lies ahead, this bland acceptance of "fate" only temporarily helps him continue to function and save face. Soon enough the emotional meanings of having failed and the realistic implications of unemployment come crashing in to burst whatever fragile balloon he's inflated to cushion the initial blow and then keep him afloat.

Men of any age will tell you that being fired figures, along with divorce or widowerhood, as one of the great catastrophes that can befall them during their lives. (See Chapters 6 and 7.) And job loss can affect the younger worker, the man just establishing himself, more than a veteran of the corporate wars, even when this older man may have more at stake. The seasoned professional may not know where to go or what to do now—he can't start over. The financial impact's formidable, with a family to support. But he can look back at least on what he has done to remind himself that at least once upon a time he was somebody. A tyro still doesn't know who he is.

Put more precisely, the younger man doesn't know just how good he is yet. He's already been sensitive to the slightest criticisms—much less the "slings and arrows of [even more] outrageous fortune." For such a newcomer, struggling to make it on his own, actually being severed from his position means being cut off from the love of surrogate fathers and from the self-esteem that comes from their recognition of a job well done.

Where a woman at such a point may experience a professional injury as a personal betrayal or a loss of love, a man proceeds to process this as an insult to his pride and self-confidence. Not only does this trauma call into question his trust, worth, competence, and independence. Not only does he no longer measure up to some ideal version of what he would like to be. Being fired also makes a man question his sexual identity.

From the time they're little boys (as I will explain in Chapters 11 and 12), men have constructed and then buttressed their manhood by linking up with other males in their world. They want to be like the men they admire and model themselves after them. It's their fathers who first lure them away from mothers and all that female stuff, teaching them what and how men are through what they do, and do together. Fathers keep boys from tumbling right back into their mothers' arms, reminding them that they have "balls" by demanding that they use them.

A boy's and later a man's masculinity is secured and repeatedly reaffirmed by his shared activities with others of his sex. Pals and buddies in grade school and high school, teachers all along, advisers, bosses, and colleagues in college and at work—all fill in as father figures for the parents of childhood. And they do so by helping a guy have a demonstrable effect on his world and by rewarding him for it. Men learn to be men—and will be men—but only if they can be with other men and together they can do—do, do, do. And Paul Mandell was no exception.

• • •

Paul closed the door to Marian Montclair Mercedes behind him. It was one year to the day since he had purchased, or rather leased, his car—the earliest point permissible for terminating his lease on it. The dealership simply reabsorbed the vehicle, preparing to refurbish it for the delight of some stranger who had bought it "used . . . but almost new." As if a little old lady from Queens had been driving it.

Paul thought he heard its engine turn over for one last time somewhere inside these glass and metal precincts before proceeding to the bus stop at the corner. He'd be riding on from there to the City and by train onto the Island to pick up his parents' Honda for the transfer price of $1. Nobody out there could drive it anymore so nobody needed it—the deal made sense.

Anyway, Judy had said she didn't give a damn what kind of car they drove. Cars were men's toys, she added. She loved Paul, she went on, loved him not his job. It didn't matter he'd been thrown for a while. He'd come back. She just needed him.

Tomorrow he'd drive the zippy little red thing farther east, out to the Hamptons to go over the documents for the sale of the Amagansett property. And just in time, too, his closing on this staving off a foreclosing by the bank.

Paul had convinced himself, with Judy's help, that he'd find a new job before he officially left the old. Not so. The tough times touted by the media were for real, and even when a door opened a crack, no more seats were to be found inside. Besides, he learned to his further horror, the promised recommendation from Amie proved never to have been mailed. Uncle Amie had let him down and betrayed him.

Returning from the interview in which he'd learned about all this, preoccupied as well by his father's latest recurrence and admission to the hospital, Paul had found himself propelled down the hall to Stein's sanctum. He was impelled by something deep down inside—truth, justice, maybe—to knock on the door, enter when only half-bidden, sit down, let the coffee cup spill, and ask him about the letter never sent. And when ten minutes later Stein had acknowledged the lapse, and with no excuses either for having forgotten to send the "damned thing," Paul was further moved to inquire, much in the mode that Amie asked his questions and against his better judgment:

"Do you ever think about anybody but yourself?"

That was it. The word went out, quickly and efficiently this time, turning very bad to much worse.

Only Judy's loyalty had steadied him. His mother and his father—or what was left of them—were no help. But Judy was always there, never straying and never doubting. Yes, she loved him.

But the days had become weeks, then months. There wasn't much to be found. Seven months later, Paul was still languishing without portfolio or pay, despite some near hits that had never quite found their target. Amos had prejudiced some potential employers against him, to be sure. But his word was taken with a grain of salt by others, some of whom had also been burned by him.

The real trouble was, Paul Mandell's range was limited. He didn't have the credentials to range freely about the world of finance, management, and sales. Stock traders were fast becoming a dime a dozen. And nobody else wanted a BS—no pun intended —anymore.

These days, with 25 percent of the work force composed of college graduates, anything less than a graduate school degree was no more than a high school equivalency. Hell, Paul remembered reading, 60 percent of the kids who got through high school went on to college. And so college alumni were to be found on the road peddling their wares, installing phones, filing papers—the sort of odd jobs once reserved for dropouts. He needed something more specialized, he figured, to make him more generally marketable. But what—what could he do now? Hell, these days he just couldn't do anything right anymore.

So each morning he'd loll about in his shorts and bathrobe and close the door behind his MBA'd wife as she trotted off to work. Just like some housewife seeing her hub off for the day. He'd gotten mad at her on and off for a while, until he figured out why. Then he stopped. After all, Judy was the only thing—whoops, person—he had left.

At first, Paul would read through the want ads, make calls,

arrange lunches, and once his finger healed, play tennis for contacts' sake. But the pretenses of this networking began to wear
thin—just like the bankroll supporting them. And pretty soon he
was simply hanging out, waiting, restless.

During the afternoons Paul wandered through the Jersey malls
looking at stuff he couldn't buy now—along with teenagers playing hooky from school. Once or twice he bought some pot from
them, got stoned, and went to an afternoon movie.

Another time he tried cocaine again, gotten through an old
white-collar connection who had supplied him with his occasional
packets for New Year's Eve and other celebrations during the
years when he was on the rise and flush enough to shell out for it.
The snowy stuff really made him feel good. While these grams
lasted, on the nights Judy was called out of town, he even went to
clubs and danced his head off.

And at one of these, he picked up a girl and got himself laid,
betraying his marriage vows for the first time. Afterward Paul
couldn't remember just what had happened. He got scared and
scoured his balls off with the Bettadine disinfectant he'd used on
his plantar wart a couple of years ago, cramming some tetracy-
cline into his gullet just to make sure. He couldn't do it again—not
to Judy.

At any rate, the money for the coke also ran dry. Without his
powdery courage, he didn't have the heart for any more escapades. So he stayed home, watched TV, drank a little beer, and
made plans. Judy, he figured, would have been all over the place
with her friends if she were in a similar predicament. But for him
it just got worse—he couldn't go out and face people anymore.

Even his father. Paul had thought he should "help" his dad
die, even find out what it was like to be dying. But he got so
ashamed, it was hard to see him. Hard, that is, to keep the secret.
Jake Mandell didn't know his son had lost his job—too much of
a strain, they'd decided. And the questions and responsive lies got
to be too much.

Jake had been a man of huge "vital capacity," as his internists
put it. There had been a lot of him until two years earlier—too
much in fact, so that his family and doctors were always telling
him to lose weight. The cancer and chemotherapy had done the
dieting for him, and now at maybe 125 pounds he'd just lie in bed,
holding Paul's hand, waiting for the good news his son made up
to tell him about his successes, his life, which was still ongoing.
Paul hoped his brother and sister wouldn't be stupid and vindictive enough to confront the old man with the truth.

The drain, the sense of death hovering everywhere, made these hours together suck at Paul's pores. After a while, they stopped talking and just sat together. After that the visits dropped down to one or two a week. Anyway, both his parents had aides at home—both—and didn't need the kids around to make things work.

But he called every day.

• • •

Take away his work, then, and the "fathers" to be found there, strip his daily existence of action and a sense of purpose, and a man is in trouble. Retirement, we know, while longed for as the rest area down the road, often brings instead depression and even physical illness. Earlier on in a man's career, when his body's more sound, it's the mind that suffers, a malady often manifest in impulsive and compulsive behavior.

Such a man feels infantilized and effeminized by his failure, cut off and adrift, yes, "castrated" once again. (Men are always prone to feeling so, it seems.) And he is further deprived of avenues for the expression in constructive action of the aggression that also goes along with acting like a man and fighting for his territorial prerogatives. So he finds himself struggling not to fall into some abject and amorphous state of mind in which his only option is to beat up on himself emotionally.

A woman in similar circumstances will tend to her appearance. Sometimes she'll seize the opportunity afforded by enforced leisure to immerse herself in clothes and shoe shopping, aerobics, manicures, facials, massages, and other sensuous indulgences for which she didn't have time when she was working.

Less preoccupied with the condition of his body than his performance and its results, the "disemployed" man sometimes plunges into defensive and other aimless activity. He just has to keep going and doing. Disappointed in himself, he tries to avoid himself—unlike a woman.

He rushes about in search of a new job. When and if these efforts fail, he still keeps moving, networking. He pounds pavements, wheeling and dealing, enacting in his mind grand schemes for new and better enterprises and endeavors. These failing, a man out of work may resort to "acting out"—alcohol, drugs, sex, any inebriant that will take his mind off his condition.

He may have fantasized about getting out of the rat race or off the treadmill. But once he's sidetracked, the passivity proves intolerable. He finds himself terrified that he won't ever get back on track, that he'll never be a "real man" again, or at least never be seen as such. He feels like a little boy after all, a man manqué, reliant on his parents' protection, perhaps even indistinguishable from the woman who bore him and on whom his survival once depended. A sissy, an aimless androgyne, an infant, a g-d woman. It's unbearable.

So he spins his would-be big wheels in the sand. Often he creates ruts for himself, sinking in deeper and deeper until people and opportunities extend themselves to him at last to pull him back onto solid ground and set him in motion. Rescued from impotence and despair, getting on with it again, he may have learned a hard-won lesson or two that will stand him in good stead.

First of all, you *can* count on others—but only up to a point. If you can fail, others can fail you. They, too, are not what they should have been.

Second, Paul found out, you can come back from the "dead."

• • •

Paul swung his car into the driveway of his Montclair home three days later, thinking how incongruous the tinny little thing looked against this grand backdrop and when compared to the other more German denizens of the suburb's streets and parking lots. Remembering his resolve, he then banished the thought as he slammed its door, even though he found himself waiting just for a second to hear that satisfying thud that never came.

He opened the front door and was greeted by the pile of mail deposited through its slot. Judy was away on yet another trip, and so three days' worth had accumulated while he was away selling everything off. Mostly bills, many past due, he figured. And then he saw it—there it was. The LSAT results.

About four months earlier, and four months into his exile, Paul had been staring through a malt-and-hops haze at ads on the TV for New Jersey Tech Institute when the idea first occurred to him that *he* might go back to school. He'd always wanted to be an attorney in serious pinstripes, with solid briefs under his arm, and more than computer screen money to deal with. The law. But Paul had never thought that he had the academic smarts.

Darryl Landsman, his rather conceited Huntington High School crony and erstwhile tennis partner—he had had them. Cornell had served him well, and Columbia Law after that. But Paul told himself, he was only street smart.

Now, however, with nowhere else to go, he'd decided to take

the aptitudes and to apply to Rutgers' and Fordham's night programs, while arranging to get a stopgap job during his days. It was, he reflected in his less than self-confident mood, a long shot. Still, Paul had attacked the new project. He'd taken a Kaplan cram course on taking the exam, binged on fortifying coffee and steadying Librium over breakfast before it, and sat for it. Now there they were—the results, and with them, one possible future. Another write-off, probably.

Though he'd gotten inured to disappointment, Paul found his hands shaking as he tore at the envelope. It wafted in several strips to the floor to reveal the computerized little card inside. The figures danced before his eyes, and the explanations in finer print about how to interpret them, and for a moment he felt dizzy and awful when he somehow thought the total came to 49. But no, there it was, 91st percentile—ninety fucking first percentile! Holy shit, Paul was going to law school!

• • •

Excitement such as Paul's is short-lived, stemming from the temporary illusion that a new beginning, or rather his beginning again, is a magical rebirth. In fact, starting over requires lots of hard work and deprivation. It's not easy to be treated like a kid again. There are new strains to be placed on a marriage. Law school, for example, is tough, especially for a man unused to the academic grind. Lawyering is also stressful—and the job market here may have a glut as big as anywhere else.

It's just that in touching what feels like "rock bottom," as the psychoanalyst Erik Erikson used to put it, a young man such as Paul has discovered more about his "work identity" and all that goes with it. He's become internally less dependent on patronage, the public form of fathering. He's come to seek security within himself rather than through the approval of others. He's felt the void of an upscale but still Willy Loman–like showiness, searching for greater discipline and substance with which to work. He's learned that a man can fail and become broke but still keep his balls and pay his dues. And above all, he's found that he is not entirely defined by what he does—by his position, his occupational role. He's a man, he discovers, and a man willy-nilly, young enough to change gears, to try something new.

Losing a job is hardly a lark—as getting an F on a physics final might have been ten years before, even when summer school was the price of failure. Yet it is not in fact like losing a life or a body part or people or a whole future. His bosses may not want or love him anymore, and never did, he discovers, but a man's intimates and relations still do.

Even the woman who was initially drawn to him perhaps because he was so ambitious, promising, successful, so manly—even she may not turn her back on him. Her love has grown as tender as it once was passionate, and it's his flesh and his being she cherishes for better or for worse—not his achievements. And when and if she doesn't, then this means there was something missing there to begin with. Each time a wife or lover touches him, each time the aging parent or other relative smiles upon him, each time the child he may or may not have yet admires and imitates him—in each such instance of unquestioning love a man stripped of his work is told that he's still there.

And so being fired informs us of two more truths about the mystery of masculinity, the sort of revelations that once again come to light when the crystal breaks and we can see its structure. First, take away the performance, and yes, a man's manhood feels fragile. But no, it really isn't, and like women, men are in fact more resilient in their ability to endure and at times to transcend suffering than they realize.

Men stay men—no matter what.

More of this in the chapters still to come.

9
• • •

B alls:
Illness and a Man's
Fight With His Physical
Self

They may have had fantasies about being laid up and discharged of all responsibility. But really getting sick is the last thing in the world men want. Quite the contrary, illness brings them face-to-face with the reality of their greatest terrors: annihilation, loss and isolation, emasculation, and yes, guilt.

Maybe men in their mid-fifties and beyond must collide with their mortality, as they come to anticipate heart attacks, strokes, or colon cancers, or when they are actually laid low by them. But young men expect to be healthy.

"Omnipotence," total power, psychotherapists call this illusion of man's impregnability and immortality. Unlike women once again, men begin their adult lives trusting that their bodies will remain intact. They will stay bounded, inviolate, reliable, and uncontaminated by the dirtiness of disease. If and when they do succumb, they feel that it's their due to get better—all better and right away.

Sickness and death don't discriminate between the sexes, of course. Both men and women fear and suffer them. And both try to ignore them. It's just that men, the younger ones especially, may generally be less aware that their whole life depends upon their bodies. Sudden illness reveals to both sexes, but to men especially, just how fragile this life is.

Once again, men interpret the experience in terms of their manhood and its vulnerability. To suffer illness or injury is to be suddenly and unceremoniously castrated. And this in turn is linked to the prospect of a living death.

So it certainly seemed to Jeremy Hurst when he confronted the ordeal of his still-young life.

• • •

Jeremy stood at the Thirty-third Street IRT platform. "Toidy-toid," the announcer of childhood days gone by used to squawk through the dilapidated public intercom, much to his grandfather's delight. Born in Brooklyn a generation earlier, Milton Hurst had become a famous and fancy East Side doctor by the time Jeremy had appeared on the scene. According to the old man himself, he'd also come to sound and look just like Eddie Robinson in *The Ten Commandments!* En route back from NYU Medical Center to his own City University's Midtown Graduate Center and then on to its inner-city campus, where he taught remedial comp lit, Jeremy sized up his fellow travelers.

Julio and José and Ricardo, or so he surmised from the tidbits of Hispanic banter coming his way, were engaged in animated discourse about their party the night before, more specifically about just who—*cuyo*—had balled whom. They stood there with their heads diving like penguins toward one another as they exchanged stories about deeds done and others aborted. And each one of them, each to a man, had his hand on his cock.

The *muchachos* punctuated every story, even the beats within it, with a careless, yes, carefree, pull at their organ—of course, and thankfully, Jeremy went on in his head, picking absently at their own and nobody else's. Their gestures seemed to define cock, or dick. The hard *k*s, the tough tug, assured all potential onlookers along with its possessor that the thing was still there—ready, willing, and able to meet and "do" on a moment's notice any female soulmate, her labia grinding between the seams of the poly-cotton denim of her too-tight jeans.

Their own britches were stretched tight enough to reveal mounds of macho manhood. Or rather three mounds in one—a head or tip and two bulges accenting God's eternal phallus and

Everyman's family jewels, the collective organ. Three. The trium-
verate, three.

And this was a whole lot more than Jeremy could say, for all
his smarts. He bit his lower lip.

He was feeling angry. Still.

Jeremy's uptown train screeched into the station, opened its
sliding doors, and admitted him. He slid into a seat near the exit
and then slid his right hand into his pants pocket. More surreptitiously, decorously than his Hispanic *compadres*, who had entered
with him only to saunter down the aisle and through the doors in
search of another car and maybe more action, Jeremy, too, felt for
his balls. Anyway, at this hour the car was almost empty and
nobody could be offended by a young guy with his hands dis-
creetly in his pockets.

So without further ado he reached down—pushing against the
tissues of the cotton lining and the Jockey briefs, which had replaced the boxers preferred by him in the past because the tighter
garment afforded greater support—to squeeze or, as the physicians put it, "palpate" his penis and testicle. Yes, testicle, singu-
lar. One of them was gone, definitely—gone for good. So next to
the penile shaft, encased in his scrotum, there was only one sphere
to be felt.

Jeremy supposed one might look at the bag as half empty or
half full. He should feel lucky, too, grateful that no other mysterious bumps had invaded his private parts since that awful one
had appeared there, oh, God, just about a year and a half ago. No
recurrences—yet. And only six months to go. But his sac felt so
naked from the inside.

And lest his remaining—and remaining for how long?—testis
feel lonely, well, pretty soon it would have a companion. A pros-
thesis made out of some kind of gel would soon be plopped into the
crinkled pouch—a benign and man-made orb this time, inserted
there surgically rather than erupting from the hellish depths
within. And with this lump there would be "no health consequences one way or the other either." Just for "cosmetic and
emotional reasons," as Dr. Lucille Sapperstein—urologist, tumor
surgeon, and erstwhile student of Milton Hurst himself—had put
it with characteristic terseness.

Some men did this right away. Others, who had partners,
didn't bother. Jeremy had waited, but he'd found the incompleteness unbearable.

In fact, that's what this appointment at NYU Medical Center

had been about. To check things out and set up the date for the next procedure. Nothing to be cut off this go-round. And no nauseating chemotherapy either. A "routine" visit. No taxi needed —he could even take the subway after it.

Still Jeremy could feel the tears welling up. He jammed his eyes shut, as if trying to blacken out the last nightmarish year. No sooner had he done so, however, than the subway catapulted itself and him into Forty-second Street, the internal concussion forcefully calling Jeremy's attention to his stop. He'd be picking up a graduate student's dissertation on Márquez at the Center before proceeding uptown to give the last undergraduate class before Thanksgiving. By the time he left, heading home for the Upper West Side one-bedroom apartment and another VCR night, it would be dark enough to last a lifetime. So he opened his eyes.

The doors opened as well and Jeremy walked out onto the platform. As the train snaked out of the station, he turned around to watch its departure. Through the windows, Jeremy caught sight of Julio and José and Ricardo. They were still walking and talking and laughing. Though he couldn't actually see anything below their waists from this vantage, he imagined nonetheless that they were still holding on to their balls.

• • •

Testicular cancer probably represents the most dramatic and obvious of assaults on a man's manhood. It imperils his sexual functioning and threatens his future as a father. And though the prognosis may be better than in many other malignancies, nonetheless it still looms as a potential death sentence. It's not particularly common, but it is a young man's disease. A low blow indeed, it hits him right in the balls. And thus it can also serve as a poignant metaphor that captures the unconscious meanings of almost any major illness at various junctures in the life cycle.

As I've noted in the previous chapters, men greet the traumas life brings with shock and denial before anxiety and anger set in. "It can't be happening." Then, "Why me!" they cry, like a little boy in a playground who's fallen and skinned his knee at the very height of his imaginary overreaching. It's unfair just because I never expected it. I shouldn't get sick. This isn't what I wanted. "Goddamn!"

Along with the righteous rage at having been unjustly singled out comes the terror. Nature and God no longer are on their side.

"Will I ever recover, ever come back from the dead?" men such as Jeremy, stricken so suddenly, wonder.

• • •

For a guy who had been something of a hypochondriac until his analyst got ahold of him four years earlier, Jeremy found his vision and recollection blurred when it came to the real thing. In his more despairing moments, Jeremy wished he were dead—wished that he hadn't discovered anything and had simply fallen into numbing eternal sleep, dying without knowing why and how.

But he had discovered it. It was six months after Meredith had left him for a nephrology fellow at Mount Sinai—with better financial prospects, he figured, than an assistant professor with expertise in Spanish and French literature but only an academic's salary. At times like these, Jeremy felt he should have done what his college tutor Ray Slavin had managed: leave graduate school, enter the publishing world, and make a bundle rather than limp along the academic tenure track like a junior gelding. Well, the hell with regrets.

Anyhow, Jeremy had started dating. And for the first time in two and one-half years, he had had intercourse—"intacoss"—with somebody other than his elegant and subdued girlfriend from Newport, Rhode Island. Her name was Gloria, she came from Massapequa, Long Island, she was twenty-three, and she helped run the CUNY Admissions Office.

Gloria spoke with a "Gisland" accent and was by her own admission forever fighting off the impulse to say "Yuz Guyz." But she had always found Jeremy attractive. And when, after much fingernail filing and eyelid batting, she had managed to get the despondent "ex-fiancé type" into bed with her, she proved it by being multiply orgasmic and moving him, with the aid of a little marijuana, to do "likewoise."

It had been about three A.M. on Saturday morning, they were at it for the second time, and Gloria was squeezing his balls when she exclaimed:

"Jerry, someting's funny heah. You gotta bump. Hey, check it out."

"Huh?"

"Checkitout, Jer."

And he'd gotten up, wilting in an instant, and reached down to feel himself. Sure enough, there it was, a mound of mysterious tissue emerging from the top of his right testis, like some Siamese

twin. Extra virility, he would have liked to have joked. But hardly
—and his humor immediately deserted him as he started to sweat.

Stoned, Jeremy became terrified. He would also have liked to
have said "paranoid" over and over, but the bump was real.
Inspections by mirror and hand, his and hers, verified the perception: a bump, an unmistakable and palpable bump that was
beginning to ache and throb with all the unerotic attention it was
getting. Maybe the sudden intensity of the pain was an illusion, he
reflected, but the bump was real.

Poor Gloria, ill-fated messenger of doom, now faded into the
background, except when Jer asked her, repeatedly, to "checkitout—again." It was as if he hoped the eruption was only temporary. Like a burst blood vessel—in which case, however, he
should get himself to an emergency room. Nonsense, it was solid,
hard, cool, not blood hot. No, don't succumb. Don't be a pussy.

Maybe he should call Grampa in Palm Beach. No, it was still
only five A.M. Milton would be asleep. And with his congestive
heart failure and his old-age diabetes, he shouldn't be disturbed.
His days of being on call were long gone. He was the patient now.
But yes, when it got to be about seven, he would call. He wouldn't
go anywhere, act or bawl like a baby, and thus again prove his
critical father, Milt's son Sam, right. He'd just call. Wait and call.

So Jeremy reran his tortured monologues until at six A.M. he
finally asked Gloria to go, leave, with as much composure—he
still had to see her at work—as he could muster. No, he said with
more clenched hysteria than compassion, she couldn't help. Sorry.

At seven A.M. he did call Grampa, who said it was probably
epididymitis (an inflammation of some cord wrapping around the
testicle). But he should go to the emergency room at NYU Hospital, right away, just to guard against "strangulation." Against
strangulation! Milton would call Lucille Sapperstein, his mentee
and vice chair there. She'd meet Jeremy, he was sure, and in the
meantime have the house staff alerted.

Looking back, Jeremy remembered the leaving of his apartment that morning more than the hospital ordeals to follow. He'd
showered once again, even packed a robe and toothpaste plus
books, and rushed to the cash machine. Then he grabbed a cab
and had himself deposited on First Avenue and Thirty-second
Street. There was no traffic on the streets at this hour and on this
day, and so he found himself alone before he walked inside.

Jeremy had sat around for hours, it seemed, before the chief
resident, looking more like a college fullback than a grown-up

doctor, had sauntered in and grabbed his balls without so much as a by-your-leave. A studied impassivity clamped his face in place to cover up any signs of worry. He was the first of several to do so before Dr. Sapperstein finally arrived, did more of the same, and ordered all the tests to follow.

Over the next few days Jeremy was poked, prodded with needles, and bled. His veins were filled with radioactive dyes, and he was shoved like a tremulous torpedo into the CAT scan. He was pierced and sliced in the scrotum. Before the final verdict came, annihilating memory, he'd been "prepped," doped up, and having said good-bye to his favorite ball, wheeled away to a place from which no traveler returns . . . the same.

Now it all got even foggier.

He recollected not feeling anything from the waist down after he came to—as if everything had been chopped off. A "total" amputee. He'd remembered the bandages and blood, the unwrappings of the gauze, the swollen and black-and-blue sheath. He could hardly look. But when he did, he saw a jagged scar lying across the place where his ball had been encased. There had been no choice. "Not elective."

Jeremy used to pride himself on his genitals. Meredith had called them "a great dove" before she fell out of love with him. And even sweet little Gloria, who more than once visited him in the hospital, had complimented him on their amplitude and form. But Jeremy couldn't look at himself now. He avoided doing so as best he could. And he thought about being alone. . . .

• • •

In a case like Jeremy's, the interwoven threats of death and castration are real. But these specters haunt the fantasy life of all men—especially those who have fallen ill. In the unconscious mind, according to Freud's disciple Sandor Ferenczi, images of dying serve to represent castration—a phenomenon every male has worried about more or less consciously from boyhood on.

A life-threatening disease such as testicular cancer, the aftereffects of chemotherapy in treating various lymphomas (sterility at least temporarily), and related problems clearly imperil a man's procreative capacity. Men's balls are there for a reason. They're bigger than he is. We are, a guy learns through the impact of illness, way stations in the passage of generations. Not only is his individual existence threatened with extinction, but if he expires or deteriorates, his "line" may also die out, confronting him with the loss of his "raison d'être" and putting his life in perspective.

In fact, men tend to "phallicize" their entire physical selves, equating their general vitality with their abilities to perform sexually and to compete aggressively. In other kinds of debilitation and injury, it's the whole body that's in jeopardy. Lose this body, and you forfeit your sexual, aggressive, and paternal prerogatives.

That is, a sick man articulates such existential dilemmas if and when his emotions let him. At first, he's just too nervous to think straight. His angst is hardly contemplative; the sick man feels his illness as a matter of life and death.

Laid low in his prime by this body's fallibility, a man thus fears for himself as well as for his ability to conceive children and/or take care of those he already has. Disabled, he's further afraid of being cast out and left to die all alone since he may no longer be able to fend for himself and because he has become useless to others. Rather than a provider, he'll become a drag, draining the resources of those who need and love him. So not only does being diseased mean being damaged, it also portends loneliness and loss. Like a wounded and stray animal, he's scared of being left out in the cold.

However much they may protest to the contrary, most sick men will then reveal two sorts of irrational responses to their misfortune. First of all, unable to keep up much less progress, they regress. Second, along with self-pity, they start blaming themselves.

Incapacitated like the old and the infirm or the young and helpless, they have little choice except to turn their attentions toward themselves. Their pressing and primitive physiological needs absorb their interest. They become irritable, cranky, ungrateful babies. Realistically out of control, they are forced to cling to their doctors' words and caretakers' ministrations as if these were magical incantations and sacred amulets.

Manly men hate themselves for such displays of weakness, of course. They see in their helplessness the foolishness and self-indulgence of old women. "Sissies," they think, "pussies." Not men. They embarrass themselves—unable to do otherwise.

With this, the self-blame sets in. Their physical and emotional backsliding justifies and intensifies their feelings of guilt. If they're sick, they think, then they must have done something wrong. Or maybe they've failed to do something they should have done. They're being unmanned because they haven't been man enough—strong, tough, and resilient. Or conversely, they're being punished for their sins—for being remiss, deficient, bad, prideful, and careless.

Sometimes they are responsible for their distress. In so many ways, these days, we've come to see a variety of illnesses as punishment for overindulgences.

Sexually transmitted diseases emerged in epidemic proportions during the seventies and eighties as I have noted especially in Chapters 3 and 4. Hitherto silent and undiagnosed chlamydia infections, herpes, and genital warts were all found to compromise the health and fertility of many sexually active men and their partners. In the 1980s, AIDS then entered the scene as a plague for this *fin de siècle*. Sufferers and witnesses alike saw the ghastly death HIV brought as an inescapable punishment for the abuse of substances and for sexual deviance. All that "Puritan claptrap," which modern-minded men and women had tried so hard to challenge or evade, seemed to be vindicated after all. Sex could kill you—not only magically because of the taboos being broken but because exchanging bodily fluids was in fact dangerous.

And there are so many other abuses of the flesh, of which physicians, the media, and the public have become aware. For instance, a lung cancer sufferer (such as Chuck Watson, Sr., in Chapter 13) must rue the two packs a day that he kept smoking even after the Surgeon General's report came out. The heart attack patient (Abe Feigelman, for instance, in Chapter 2) or a man suffering from colon cancer nowadays regrets all the red meat and gristle he's consumed over the decades, the lack of fiber, or some other alimentary indiscretion—all the dietary little sins of commission and omission we've been discovering in the last decade. Too much sunshine, and you risk melanoma. Hell, these days you can't bite into a hitherto healthy hunk of noncholesterol fish without inviting parasites. Nothing just happens to you anymore; the causes can all be found in your behavior.

For some there's even a collective guilt to be reckoned with, given our growing sensitivity to the environment and the noxious by-products of the technology with which we've all been pampering ourselves. Toxic wastes in the world around us, in the air we breathe, in our food, in ourselves, have all been implicated as causes of Hodgkin's disease, other lymphomas, leukemias, and a host of cancers that don't discriminate when it comes to the victim's age or sexual and dietary practices.

Everything has its price, it seems, especially when it's fun. So precautions must be taken.

Fair enough. Men have responsibilities. They should monitor themselves and not endanger themselves or others. The trouble is, even men who can find no discernible cause for having fallen ill—such as the testicular cancer victim whose malignancy has nothing to do with what he's done—often blame themselves for succumbing. In their scheme of things, there's no such thing as chance or mischance. They've lapsed somehow, done something wrong. Fate's in their hands. They're only getting what they deserve.

Yet in this misconception lies the sick man's initial route to recovery: control. Quality control.

• • •

Months later, rather than inspect his body, Jeremy read about his illness. Abstractions and statistical probabilities danced optimistically before him. They seemed safer—less hideous. He kept coming back to the pages on which these numbers were engraved in repeated efforts to reassure himself that he had a future—and a future as a man. Intellectually at least, in his mind's eye, he wanted to take charge—to understand.

Yes, Jeremy Hurst had had testicular cancer, a malady befalling men most often between the ages of twenty and forty—at the height, that is, of their work activity, sexual drive, and desire to procreate. Though it was rare to be sure (a few guys in every one hundred thousand get it), still this is the second most prevalent form of malignancy found in men this age, ranking third among causes of death. And this diagnosis had required the surgical removal of the runaway ball—a "unilateral orchiectomy."

God, could you believe it—they cut his fuckin' ball off. No, not they—she did!

They, she, had then gone on to tell him it could've been worse. Jeremy had cancer, "stage I, contained," limited to the one testicle, not even II much less III. No metastases—near or far, she repeated. This meant the disease hadn't spread. The cancer cells were "nonseminomatous," which meant they could be killed more easily. Properly treated, he had a better than 80 percent chance of surviving. Even men who were worse off than he was had a good chance of making it. Two years he'd have to wait—twenty-four months without a recurrence—unlike your typical five. After that, he was home free!

So all they'd had to do was ablate the one offending glob rather than perform some more gruesome procedure called a ret-

roperitoneal lymph-node dissection. This was the male equiva-
lent, as Jeremy analogized it, of a radical mastectomy. It was an
operation in which these knife-wielding medical men, or women,
would also have gouged a whole lot of stuff out from between his
legs. No radiation either—he was doomed to just a little course of
chemo. Some vomiting. Not even much hair loss. He was lucky.

Yes, all this indicated that Jeremy could again achieve "normal sexual function." He would or should be able to impregnate
somebody someday soon. Other testicular cancer patients might
reveal a decreased sperm count and impaired sperm motility as a
consequence of the disease. Not so Jeremy, the doctor smiled
almost in congratulation; he had ranked up there with the rest of
"normal" mankind on these counts. And once the traumas of the
curative interventions wore off, she added, he'd be able to get
down to getting erections, making love, making a marriage, and
making babies.

Normal. He'd come again. He'd become a father. He'd live,
probably. He was lucky.

Lucky. "Fuck them! Fuck you! Fuck me!"

• • •

Like all life processes—like labor, birth, death—disease tends to
run its own course. However, to the extent a stricken man takes
responsibility for his state, even when he is unrealistically hard on
himself, he is preparing himself to take charge as best he can—and
to fight. Mad at himself, he gets angry at his body and at the
medical establishment for potentially mismanaging it.

By and large, men's consciences are more promiscuous and
cruel than are women's. They get guilty over the oddest things,
and this self-criticism can paralyze them. Yet men also exploit
such guilt to get going. Where people and their needs move a
woman to recover from sickness, a man relies on principles to
make him do battle for his life.

According to physicians who treat the very ill, indignant and
high-minded patients tend to do better than others who acquiesce
to their illness and their doctors. There may even be certain physiological concomitants of this more aggressive attitude. But in all
events, the desire to fight reactivates the will to live, helping heal-
ing happen, according to internist Eric Cassell.

Demoralized, "castrated," and potentially isolated by illness,
many men patients may initially capitulate more than women.
They should be perfect, they feel, and when they aren't, when they

fail to measure up to their fantasy about themselves, sick men can become utterly depressed. But when they engage actively in a campaign for their lives, they begin to feel male once more. Their attitude toward their physical selves has changed. They become more detached and more determined—ironically, like women at their best.

Kicking and screaming, a man claws his way out of the valley of death. As always, a man must act on his aggression to feel like a man—to be alive, to live.

• • •

Jeremy had had a dream in the recovery room in the hours after Dr. "I Love Lucy" made him whole again. (He'd figured out why he had to make her less, diminishing her, too, but still had to do it anyway.) It was quite simple really, but pretty ghoulish.

In it, Milton Hurst, as if in his prime, and Dr. Sapperstein, who looked younger and prettier than she was, were playing Ping-Pong. He, Jeremy, was waiting his turn in the round-robin. But they were in no hurry to hand their table over to him. He reached toward the net, and the next thing he could discern was a testicle, his testicle, he assumed, larger than life. It was bloody, maybe like a sweetbread being hurled about. And Grampa Milt was "Uncle Miltie" now, and at last Lucy had evolved into *the* Lucy, Ball, that is—"Ball, get it, Jer?" And they were laughing. He felt like a pathetic little kid again—like a monkey in the middle.

Berle, Ball. He was getting a burled ball.

Except when Jeremy thought about it later, lying in his hospital bed, and still later, back home, the dream still didn't quite make sense. You see, Milton Hurst had been a good guy—his "good guy" at least. Rumor had it he could be an SOB, tough as nails, in his department (and Jeremy shuddered to think of a nail being driven through a scrotum). But when it came to his youngest grandchild, Milt was a soft touch and had only love to give.

He would never want to hurt or taunt him. Quite the contrary, he had fixed things for Jeremy when they went wrong—such as now. . . . After the fake ball was inserted, Jeremy thought that night, over his Orangina and popcorn, he'd probably feel better about himself. He might even get a voluntary erection again. There wasn't any organic reason for his being so totally impotent. Other hemicastrates did fine, after all. Not Jeremy.

Funny, with all these people fondling him, especially Dr. Lucy, he'd had some passing worries about getting hard and embarrassing himself. Quite the contrary, his penis had simply shriveled up, as if it were turned inward—"invaginating."

"Koro," or something like that, the Chinese or Indonesians called this form of hysterical conversion. And they prescribed as a remedy the devotion of an old man, who simply held on to the patient's penis day in and day out in an effort to keep everything aboveboard. To keep men from becoming anything less than men—Jeremy mused.

It was *Blade Runner* he had rented, the movie about the fake people, the "replicants." Its familiar images played themselves out across the TV as Jeremy sprawled in his bathrobe, almost spread-eagle on his bed, chomping his popcorn and sipping soda. He'd gotten used to this position, hadn't he, over the last twelve months? Like a woman about to be gynecologically prodded, poked, fucked, fucked over.

But, he went on, he was alone. Who would want him now? Oh, yes, Gloria would, did—but nobody else. . . .

It was, Jeremy thought as he lay naked on the top of his bed in his apartment, oh, maybe a month later, admiring his refurbished equipment—it was his father, Sam, who was the problem. Sam—balls of brass, litigating Sam—was the guy who'd scared him. All along. Excluded him, too. All the trips away from home with a mother who, though decent enough, made no bones about owing her first allegiance to her husband, not her kids. And then when she died, there was a stepmother who had no reason to care—no duty much less inclination toward their welfare and peace of mind. And an older brother, Sam, Jr., too, who went into his father's field and then his firm.

Jeremy remembered Sam's thundering, "The kid's got no balls." That was the time he had stayed home "sick" rather than freeze in the middle of the middle-school piano recital. Uncle Milt (everybody called him Uncle—even his own kids) had signed the note, too, saying he had the flu and so excusing him. But Sam, his son and Jeremy's father, had been tempted to call the school office and blow the lid on his son's malingering. He didn't, but he glowered at him. He made Jeremy feel he wasn't a man—a man in the making.

Maybe half a man. A man with fake balls. That was all.

But Jeremy added to himself, before at last granting himself sleep, Sam had never had to deal with anything like this.

• • •

According to psychologist Susan Tross (who has studied testicular cancer survivors as well as AIDS sufferers), beset by the threats
of castration, sterility, and death, many men can discover reserves
of strength they had never known they had. During the two years
orchiectomy patients maintain their vigil over a possible recurrence, the strain may seem unbearable. They feel abandoned by
their doctors, having been told they're "normal" again when they
feel damaged and still at risk. They ruminate about retaining their
jobs and holding on to their health insurance. They worry about
their remaining ball. Life has contracted for them.

Yet if they survive, Tross found, cancer victims such as these
young men emerge from their ordeals with renewed endurance
and a precocious sense of the preciousness of life. Each moment
counts, each sensation. Simply feeling something other than pain,
numbness, or terror.

Generally more removed from their bodies than women and
intent instead upon what they do, men don't usually feel things as
fully and directly. But coming back from an illness, they become
less goal oriented. Results don't matter so much anymore. Being
becomes an end in itself—being and feeling alive.

• • •

"Ach, Jer, it's beautiful."

Gloria grinned and clapped as, high again, Jeremy strode
nude before her. Maybe he shouldn't have been so bold—something might get tangled up after all. But he whirled and twirled.
He imitated a ballet dancer doing leaps and pirouettes. His penis
and testicles swung through the air with the greatest of ease.

"Oh, ya gawgious hunk," Gloria squealed as she drew Jeremy
toward her, yes, by the balls. She began with his penis and then
let her hand slip back to cup his testicles—both balls, that is,
shaking her head happily to indicate that there wasn't any difference between them. She bent down and pulled him toward her—
even closer now, kissing and sucking on him, mouthing him all
over.

And Jeremy began to grow hard, erect for the first time in over
two years. He did it for her! But his excitement was so intense that
he wouldn't have been able to contain himself for long. His sweet
lover knew this and released him for the moment as she fell back
onto the bed and beckoned him. Jeremy did her bidding and
kneeling, plunged his penis into Gloria's vagina. "Glorious! 'You
can find your way back home.' "

"Yeah," Gloria said, cheering him on, giving him the high sign.

He thrust, feeling her warmth inside, feeling his scrotum slapping gently against her inner thighs and pubic bone, almost imagining the sensation in the right testicle.

Yet it didn't matter. Reality or illusion. Either one meant he was alive.

And soon, sooner than he would have liked, because the tension kept telling him that he and it could feel, Jeremy began to come. It welled up from within him. He felt his pelvis and anus and vas deferens shudder and begin to contract.

He felt he could feel the semen gather at the base of his penis, and in his mind's eye, he seemed to see the sperm amassing. And he was coming now for real, pushing life out of him from the core of his body, from the base of his spine. Semen, rich in wriggling sperm, was shooting forth the fountain of youth, of everlasting life, his gift to and his part within the cycling generations. He was coming, and so was his Gloria, whose genital seemed to grip his in gratitude and delight. As he groaned, she laughed.

"Oh, Jer, oh, Jer. You're so happy—aren't you."

And she hugged him—harder than anybody ever had. . . .

It was four months later, and Jeremy stood facing Gloria on the front steps of their CUNY compound, City College itself, on Manhattan's upper Upper West Side. She had already said what she was going to say. However, since Jeremy had greeted her announcement mutely, simply staring back at her for a minute or two, she felt forced to repeat herself.

"Jer, I'm not coming home with you tonight. That's it, Jer, no more makin' luv."

"Why?"

"Oh, I, uh, met sumbuddy—a guy like me. You know, stick to your own kind, as dey say in da movies."

"Wasn't I enough—"

"Look, Jer, I'm never gonna be able to keep yu . . . zzz." She laughed. "You needed me, Jer, but you also threatened me. I'm scared of yuh. Okay?"

And she kissed him under the ear and walked away.

What Gloria didn't say was that she'd read on Jer's desk the note from this Molly—yeah, Pritchard, a genu-wine WASP name—about how great his talk on the "Marquizee" guy had been. She had known it was the beginning of the end and left before things could get bad between them. Gloria would let herself be used, but she couldn't stand being dumped.

A guy like Pat—a hometown boy even if he wasn't Jewish and had had his problems—well, still he could be hers. Yeah, Pat Davies was her "own kind."

And Jer, well, he just stood there and watched her walk away from him. He felt sad, relieved, and frustrated.

For a moment Jeremy felt himself become petulant, the victim again. It seemed, he complained inwardly, that things were always happening to him and that something or someone was always being taken away.

Still he had changed. When you fight for breath and win, when you see your body begin to desert you, when you almost die, you can become less selfish after all. Self-absorption, a potentially dead man learns, is a dead-end street. So Jeremy was also thinking about her. He did love Gloria, sweetest soul he had ever met, but couldn't talk to her. At least not with anything other than his balls and his heart. She was right—she couldn't keep him.

He gathered himself up. Giving Gloria enough of a lead so that they wouldn't collide on the platform, he, too, headed toward the subway. He was thinking of Molly now. She was a lady. Like Meredith. Before his ball had gotten cut off, Jeremy had loved ladies. He loved helping them find their sensuality, taking the time to do it and making it erupt in them and burst the buttons— just as Gloria had been doing for him in these last few months. His erotic convalescence.

The trouble was, he didn't quite have the old confidence and savoir faire back. Waiting for anything these days conjured up waiting for life or death. He couldn't take no's for answers anymore—not so easily at any rate, because they had cut him, sliced him, hurled him into lonely helplessness. Yes, he'd been using Gloria to give him what the new woman in his life couldn't—not yet. Balls.

Jesus, it still hurt.

But once again, he had learned to get out of himself, and so he thought of Molly, whom he was seeing for the fifth time on Saturday. Tomorrow. She also had every reason to be scared from what he had begun to know of her. Her life had been pretty terrible, especially the sex parts of it. Molly was also a victim, and a survivor.

• • •

Illness and the threat of death teach men what's important in life, what passes and what lasts. Like any great ordeal or challenge to one's expectations they also show that there are no easy equations to be made between what one wants, what one can count on, and what's valuable.

And there are other stresses, too, that set in relief our moral limits and powers. Threats to our children, for example, and our more selfish expectations of them.

10

A Serpent's Tooth: The Damaged Child

However seriously they may take their own lives, all men realize that their hope for eternal life resides in their children—and their children's children. As Sigmund Freud put it in a paper, "On Narcissism," men are merely "vehicles for the transmission of the immortal germ plasm."

Threaten a normal man's son, and you jab at his groin. You know, "Fuck with him, and you fuck with me." And not only is such a man's personal manhood called into question, but also his role as the guardian of the family and the race. Noble or not, all sons are scions, embodiments of fathers and forefathers. It's a matter of honor, of identity.

It was with this sense of mission that Professor Thomas Robinson, accompanied by his wife, Professor Audrey Robinson, had entered classroom 1C on the first floor of the Miami Day School.

• • •

Mrs. Berger twisted up the corners of her lips into one of those ever-present teacher smiles Tom remembered from his own nursery and elementary school days in Jacksonville. It was Nathaniel's very first school conference. Nathaniel was the Robinsons' first child, Tom's firstborn son.

As Adele Berger intoned her introduction, Tom found himself flooded once again with memories of his own school days and the great expectations that had attended them. Great-great-grandson of a slave, grandson of the last in a line of Georgia sharecroppers, son of the first black deputy chief of the Miami Police—Tom had been everything anybody had ever wanted him to be. A wiz. A schoolboy star. It all followed from there. Tom sometimes felt like the American myth.

But now Tom's mind was less occupied by his past and the sense of future that had haunted it than by his anticipation of what this teacher would say about his son. He stared at her lips, and the picture of little Nat superimposed itself on the classroom tableau before him. Nat, with his wide white eyes and trusting hands, whose pinky caressed his daddy's palm when he took the boy's in his. Tom even imagined the boy sitting in the undersized chair on which his adult body was tenuously perched, wriggling with impatience, eager to answer the questions put to the class before anybody else did.

"Your son's an awfully dear child," Mrs. Berger began with a slight cough. And immediately Tom's heart sank.

He should have known better but hadn't wanted to. That Nathaniel had definite problems.

"Yes, a darling boy," Mrs. Berger continued in the singsong tones and studied elocution of the early-childhood educator, but still there was no mistaking what she said.

Not for anybody there wasn't, but especially for Tom, the neurobiologist who at twenty-nine knew just about everything, everybody said, and Audrey, the psychologist who shared his year of birth and had an assistant professorship at the same university. The development of girls, black ones particularly, was Professor Audrey Robinson's specialty, but she still knew enough to recognize a learning disability when she saw one in a boy such as her Nathaniel.

"He's really very creative. The other children love him. His paper constructions." And Mrs. Berger gestured to some Scotch-taped colored paper, mumbling faint praise as she did so. "I wouldn't put too much pressure on him to read."

The words drifted into a hum in Tom's head. Instead of hearing Mrs. Berger, he was remembering again—Nathaniel this time, his beginnings.

He and Audrey were back in the labor room, panting and counting. The fetal monitor blipped away. And then, so many short hours later, the crazy scrawls had suddenly straightened out, a sign the contractions had precipitously ceased. In the frenzy that followed, Tom, husband coach, was abruptly excluded from the potential disaster scene as nurses and obstetrician rushed to prep mother and baby for the knife. Lacerating her drum-tight skin as they shaved her, muttering about the urgency, calm no longer but yelling at one another now—they whisked Audrey into the operating room and ripped Nathaniel out of her.

Just in time, or so they said later, because the cord had wrapped itself around the baby's neck. Even then, when he saw his son dangling upside down in the operating theater's antechamber, Tom had noted how ashen he seemed. They said an initial Apgar score of six was fine, but still this black kid was white. White.

". . . reading readiness is an individual matter . . ."

Berger's words stung his earlobes. And as he had in the occasional Friday-afternoon detention he had earned as a boy, Tom found himself restless to get out of the classroom. Now as then, hands folded on his desk, unable to escape prison until the appointed hour, he had fled mentally instead. But this time the visions were not wishful ones. Rather they were memories and sad ones, too—images of little Nathaniel again.

With those perinatal complications, things could've been terrible, and thank God he didn't have cerebral palsy or some severe retardation—though there are some infancy experts who link learning disabilities to a mild form of cerebral palsy. It could have been worse.

Tom and Audrey were tuned in to the danger signals, of course, and how! Physical and occupational therapists were brought in early to check Nat out for development gone awry and to intervene where they could. His weight had been within normal limits—and so there were none of the problems associated with being undersized. Visually, he didn't track so well early on. He was sort of bloblike in the body and tight in the limbs. His legs and feet tended to contract just a little too much. But the therapists helped him with this. Most of his reflexes were, once again, within what the experts called reasonable parameters. He tended to smile when it was expected, around two and a half months, but then he stopped. He only got scared of strangers when he was

about twelve months, just about one-quarter year after most babies.

Yes, Nat was meeting most milestones—even though he was
taking his time doing it. It could have been worse, indeed. But he
was slow, no doubt about it. And the older he got the more it
showed.

Tom had walked at nine months, and God knows he was no
superjock. It was almost two whole years before his son rose and
let go of the steadying support of a kitchen chair to wobble and
lurch across the floor for the first time. And this when many black
children move about at far younger ages than their white or Ori-
ental counterparts, according to pediatrician Berry Brazelton.
And to do so you didn't have to have an intelligence quotient
upward of one hundred and fifty-five—such as his father's—to
show precocious motor development. Just be normal. Shit, that's
all—just normal!

You see, Nathaniel didn't talk either. Not on schedule. The
words didn't come once again until almost that second birthday.
And they weren't fit together into rudimentary sentences until two
more years had elapsed after that. So he asked none of those two-
and three-year-old's questions he was supposed to. In fact, little
Nat was slow across the board. Didn't look. Didn't listen. Couldn't
pay attention.

"Professor Robinson," Mrs. Berger snapped. "Tommy Robinson! You hear me!" The words cracked their benign whip from
his schoolboyish past. His inner litany interrupted, Tom looked at
her again, blankly trying to snap to.

"I'm sorry, but you don't seem to be hearing me. I know this
is hard, but it's also complicated—even for a man like you." And
she gestured with a wink of her right eye toward the person beside
him, Audrey—at whom he'd been staring but whom he hadn't
seen. She was crying. Once again, Tom saw how beautiful she
was. Audrey was crying because she had heard what Tom, in the
haze of his unhappiness, had not:

"Miami Day really isn't right for Nathaniel," Mrs. Berger
had said.

Continuing to explain, she went on, "Oh, yes, we could go the
route of tutors to deal with his lags and get him, maybe, to barely
keep up. However, let me be frank. He'd always be playing
catch-up ball here, so to speak, and he'd compare himself to the
other children and so couldn't help feeling terrible about himself.
I've been in this field a long time and have gone just about every

alternative route with boys like little Nathaniel, and this is what my wisdom tells me is best. Of course, we do have a commitment to your son and his family, and we will stick by this—unlike other schools perhaps. We're Bank Street and Sarah Lawrence educated mostly, and we believe in education for all kinds of children [all kinds]. Still, most of our parents are professionals, academics, intellectuals like you. The children are bright and know it, and they are very competitive—"

Audrey Robinson was crying not for herself but for her son, and maybe for her husband, too. She would come later. The self-accusations, the blame, the disappointment for herself, all those terrible feelings would hit her when she was alone. In the meantime she pictured her little boy, with his soft cheeks and dreamy smile, and saw the fear and disappointment in his eyes when he was told he'd have to make a change. And she imagined what was to come—what would evolve between father and son, between this future Nobel Prize winner maybe or university president and the kid who would never be able to do his algebra. For Audrey, reality had fallen heavily into place. It hadn't dislodged her love, though it had saddened her, and so she had no need to deny it.

Not so for Tom, who had "left" again. Fading Mrs. Berger into the blackboard behind her, he saw instead the dumb kids of his junior high days, all the sixteen-year-olds in seventh or eighth grade, dancing before him with their muffled monotones for speech and jive for language, the kids his father had busted for dealing drugs because they simply couldn't do anything else. He imagined his dear little Nathaniel—"a boy like little Nathaniel," that's what she had said, yes, "little"—slipping back into the wretched of the earth, after all. And anger then seized Tom Robinson.

"Are you sure?" he interrupted, it seemed for the first time, suppressing his temptation to hiss or bellow, instead evening out his question into an inquiring and dispassionate monotone. He was a scientist, he reminded himself, after all.

"Are you certain," he repeated, glancing at his expert-wife for reassurance, "that you're assessing my son accurately? What I mean to say is, have you tested him? Do you have evidence about his baseline intellectual functioning? I, uh, I mean"—he paused—"Natie's always been shy, reluctant to perform in front of people."

Tom tripped over his words because as he uttered his challenge, he was picturing his son's inability to catch a rag ball at

Stan's birthday party the weekend before and remembering how Nat had fled in shame from the makeshift playing field. Yanking his father's arm, Nathaniel had demanded to be taken home with a steadfastness not usually found in his otherwise halting and docile manner.

The fact was the egg had come before the chicken. Nat couldn't perform, and that's why the boy had performance anxiety. He was, oh, hell, a born loser.

It was different with Tom. Very different.

Tom was the opposite of his son. And so now he couldn't help noticing the trepidation creeping uncharacteristically into his awareness, disrupting *his* concentration. He didn't know what was going on. He was just so upset, he couldn't figure anything out.

"Yes, we have. Tested him. Right, Mrs., er, Ms.—Dr. Robinson?"

"Tom," Audrey whispered as she tried to smile, settling her hand on his.

His eyes blazed, and he felt them. Betrayal and surprise. He hadn't been told. He hadn't been told.

"We, no, I felt I couldn't tell you," Audrey answered her husband's mute accusation. "Not yet. We thought you'd get too upset—no, I did. I was afraid you'd start to worry, pressure Natie, and uh, he would just fall apart. It was hard enough for him already."

Tom started to rise. He struggled to free himself from the miniature chair that now seemed stuck to his rear. He pushed down with the heels of his hand on an adjacent desk as he stood up.

"Hold on. We had a learning specialist here do the testing, just focal stuff, about school. Not a whole evaluation. Emotionally, he's okay. The point is"—and Mrs. Berger was stretching her voice to catch up with him—"the point is he really can't—"

But it was too late. Tom had gotten up and, freed from his seat, had walked out the door.

His eyes were filling up. And he had that acid taste of desperation and helplessness as he strode down the marbled-linoleum corridors. Down the halls he hurried, hoping nobody was looking, and out the double metal doors separating Miami Day from the rest of the world.

What could he do? What was Nathaniel going to do?

• • •

The damaged child threatens to rob a man of what he wants for himself—forever. All loving parents, even superstars such as Tom and Audrey Robinson, have to some degree subordinated their needs and their sense of their personal importance to their child's happiness, beauty, and accomplishments. The sacrifices these children demand of them are such that most mothers and fathers must put themselves last, or lower down at least in the hierarchy of priorities ordering daily routines and governing longer-range plans for the family's future.

The concrete payoff comes in the expectation of being cared for in turn—tended in our old age by the children we have reared, as I've noted earlier. Most selfishly and traditionally, we conceive children so that they can help out in life—feed and shelter us when we get old. Yet, as I've also implied, the sense of connection goes deeper than that. It's less pragmatic and more powerful. The less tangible but more compelling compensations for the sacrifices a parent makes when he or she subordinates personal interests to the welfare of the child are to be found in that parent's profound identification with that child. Again, as Freud remarked in his exploration of "narcissism," the boundless and altruistic love a mother or father showers on a child is in the end a disguised expression of the adult's self-love.

As we grow up, most of us relinquish the sort of "egomaniacal" absorption in and overestimation of the self seen in very young children. We give up this self-importance because it seems inane and immoral. But then we find these childish feelings and fantasies reborn in our utter fascination and delight in our child and the expectations and illusions he or she stirs up in us. "His Majesty the Baby" comes to embody all that we once were in our eyes and all that we might have become.

Physically bound to her baby, having given up her body to it, inside and then out, a mother is possessed of a more elemental and unthinking love for an infant. To be loved by her, her baby simply has to be. After all, because she's a woman and his mother, he's already part of her.

Fathers, in contrast, have been said to love conditionally (as I've noted repeatedly in one context or another). To do otherwise is not in their nature as men. They don't have the anatomical equipment and physiological wherewithal to make babies or simply to let their children just be there with and for them. Men's satisfactions in rearing children are less sensuous and palpable, more mental than physical. Goal oriented and future directed, they have ideas about their children, who they are, what they should become, and how they as fathers can help them.

Even when they stay home with the kids, researchers such as Kyle Pruett or Michael Lamb have found, "househusbands" *do* more with their kids. Despite the role reversal, their sons and daughters in turn relate to them as men, seeking them out for roughhousing and imitating them as best they can. These children accommodate to their fathers' greater demands by performing accordingly. Initially at least, they learn at a greater pace and higher level than those of their peers brought up in the more traditional way, with mothers as primary caregivers.

More so than most mothers (and there are notable exceptions), then, fathers project onto their progeny their egotistical and specifically masculine aspirations. This may be true even when the child is a girl, a fact to which many women overachievers can readily attest. Indeed, more often than not such women attribute their ambition and success more to their fathers' than their mothers' encouragement and presence as role models. And not infrequently, they may feel that their femininity has been compromised by a father's stress on academic and work achievement.

But the potential for conflict becomes poignant when that child is a boy. He may resist being superseded by a son, but a father also wants to be surpassed. He wants to be validated and honored in all that the child attains in the here and now —those first toddling steps and at bats on the Little League diamond— and in the promise of more to come after he is old and then gone. A father feels responsible for the development of a son's masculinity. And he relives his wish to outdo his own father through his son's accomplishments.

So when there's something wrong with his child, a man may have a much tougher time adjusting to the crisis and "doing the necessary." It's harder for him to accept the unwelcome reality than for a woman, for whom any baby's helplessness has been par for the course. The damaged, impaired, diminished, or inadequate child becomes just that in the father's eyes. The child becomes a ruin, the broken reminder of all the father's hopes come to grief. Already displaced by this child in his wife's affections and in the cycle of the generations, he is dealt a further blow to his self-esteem when the child himself fails him. "Has it all been worth it after all?" he asks himself.

Worried about the child, grieving over a living loss, perhaps concerned about a future of endless financial demands and privations, he also takes it personally. For no fault of his own, he has "failed" as a father. And the father of a son like this must contend with the feeling of being castrated (once again) by the child's imperfections.

Though this fear has been energetically repressed by most men, its ghost, as I've reiterated, is ever present in all of them. And when, as they must, the facts become inescapable, and still nobody else can be blamed for misperceiving the truth or having caused the harm, men become enraged. "Narcissistic rage," psychiatrists have called this sort of seething anger about one's felt injuries and helplessness to heal them. The alternative, in all events, is despair.

And this is a typical sequence when men find out that their children, again their sons in particular, have been compromised by misfortune—congenitally defective, learning disabled, emotionally handicapped, or later on, sexually deviant, socially delinquent, drug addicted, HIV positive, and more. In an effort to subdue themselves, fathers first try to deny or minimize the truth. This failing, as inevitably it must, they then get angry—at the doctors, the schools, God, their wives, themselves, at everybody else. But in the end, it's the kid who's faulty, the child whose presence is a constant symbol of a broken genealogy and of a personal failure that can't be explained. Finally, fathers get angry at them—their kids.

As developmental expert Francine Stern has stressed, while there are many individual differences, fathers tend to oscillate between unrealistic fantasies about what the child can and will be able to do one day and irrational anger—often enough directed at the bearers of bad tidings, at teachers, at the practitioners who have diagnosed and must then treat their children. Unlike mothers who are around these children so much of the time and can see both what is true and what is good about them, many such fathers either see or don't see only the defects.

And for all his brains, Tom was no exception.

• • •

Thomas Robinson stared at his son, studying him as he had so many times in the seven-year-old's young life. There were no other kids at home to compare him with.

Audrey had her fledgling career. And even an up-and-coming superstar research and teaching scientist (the accolades reverberating in Tom's head, especially now) had only a young academic's earnings to live off. Oh, there were the perks from the grants, the expenses, travel, and some such, and some consultancies, but not enough. And Audrey had only her assistant professor's money, less than the salary of a doorman at one of those deco palaces lining the Beach.

Tom expected his full professorship next year. God, at thirty, could you believe it! They hadn't taken this twenty-three-year-old Ph.D. too seriously at first, not because he was young, but, he'd known, because he was black. Now they just might be promoting him because of his race, not the thirty-nine publications in a half dozen years. But so what, opportunity, equal or not, may get a foot through the door, but the rest's up to you—just you.

In the end, life's a solo trip. Yeah, for Nathaniel, too.

Jeez, money. What was this kid gonna cost? Where would Tom get it? Would he have to give up academia for the private sector, as they said euphemistically? Give up that big one. Tom had already sacrificed the higher reaches of his career for family, for the ties that bind, turning down positions at more prestigious universities in the Northeast and West to stay close to Audrey's and his families. For the kids. For the grandparents. Especially after the tragedy with his sister, Thelma. How much more would he have to lower his sights now?

So he narrowed his eyes and bore down with them on Nat as he sat cross legged on the floor, TV blaring while he colored away in some preschooler's book. Yet again Tom sized up his son. The boy looked and acted, he thought to himself, half his actual age. Each time he smiled up at his daddy, Tom felt his heart as it sank. Yes, exactly—"sank"—that was the sensation of heaviness that came with sadness, disappointment, unwanted anger, the futility of asking for more. And the guilt.

Before now, he'd watch the kid waddling after a cousin his age and try to comfort himself with the pronouncements and jargon he'd acquired about different timetables of development. Audrey had set him on the track of certain readings, and he'd followed her lead before moving on to more—assimilating two years of doctoral course work in mere months, it seemed. (More plaudits, please!) But what they called "clinical judgment" came with real experience, and so he would check Audrey out for the truth, and the flicker of an eyelid gave a quick lie to all the smiling platitudes. Besides, Tom remembered from his mother's and father's accounts, he had been reading at three and a half, when he entered nursery school, so much and so fast in fact that teachers had advised his parents to slow him down.

His parents. Tom was their only child now—his younger sister having died in the Lockerbie bombing over Scotland. Yes, that Third World, of all things, had risen up to destroy Thelma and those other young kids. Forces beyond their control seemed to be hurling this family—yes, family, a *black family*—back into the abyss.

Harry and Louise didn't know much about learning or congenital problems, Tom knew. But he knew they knew that Nat wasn't like him. His father would arrive at their house beaming, that jovial get-along politician style of his just radiating out of every pore. But then he, too, would subside into dull silence when his efforts to get Nat to read failed. And when he couldn't do something, couldn't learn, Nat would then posture and push. He'd just push anybody away. Even Big Harry didn't stand a chance.

Now this, the latest verdict would confirm his fears, too. Tom never liked to let his father down. . . .

A tough guy, cop and ex-jock, nonetheless Harry Robinson was an obsessive worrywart when it came to the family he'd made. He'd built it from nothing, from the dirt ground under his nails as a kid working the fields, a boy with no father in sight to model himself after. So he had fretted over everything his kids did or didn't do growing up. Inwardly he had written Thelma off as a "girl" nonetheless. She was bright enough, kind and decent, but not headed for stardom like his son.

There was truth to this perception. But he'd been on Tom's back. God forbid he got a B− or C+. He wasn't punished for it, exactly. But still Harry didn't disguise his disappointment and disapproval of mere mediocrity. And it had taken him years to accept the fact that, while he'd been a superstar in college sports, Tom was a mediocre athlete at best—the only black kid on the block who couldn't play basketball.

Harry had wanted the world for his children, a place very different from his father's universe. But, it seems, everything a person can dread in life can happen. After all, of the five children his mother had given birth to, only two had survived more or less intact. Harry had brought his brothers and sisters up only to see two die and another, well, just disappear. The worst was when his brother Robert—having escaped the Klan—got killed in that car crash. After Bobby died, Harry's sister-in-law Lil moved up North with those "mix and match" kids of hers. He never did see them again, and his childhood seemed to vanish with them.

Harry'd tried not to think about the past after that. But he couldn't get his kids out of his mind, and they knew it. Tom, for one, had wanted to make it up for him, make his father's life special forever. To give him his childhood and that of his son.

"First Thelma. Now Nat. Of course, they aren't the same, death and disability, or are they?" Tom growled to himself as he coughed and padded back to bed. It was the fifth time he'd urinated in three hours. A trickle each trip.

At least for Harry, though, there'd been hope. A struggle, but lots of hope. A future in his kids. For Tom now there was only grayness. It had stopped. No, even that wasn't quite fair—his father had had it harder by far. Again he felt mixed up.

Like his father, Tom was worrying. Like him, he couldn't contain himself. His private thoughts had been translated into a hoarse monologue and this into a bombardment. Predictably, Audrey was its recipient.

It was two o'clock and silent save for the drone of Tom's lament. Several times Audrey had reached over from her side of the bed to him, but he'd simply brushed her away.

"He's still a person, same one he was before. You heard Adele. He's darling—" Again she was talking to her husband's back. Once again he got up and away from her, her and her words. Grabbing his pillow this time, Tom walked out of their bedroom to sleep on the sofa in the living room.

He was mad at her. Maybe he shouldn't feel that way, but Tom couldn't help blaming Audrey for her intrusion into the Robinson legacy. The Saunders genes. Her uterus. Something. He hated himself for the idea, but Tom couldn't help thinking that things might have turned out different if only he hadn't married her.

Banishing these thoughts, he turned off the lamp, positioning himself like a fetus on the lonely couch. He waited for the Benadryl to take effect and submerge him and his thoughts in sleep. Down the hall, he knew, Nat was sleeping, or maybe wondering why his parents had looked so sad and nervous and had talked so late into the night and why his dad was peeing so much. Tom pulled up the edge of the blanket he'd retrieved from the linen closet and snuggled into it.

"Come to bed."

It was Audrey. She had turned Tom over with the gentle

pressure of an index finger on a shoulder that no longer had the will to resist. And so he obeyed it and her, following his wife back into their bedroom. He left behind the pillow and blanket, making a vacant berth of the sofa in the dark room, like an empty cradle. . . .

• • •

Eleven A.M. the next morning. It was cobra venom Tom was about to suck up. Pipetting the lethal stuff, a neurotoxin with infinite research possibilities, was part of the experimental procedure he was demonstrating to his new graduate research assistant. It was a pain, he grumbled in interior silence, having to teach this dork the ropes.

Tom drew the liquid up through the narrowest of glass tubes, with greater finesse than the deftest black sax player. And then he was back at Bickford's. A chocolate frosted or a cherry Coke was laid out before him on the counter, two candy-striped straws awaiting the suctioning power of a thirsty kid's lips. In his mind's eye, he was bending over, poised to suck up the sweet stuff in one gulp.

It was in that instant that Tom thought he might just keep on going, inhaling death through his chapped lips. Poised before it, he remembered a scene from a James Bond movie. Bond rolls over, and the girl he's with for that night receives on her slightly parted lips a hideous hemlock meant for 007. Except that it wasn't she who received the grim elixir in Tom's vision, but Nathaniel, sweating and smelling of milk as he slept.

No, Tom didn't spit the stuff out. He simply stopped and asked Jerry Cushman to give it a try.

• • •

Families and the vulnerable members within them need these fathers like Tom. They need their composure and realism, and yet, Francine Stern has noted, their irrational reactions can turn trauma into tragedy. Emotional pressures may make it impossible for such men to fulfill their roles as providers and mainstays of the family's morale—often at a time when their wives have given up other professional options and sources of income to devote themselves to the daily needs of a demanding child. Separation and divorce, Stern continues, are not uncommon under the circumstances.

Intelligent and moral men are made uncomfortable, to say the least, by the fury roused in them by a child already at risk, a child all the more dependent on their unwavering goodwill and protection. So they may at first try to join with their wives in subordinating their personal pleasures and freedoms to the care of this child over many years. Marshaling what psychoanalysts call "reaction formations" to do so, turning emotions such as hatred or resentment into their opposites (love and unblinking concern), still such men find that the life has gone out of their families. Missing are the unalloyed joy, the fun, the highs that come with being a successful father to a kid who glows.

They continue to measure their children against their more successful peers in unconscious and magical efforts to heal the hurts. Failing each time, repeatedly confronted by the great gulf between an ideal and the reality before them, undeniably helpless, these men become depressed.

Yes, they tend that kid, and love him (or her.) But as developmental pediatricians dealing with children and families like these have noted again and again, they can't turn from looking at the damage to seeing the child himself. The lot of such men is reduced to one of wearisome obligation, torturous prognostications about an ambiguous future, and worst of all, obsessive efforts to undo what can't be undone: "If only . . . then . . ."

Or unable to accept his impotence to effect radical change, such a father may turn off and give up on a lost cause. Sometimes he may abandon the whole family, especially when the defective child is the first in a series of children that seem never to have been meant to be. More commonly, he may act to maintain the structure of the family while retracting his daily investment in the specific problem child. Such fathers go on to make more and better babies or absorb themselves in work or have affairs, while leaving "it" to their wives, institutions, or health care professionals. They let others take care of a son or daughter who is no longer a person, much less a family member, in their eyes. For them, out of sight = out of mind = out of existence.

Maybe that's why Tom ran—full steam into a career that was advancing far more rapidly than his developmentally stalled little boy.

• • •

A half dozen years later: Tom spooned out the Cremora into the not-bad coffee. The coffee, like the gracious secretary, was provided for the National Science Foundation team of site visitors, of whom he was a member. Department? Which department? He'd been on so many of these expeditions in the last three years, he hardly knew where he was.

Travel. Nice lunches. New people, new programs, not bad. Necessary, too, for a chairman-to-be.

So far he'd done no cohabiting with any fellow inspectors—female sex, of course—but had come awfully close once or twice. He remained bound to Audrey, who, at home and no longer employed full-time herself, had stayed tied to the kids (two now)—more and more in fact. Like many professional parents with troubled children, she had reorganized her career as well as her life around their problems. So Audrey had drifted from black studies and female development to perinatal complications and their cognitive, or intellectual, consequences and emotional impact later in childhood.

An expert in learning disabilities now, Audrey had served as a consultant at Miami's Mailman Center and had just been approached to be the new director. She'd been interviewed by the board and had made a good impression, particularly on one of the co-chairpersons, Barbara Whitford, who was fast becoming a new friend. Her only compunctions had to do with the time that would be taken from her kids—especially with Tom's spending so much of his on the road these days.

Nat was twelve now, and Julie was a sweet little three. Tom didn't actually see them a whole lot, but still their images were in the forefront of his thoughts—always.

"That stuff's poison," he heard from behind, "with a cholesterol like yours. Read the ingredients. Coconut."

One scientist to another—like doctors who couldn't find an aspirin at home.

Roger Cummings had been waiting his turn at the urn behind Tom. In the last year an unexpected friendship had developed between the two. Cummings, who held the august Gold Chair at Yale and had already garnered his Swedish trophy (actually for work done when he was about Tom's age), was fifty-eight, older, it turned out, than Harry Robinson. The difference was that Roger had married late (his younger brother, Don, was still a bachelor) and had a good deal in common, besides shared research interests, with a colleague young enough to be his son.

A son, that was it. That was it; each of them had a son. In fact, both their sons were in trouble. And Roger's more than Tom's.

Oh, yes, one might say that Roger's son wasn't really his.

Preston had been adopted. Roger and Pud (Pauline, actually), having started the process in motion late in their life, had proved incapable of conceiving. His sperm hadn't been all that lively, he chuckled, with truncated tails to boot, and the "old girl" hardly ovulated anymore. So they'd started their search through the agencies.

One would have thought the process would be easy, with a couple as stable, distinguished, and desirable as the Cummingses. Yet it took two years before they located the first of the two children. And even then the circumstances weren't ideal.

Preston, named for Pud's grandfather, was nearly two when he arrived. He was unruly and unkempt from the start, stubbornly lacking in language, relatedness, and a host of the prototypical social skills that one might expect in a toddler. Then again, he had mysterious scars on his scalp and underarms, puckered creases where, it seemed, he'd been branded somehow. And these told of an early upbringing that was harsh at best and no doubt filled with terror.

Hugh, whom they adopted a year and a half later and whose unwed mother had interviewed the Cummingses before she decided on them, would prove to be a different story. Having arrived in fairly pristine condition, fresh from the womb, he was more of a blank slate on whom his gentle and civil parents would write. Few problems there, though Hugh was hardly the "rocket scientist" his father might have been had he just happened to choose another field.

Like Nathaniel, the second boy was rather slow—with similar lags in receptive language, dyslexia, and low muscle tone (hypotonicity, the experts called it), which had made walking and activities emerging later on bigger problems than they were for other children. Still, physical therapists and tutors had helped Hugh along (like Nathaniel), eventually launching him into the mainstream.

It was Pres who terrorized the family as, it seemed, he had been brutalized during those first months by his biological parents. Always at odds with his classmates, by ten he had become the scourge of his schoolroom. The fighting with peers, the truancy, and the physical attacks on his teachers and parents had become unbearable. The boy had begun to make the mental health and special education rounds—therapists, special schools, stabs at medication—all the very best, all futile.

By fourteen Preston had nothing in common, it seemed, with

the parents who had reared him. Maybe he did with the mysterious crew who had first brought him into the world. One of his
therapists had wondered, in fact, whether what was called Pres's
"acting out" didn't in fact represent some symbolic search for his
identity and for his past. The trouble was, the boy was so wild, so
out of it, so uncommunicative and unreceptive, that imparting
insight of any kind to him was to no avail.

Not only pot but cocaine and eventually crack made their way
into Preston's repertoire of substances to be abused—along with
the beer and hard liquor of earlier delinquent generations. Physically, once he became an adolescent, he looked more like a Hell's
Angel than a scientist's son. Pres towered over his parents, his
height matched only by an advancing beer belly. The girth and
general bloatedness were accentuated by the mounds of tangled
black hair and mangy growths on his chin and cheeks. Sundry
metal jewelry and chains capped off the menacing look of a child
whom the Cummingses—now afraid of him—had once bathed
and diapered.

It was the night he and his friends broke into the garage and
the kitchen, stealing the car before wrecking it and buying booze
with the household money, that finally did it. Preston was taken
from his "home" at this point, beginning and aborting one course
of residential treatment after another. One after another, the nation's preeminent psychiatric institutions took on this tough guy
until at last they gave up on him, or the Cummingses on them,
sending Preston on to the next financially and emotionally draining holding operation.

The toll on the family had been exacting. There were the
insurance companies to be cajoled and coerced and the expenses
not covered by them. There were clinical conferences, parent support groups, family therapy to be attended, and the travel to get
to all these harsh and humiliating encounters. Twice, the marriage had almost collapsed. Hugh had been neglected and knew it,
occasionally acting up and "out" apparently to redirect his parents' attention toward him. In fact, the three nonhospitalized
family members had been driven to seek therapies of their own.

Roger, "WASP that I am," as he put it to Tom, had been the
last to relent, to "soften up that stiff upper lip so that I could talk
about myself." In fact, he went on, he'd found the process both
comforting and intriguing. A whole psychoanalysis had evolved
out of the sessions, which initially dealt with the emergent crises
in his family life, crises that proved to be chronic.

"I began to see," he'd told Tom over yet another after-dinner drink and peanuts the night before, when their hosts and fellow site visitors had long gone to bed, "that Pres was only a piece in my personal puzzle. Yes, he changed our lives forever, and no doubt for the worst, and he injured me. But somehow, if he hadn't, something else would. I needed to feel punished. We had too much, too much of our mother—both I and then my brother, Don—he more than I, but each in our own way.

"Odd, no? But there's a logic to it. Uh, I do regret, though, that without knowing it I tried to avoid him in those earlier days, plunging into my work again, and letting Pud do what she could. Maybe I couldn't have stemmed the tide, but I would have felt less guilty had I stuck around more. Maybe all this is too telegraphic. Maybe I'm not making any sense."

It had been these last words—"less guilty had I stuck around more"—that had reverberated in the back of Tom's brain that night. They stuck in his thoughts after he'd hung up the phone and Audrey's voice and image had begun to fade, leaving him only with himself. They stayed with him after he'd flicked through the TV channels in an unsuccessful effort to induce sleep. Alone in the king-size bed of this, another strange hotel room where he'd never sleep again, Tom had wondered whether he'd been doing everything he could.

And now this visit was coming to an end. A half-hour's break before they gave some initial feedback and advice about what might be done, this debriefing session's duration, and they'd be flying home again.

"Thank heaven for small blessings," Roger murmured.

"What?" Tom had hardly heard him.

"Pres made it out of the quiet room today. Tomorrow's his eighteenth birthday. McLeans is giving him a party—"

"Congratulations," Tom responded pro forma, and thinking about his friend, immediately wished that, not knowing what to say, he hadn't said anything.

Roger simply smiled. Before Tom could apologize for what passed as absentmindedness, but was really self-absorption, Roger asked, "How's Nat?"

•   •   •

Fine. Nat was fine, Tom realized the next morning in the taxi home from the airport. He was doing great at the Hudson School, had gotten Bs (their Bs to be sure but *his* Bs nonetheless) last semester and was vice president of the seventh grade. He was also teaching his sister how to throw, catch, and bat. He was doing what he should be doing.

Tom thought about Roger, about his mental pictures of Pres and Pud and Hugh, about Audrey and Julie, and more about Nat, and before he knew it he was home. With the slamming of the cab door, the dog had barked, heralding his arrival.

The children came running as always, Julie flying into his arms and then sliding down his body. Behind her marched Nathaniel, looking his twelve years, the boy not yet turned man.

"Hi, Dad," he said, trying to be perfunctory, but rushing to hug his father. Tom felt the arms encircling his waist, the soft face burying itself into his middle, the snuggling—all before Nat caught himself in the act and eased away.

Too babyish. Yeah.

"Hey, Dad." Nat's voice had suddenly grown deeper, like that of those classmates of his who were already over the hump into puberty. "That bag's pretty heavy for you." And he swept up Tom's suitcase (which unfortunately contained some printouts plus books), trying not to reveal the unanticipated strain as he dragged it up the front steps.

"Pretty strong," Tom affirmed as, entering, he looked at Audrey and quickly caressed her hand.

"Yep, see this." And having released his burden onto the foyer floor, Nat was making a muscle. Pushing up his short sleeve for effect, he crooked his arm and tensed his biceps. And there it was indeed. A muscle, round and firm and bulging out, just asking to be felt—a palpable muscle, the strength of the man Nat, like everyone else of his sex, was destined to be.

Feel it Tom did indeed, with Audrey and even Julie appreciatively following suit. Yes, he had one more site visit to make next month. But Nat's father had already resolved to resign from the committee. Nat's biceps were incentive enough.

He'd miss Roger, but then again he and Pud would most likely enjoy a visit to their nation's vacation mecca. Oh, yes, and Hugh would, too. They'd all love his—Tom's, not Audrey's—Key lime pie.

Preston was another matter.

• • •

Most fathers take a special pride in their sons' unfolding manhood. And men these boys will become—for the most part at least.

Nature and to some extent society will have their way with them.

Indeed, like an illness of his own, overcoming his despair over a child's disabilities can help a man feel more empowered, able to accept and master at once what nature has in store for him. Contending with fate and the blows to his pride that misfortune brings with it allows for some measure of genuine self-control and self-acceptance.

In any event, all lives have their setbacks and disappointments, as the story of a more or less "normal" man's life reveals. And this takes us to the next series of chapters, and the making of a man from birth, and before it, to maturity, and beyond—to the life story of Chuck Watson, Jr., M.D.

The Making of a Man

So far I've merely hinted at the boys men once were. In the following chapters, I will start from the beginning and pursue the development of one boy as he evolves through childhood and adolescence into an adult man. In keeping with the book's main threads, I will follow the interweaving of his "primal androgyny," encompassing his feminine yearnings, and the aggressive thrust of his masculine destiny along with all the tensions these give rise to. We'll look at everybody's conflicts in fact—those of the boy himself and the mixed feelings and messages of those responsible for making a man of him.

11
∴

A Boy Is Born

Comedian Richard Pryor once depicted the wide-eyed but reluctant infant making his way out of the womb. More recently, in the movie *Look Who's Talking*, macho Bruce Willis dubbed in the voice of a smart-alecky babe seeing his world through savvy adult eyes. These fictive kids come charging into the world as if fully formed, like homunculi. They're tough guys, street smart from the start. And, oh boy, do they know what they want!

In truth, the beginnings of life remain as much of a mystery to the experts on infant and child development as they do to those of us who have lived it. When a grown-up looks at a baby during the first hours, weeks, even months, of life, something perhaps of his first longings and sensations is revived, enabling the adult observer to intuit what this little "thing" wants. Reading the infant's wordless cues, he or she can manage to minister to its needs. But an observer can't really know what this kid can't tell him.

So far what have emerged from these developmental psychologists' inquiries into the dawn of consciousness are a variety of paradoxes. On the one hand, the infant, far from being some kind of blank slate—the empiricist philosopher's tabula rasa—is believed to be all there from the start. He has much to begin with and he will have still more to come. As pediatrician T. Berry Brazelton (our contemporary Dr. Spock) has put it, the newborn is already a "socially deft and well-related little fellow." From the very start, he's equipped with the rudimentary capacity to communicate with his caretakers.

On the other hand, the baby is also ready to be made. In the words of the late infant observer René Spitz, he or she is the only person in a family without a past. Yet soon enough he's fitted with one. Even before he's born, his parents give him *their* histories, perceiving him accordingly and teaching their baby—a boy in this case—what it means to be who he is.

And so it is with a boy's masculinity. It's both innate *and* conditioned. It unfolds in stages over time as a result of both an inborn timetable and a process of social learning, with the child's parents as his main instructors. Such was the case with Simone and Chuck Watson.

• • •

In 1953 in Medford, Massachusetts, it was standard operating procedure for a mother-to-be to be anesthetized into oblivion as she gave birth, or rather as her obstetrician delivered her baby. In the meantime, her husband proverbially paced the waiting room floor. That is, his wife will tell you, if he managed to get to the hospital at all.

Thirty years later, Little Chuck, the baby boy born in this way on May 8 of this year and in this place, would serve as his wife's "coach," helping her pant and push her way through a Lamaze-style childbirth at New York Hospital. For the time being, however, his father, Charles Watson, Sr.—Big Chuck, as he came to be called—fit the stereotype of the times.

He strode aimlessly about the lounge, pausing only occasionally to light or extinguish yet another Chesterfield King. Big Chuck didn't yet know the sex of the child—again unlike Little Chuck years later, for whom an amniocentesis had told all. But the occasion was to prove auspicious, heralding the appearance on earth of his firstborn son.

Mrs. Simone Watson, née Lazarre, was a slight, fair-skinned, delicate woman. She had been a French "war bride," a child herself. And to her husband at least, she still looked the virtual waif who met, loved, and married her burly soldier eight years earlier. And so war hero Charles, or Chuck, whose "Watson" was actually an anglicization of Wysinski, was worried. He was *really* worried about his wife.

Perhaps they shouldn't have waited so long to conceive their child, he scolded himself as he roamed about. But then again, necessity and nature had had their way with them. He'd had to go to college on the GI Bill, forcing the two of them to earn money for a while before he began his own contracting business.

After this, a man of his times, he'd vowed that his wife would never have to work again. And for two years she hadn't. There had already been one pregnancy in fact, culminating in a miscarriage just about a year ago.

So this time Simone had gone to bed for two months. The man who'd machine-gunned down a dozen "krauts" now made their dinners and breakfasts. His aunt Sophia came in to do the housework and provide lunch. Simone should have been well rested. But he shouldn't have taken her to Edith and Dave's Thursday night. After the visit, she'd gone into labor—two weeks before her due date. The delivery was barely premature. However, it was early enough under the circumstances of his wife's condition for concern.

It had gone on for twelve hours—hours and hours of separate pain and fretfulness. And he felt useless to boot, not part of this process so much bigger than he was.

"It's a boy."

Chuck Watson had stopped for a rare moment to face the window. No, he reassured himself, he hadn't left his car lights on. A hand then rested itself on his shoulder and turned him about. Alone there, he would have hoped to see Dr. Heaton's beaming face instead of this nurse's. But this silly moment of disappointment was eased by the more important news at hand.

"He and his mom are doing just fine," Mrs. Spinelli continued in response to his inquiring gaze. "He weighed in at six pounds two ounces."

Again an irrational instant of letdown: only six pounds, Chuck thought.

"I'll take you to have a look-see."

"A 'look-see'?"

Even Chuck—who was certainly no literary type—even he couldn't help resenting the corn. He imagined Nurse Spinelli depositing him at the nursery window and clicking herself off with a TV weatherwoman's code word as she pointed to the kid: "Good night, Chuck, and have a happy."

For the rest of your lives.

But there he was, and there she was pointing. Behind the glass, her colleague, Nurse Kate O'Hara, had lifted up for his view the newborn, a scrubbed and swaddled Charles, Jr. He was pink, wrinkled, and gulping blankly, just as in the movies. And he hardly felt real.

The new Charles senior felt just a little wobbly for the moment, out there alone again. He had become a father, and as they say, his life had just changed forever. Self-consciously, aware of Spinelli's gaze, of her scrutiny really, he had meant to say with an initiate's solemnity, "My son . . . my *son*." Instead his utterance came forth:

"My father."

Had Nurse Spinelli been a psychiatrist and he her patient, then they might have understood the generational echoes in this slip of the tongue. Instead, they simply let it pass with a laugh and an amendment: "Er, father, uh, I mean son."

Still, Big Chuck would tell this story on himself for years after, laughing heartily each time without knowing quite why. He left it to future generations—to Little Chuck, his wife, and their psychoanalysts, "of all things"—to decode its meanings. And indeed Little Chuck, as a man looking in on himself, would return many times to the "personal myth" that evolved out of his father's narrative of this evening's successive events and images.

Sometime—he wasn't sure when, but it must have come at a time when he was able to understand such things—the boy would learn how mixed his father's emotions had been. Big Chuck was a fairly reticent man, of course, a man of his times, stoic and tough, a man's man. But he did convey to his son just how deeply scary the event was. And more: he'd been mad at him, too—at this quivering hunk of flesh who had suddenly coalesced into a son.

Chuck had sat by Simone's bed, he related later on, waiting for her to wake up. Odd isn't it, he mused, that she of all people should have been taken away from the scene of her baby's birth? And he'd registered the winces of pain that played across her face even in drugged sleep. His son had done that to her. He, their pride and joy, had torn her apart.

A generation later Charles junior had felt rather the same after his firstborn, a daughter, Agatha, had been shoved out into the world. She'd made an awful mess of her mother, he, too, couldn't help reflecting, as he watched the sewing up of the episiotomy. He'd seen and done dozens of these in his medical school and internship days, and their Lamaze instructor had told them to be matter-of-fact about it. But this was different.

"So this is what my dad meant?" the son later wondered.

"It's a girl," they had said, in unison, and though he'd known it ahead of time through the results of the amniocentesis, to his dismay Chuck felt his racing heartbeat flatten just for a moment. A cloud of lost hope, of unrenewed beginnings, wafted across the white light of the delivery room.

They covered up his naked girl, burying her and hiding her sex in swaddling clothes, and he recovered present and future and gained a measure of a past that had never been. His life as a little girl, maybe.

"Maybe," Charles's analyst—the "training analyst" assigned to all candidates at psychoanalytic institutes to teach, free, and heal at the same time—"maybe," Dr. Rachel Peterson said, "your father meant to say that your birth enabled him to identify with his father at last. As a father."

"Yes, and maybe I was his rival, too."

• • •

Long before a baby such as Little Chuck has any idea that he's an "I," a person among other people, much less a boy in a world of males and females, a baby's parents know and react to his sex. He comes naked into the world, and all present herald the power of his penis long before it will be used. Parents seize on the signs of the boy's sex—an expectant but still dormant genital or, these days in fact, when they can decide to find it out ahead of time through amniocentesis, even a chromosomal computer readout—and begin to expect and demand great and specific things of him.

From the start, parents teach their boys and girls their sex roles. They do so in the way they touch them, dress them, handle them. They talk to them as boys in words they can't yet understand, but in a language whose music, pitches, and tones, valences and cadences even infants pick up and absorb into their body rhythms.

"Oh, you darling girl, but aren't you a flirt sometimes!" a mother in one study I conducted of parents and children exclaims in mock remonstration.

"See," she continues as her four-month-old grimaces at me making the so-called social smile of an infant in response even to a Halloween mask, "see, she does that with all the fellas."

"Eat yoa dinna of beef, young fella, and for Gawdsake, be good to yoa motha!"

So intones one man, with Boston drawl and animated John Lewis eyebrows—the father of a boy almost the same age in another study by pediatricians Berry Brazelton and Michael Yogman.

The baby seems to love these manly intrusions. A father's abruptness, the deep voice, seem contagious, and the baby boy's movements and cooing begin to mirror and echo the "maleness" of his father's verbal and nonverbal talk with him. His mother offers her own pleasures. The baby finds her more gentle envelopment of him soothing and quieting, and he seems to ease even into the sounds she makes. But still a baby boy seeks out the stimulation only men have to offer.

Fathers act similarly toward daughters, these developmental pediatricians found—only less so. Where like mothers they will tend to sweep their daughters up into their arms on the note of a mere peep of distress, dads will let their boys tough it out far longer. After all, they'll have to venture forth into a cold, hard world one day and fend for themselves and their families. Adults are constantly sending signals about what it is to be male versus female.

Yet something comes from within the child as well, and it's this that primes him to receive and at times elicit the cues he's given. He seems hungry for them almost from the start. And yes, pretty soon babies and certainly toddlers act to engage their parents in what developmental psychologists call *"sex specific* interactions."

Boys turn to their mothers for food and comfort, physical and emotional, and to fathers for play. There are individual differences in style, but generally, as women mothers offer sensuous pleasures, fathers more motoric and high-keyed forms of fun. By a year or so girls are "flirting with" their fathers while their brothers are pestering them to roughhouse with them. When either gets hurt or disappointed, however, he or she runs back to mommy.

Boys don't simply "learn" what it is to be a male, then. The thrust emerges from within and drives them to be with their fathers. (See Chapter 8.) It makes them imitate their actions, finally "identifying themselves" with what is felt as their masculinity. Strutting, smelling different, tough, rough, big and hairy, active, aggressive—and yes, a man with a penis—this person is a dad. This is an adult man, and this is what the boy will become. There's a sense of movement, of motion, of drivenness, to the unfolding of a son's maleness. Being a boy seems to require *doing* something—getting up, getting going, getting away from a mother who loves him so, for whom his love is also boundless but who tends to hold him back.

Where he meets his father in short bursts of activity and excitement, the time a baby boy spends with his mother seems endless and eternal—timeless time. He came from her body and feeds on the milk from her breasts. She's made him, it seems, from herself. In the best of circumstances, a boy child spends his "leisure hours," intervals when survival needs per se aren't being addressed, luxuriating in his mother's aura, her scent, her feel, and their shared being. (Even where women work, this is the feeling, the "peak experience" in the meetings of mothers and infants.)

Thus, while his sexual destiny entreats him to move forward, on toward a man's world, a boy is forever drawn back into his mother's arms. Psychoanalysts such as Margaret Mahler have talked of an essential "symbiosis" between mothers and babies of both sexes. It is a state in which she and he are not yet clearly differentiated from each other most of the time in a child's mind for sure and, to a far lesser degree, even in the mother's emotional experience.

In such a union, one in which the two beings are psychologically enfolded by what Mahler called an illusory "membrane," the boy is primarily "one with his mother." He drinks her person in, making its odors and textures his own, immersing himself in her sounds and sights, identifying as well with what he gradually comes to distinguish as her femininity. Even when he ventures forth, it's as if he takes a little of her with him—a security blanket, a gesture, just a feeling—to ease his anxiety in the face of solitude.

Freedom is lonely. And so is masculinity.

Thus, for boys, maybe more so than for girls at first, there's a tension in this sense of himself, a sense of responding to mixed messages that somehow have to do with maleness. On the one hand, his body, his caretakers, and the fascination of the environment itself tell him he should be separate, impermeable, and male. On the other hand, mother and her womanhood are home base, and he's inclined to let himself be reabsorbed by her.

He has to tear himself away—pushing, wriggling, struggling, to be free. Later on down the line, when specific wants replace mere impulses, when he sees that actions have consequences, his wish to be man will come to mean being aggressive.

Such inherent tension is further compounded by the parents'

competing reactions to his emerging masculinity and its place in
their lives. Mothers adore their little boys and find in them their
own completion. Yet they may resent their masculinity because it
reminds them of other men and how they've been dominated,
rejected, or hurt by them—of the men who've already left them.

Fathers see in sons their own reincarnation in addition to the
boy's promise of something new and special. Yet they fear and
resent this potential because it augurs their obsolescence and
death—because their boys will replace them. Sons make fathers
redundant.

I've touched on these themes in preceding chapters (Chapters
2, 7, 8, and 10, for instance) and will return to them later. (See
Chapters 12, 13, and 15.) The point I wish to make here is that
these conflicting reactions, these *ambivalences* about a boy's maleness influence the ways in which adults charged with his care act
to enhance, impede, or otherwise shape its natural unfolding.

Mothers and fathers at first, and then teachers and coaches
later on, constantly contradict themselves about what it is and
how good it is to be a boy and to become a man. The pulls are
there from the start, as I've said, in the impulses of the bodily
self—powerful urges to sink into women for safety's sake versus
the pressing drive to get going with men in order to grow up. But
then, because of their own needs, the people in a child's life act to
refine this visceral tension into emotional conflict—many conflicts
in fact, all having to do with aspects of a child's masculinity.

Finally, adults add the icing to the cake. They tell him that
because he's a boy, he shouldn't have uncertainties of any sort.
Unlike girls, males were meant to be straightforward. It doesn't
matter that it doesn't start out like that—not with mothers who
are people, complicated people, people who tell their babies how
to be. People such as Madame Watson of Medford, Massachusetts.

• • •

Baby Charles's first days, weeks, months, were a strange time
indeed for his mother. Simone Lazarre Watson had been used to
being a person without a passport, orphaned and zoneless. But
now, just as she had begun to plant seeds and grow roots again,
working for a while, finding friends in her office and in Charles's
family—poof—it was gone. Her bearings, her points of reference.
Her new identity.

First there had been the hospital, and her awakening to see

this red thing staring up dark-eyed at her before zeroing in on her nipple, which soon got sore and bled. She was supposed to love him and did. But she, the youngest in a family that no longer existed, she, still tender and motherless herself—how could she be a mother? How could she know a child?

Simone and her baby went home, and the endless days and nights blended into each other. She couldn't bear to let him cry— the way pediatricians advised in those days (if not now). Probably, Simone thought, it was that she'd too many memories of abandoned children wailing into the ruins. Then, too, this boy was hers—all hers no matter what her doctor or mother-in-law advised. And feeling so, falling in love with her baby, she fell into knowing him. Simone and her Charles swaddled themselves in the walls of their white frame house and in themselves. They wrapped up their being—the feeding, the shitting, the diapering, the hours of pretend chatter—in the tissue of an illusion. They became alone in the world and inseparable.

Sometimes she'd undress her boy and take off her clothes, which had become limp and functional and no longer important to her. Housecoats, they were called then. She'd lay his body on her naked belly with his head between her breasts as he drifted into sleep. She'd spin up the two of them in the bedclothes, like a cocoon, lying there, deliciously fading into the darkness she'd made of the room.

Some expert had thought this was good, she found out later. Skin-to-skin contact helped babies feel secure. But Simone could feel his penis now and then—or at first, she wasn't sure, was it the remains of his umbilical?—felt it push against her belly button as they breathed together. Synchronicity or counterpoint. But always in tune.

Now and then Simone became uneasy. Little Charles's penis seemed to grow hard. "Do little boys get erections?" she'd asked her doctor. Yes, they do. Had she caused this? No. No need to worry.

Yet it was a harbinger of things to come. She would lose him because he was a boy—a boy who could love her, as the poet says, or so her husband told her, "not wisely but too well." How she knew this she didn't know. But she did. And knowing, sometimes she had the dreaded thought, "If he didn't have a penis, he would never go away. From me."

For her son the voluptuousness would be lost to memory. By mutual consent, skin and the nudity, her touch, all would become off-limits. Charles would never wholly remember the mother of these days and what his later teacher and mentor Margaret Mahler had called their "dual unity." But he would always feel good about himself. It was a goodness that came to reside inside. He would feel it in his gut even when otherwise he felt bad—ugly, mean, wounded. Even when she, his mother, or someone else hurt him later on, their first goodness was still there.

Sometimes it had scared him, though—when he was a boy alone at home and wandered into his mother's room or caught the silhouette of a body he shouldn't see. Later, when Chuck was grown and a girlfriend wanted to hang out a little longer with him, it came over him.

It. He felt his memory. He couldn't say or see it exactly. It was sensation and mood. And it stayed with him.

Years later his mother would come to visit—it was after Big Chuck had died. She'd use the bathroom, and Chuck would go into it to get something afterward. Her smell was still there. It lingered about the robe dangling from the hook on the door, extending its reach to permeate the room and enfold him. It was everywhere. He tried at these times to be laid-back and take it all in, straining to recollect what had become different. He tried to submerge himself in that proverbial "buzzing confusion" of baby life, to see impressions of himself and mother coalescing as one, and to feel a world without boundaries. He couldn't. And the mental exercise was unsettling, too—even for a guy like him. Being, without being himself. Being born as a self.

• • •

A woman like Simone isn't abnormal. A mother should be absorbed in her baby. "Primary maternal preoccupation" is to be expected. What's more, a mother's love affair with her infant evokes in him a sense of well-being through and through along with a faith in a world that begins as her creation. He'll get fed, feel good, survive. "Basic trust," Erik Erikson has dubbed this first existential achievement. And hell, life's painful enough even when you've got it!

Early on it's a father's job to provide for and to protect this pair, "the mother-child dyad." He spares them the cares of the world so that they can just hang out and savor each other, free from extrinsic concerns that might jar them loose from each other and take their minds elsewhere. But you can have too much of a good thing—too much for too long. A "protracted symbiosis" gets pretty cloying. And it goes against the grain of any child's development—but especially perhaps that of a boy. The lap baby will soon become a creeper, crawler, and finally a toddler. He'll want to move about on his own in a world that, if he has an inner illusion of perpetual safety, starts out as a benign yet exciting place.

Timing is all.

Many mothers—many but not all—might be moved to languish forever in a state of effective merger with their little boys. Depending on their personalities and their infant's basic temperament, the feelings of sensuous, tactile, visceral completion and of *maternal competence,* a competence that has to do with a woman's ability to make and sustain life itself, figure as strong temptations to stay bound together forever. Some mothers might never relinquish their hold on a baby's body and soul—and some never do—were it not for forces to the contrary: were it not for fathers.

"Midnight marauder" was what pediatrician and psychoanalyst Phyllis Greenacre once called the baby's father during the first year of life. Imagine a modest guy like Chuck Watson as the marauder or, alternatively and progressively, "a knight in shining armor"! But he is.

Plunging into the world of madonna and infant in their symbiotic clinch, a man offers himself to his growing child as an alternative source of interest and satisfaction, and as a subject of imitation. He gets in between this pair-in-one, more or less vigorously, depending on his particular inclinations. And when a son is involved, he makes him male.

He invites his aggression. He tells him to get out.

You see, a father resents that clinch. Chuck Watson did.

• • •

Simone's and Little Charles's days were punctuated at each end by the sudden sounds and sights of Big Chuck's nightly return to the house. Just one man came home, and a fairly humble and unpresumptuous one to boot, and a whole world changed.

"Hi, darlin', hey, Chuckie."

The words of greeting had become almost ritualized—Chuck Watson's Boston aloha. And as usual, he saluted his newborn family by letting the front door slam behind him.

" 'Hi,' 'hey,' and bam. Oh, those men—*les hommes,*" Simone murmured out of her evening slumber. The tone, pace, rhythm, of the household had changed.

On other days—there didn't seem to be a pattern to which ones—she would await the grand entrance in impatient expectation, perched by the door, alert to the twist of a key. She would hand over either "Junior" or "Le Tigre"—depending on their day—with sighs of relief or freedom. Or in this anticipatory mood, she might be eager to bring everybody together—relating the day's domestic events and imagining for her still uncomprehending son his father's great deeds and tribulations. She'd serve once again as interpreter, as she had during and after the war. But this time Simone would translate her two lovers'—"*mes amants*"—languages for each other and animate their knowledge of the other. She'd make her "men" important and real.

Today, however, molding to her baby and he to her, swathed in her cocoon, Simone was feeling particularly languorous and had to drag herself from the haze of half sleep. Little Chuck was nine months old now, and larval no longer. He was standing and about to walk, beginning to wean himself as well from breasts that, had his mother not been told otherwise, would still be freely offered for his pleasure.

Actually, he was forever on the go, grabbing and groping, and seemed hardly interested in his mother anymore. Usually she had to wait for him to sleep to get hold of him, and moments such as these had become precious indeed. She felt loath to let them go. Maybe she was feeling pressured to say good-bye.

The slam did it, however, jostling the whole house and waking up her Little Chuck. At its sound, and just as his mother stole from her place beside him, he erupted out of slumber. Simone had started to soothe her son, hugging him and cradling his head, when another of Big Chuck's shouts, this time from the foot of the stairs, riveted the boy's attention. He pushed her away. Little Chuck turned toward the door, strained at the sounds of his father's voice, and arching his back, pushed Simone away. Yes; *mais oui.*

Chuck strode in on his long man's legs and swept his chortling boy away from his mother, his wife. He just grabbed him in his large hands while bending over to plant a kiss on her stunned cheek. Up and around, around and around, he spun the baby, spiraling him into the air as he had his tattered football when he was a kid. When he was a boy.

Simone sank back, not needed but trying not to worry—trying, though, to hold on. Little Chuck had sucked his bottle dry a half-hour before. Roused from sleep, he should have been distressed by all the rough handling—spitting up maybe. But he loved it. Loved it! Higher and higher Big Chuck tossed him, the little body arcing just short of the overhead fixture. Simone could feel her pulse begin to pound. She bit her lip, frozen, hoping not to drown her "men's" enthusiasm. And just before she could no longer contain herself, they stopped. Chuck caught his kid in one crooked elbow and made a move with his other paw, as if straight-arming an invisible opponent, before he handed the baby back to his silenced mother. Bouncing back out of her arms, like a fumble on the field, Little Chuck reached for his daddy with outstretched and insistent arms. "More," his body said in these months before the brain found the words. More.

But now it was Little Chuck's turn to fade into the family's background. Unheeded just for the moment, he scrambled about the mussed bed. To no avail, however, since his father was kissing his mother, his wife.

Yes, Big Chuck had smothered her, planting his big body on hers, pinioning Simone, immobilizing and possessing her while he drove his tongue deep into her open mouth. It was *his* body that spoke now: "Mine! Mine!" and all she could do otherwise was peep, peep through her husband's huge arms at her child—*her* child, demanding at that moment not hers but his father's focus.

Everybody was about to be forgotten.

"Tonight's the night," Chuck announced as he disengaged from his wife, unkissing her with the smack of a suction cup.

• • •

A woman's husband and her boy's father, a man such as Chuck, makes his own demands. That is, if the family is lucky enough to have him. More so than with daughters, most men believe that they have a special role in a young son's development. It's their job and their desire to prevent this kid from becoming a mama's boy. It's their role in life to make a man of him, so they hand him bat and ball as soon as he's ready to stand on his feet.

And from early on they do have fatherly functions to perform. According to observers such as Robert Stoller and Ernst Abelin, when the father's absent from the scene, mother and son simply sink into each other and stay stuck together. It's then that a boy's male "gender identity" is at risk, their "blissful symbiosis" eventually producing an effeminate or "transsexual boy"—a male who wants or even believes himself to be female. Other men would be utterly appalled to see their boy suffer such an ignominious fate—one that reflects directly on their virility.

Then, too, this son of his—he has a penis, doesn't he, even if he is a long way from using it? Well, this kid's also his competitor. The woman he loved, the woman he gave that baby to, often seems forgetful of him. Why, mesmerized by that kid, she hardly shoots him a glance anymore! And so he gets downright jealous.

Of a kid? A baby!

So, Son, he thinks beneath the surface of everyday common sense, get going, leave *my* woman alone, give me back her breasts and the rest of her sweet body, and—someday—find someone for yourself. I'll even teach you how—how to be a man, man enough for a woman. But leave the real McCoy, your mama, to me. Yes, "marry a girl just *like* the girl who married dear old dad." But that's it—no closer to home.

And a father's jealous on another head. He envies women and their ability to mother.

Husbands unconsciously begrudge their wives their womanly abilities to get pregnant, give birth, and nurse the babies they make. Imitating them, they often gain as much as twenty pounds during the months before a child is delivered into the world. This has been called the couvade syndrome by psychologists and pediatricians, so named after the ritual sympathy pains of the Basque peasants during their wives' labor. It's a practice found all over the world, incidentally, from the shores of the Amazon to the plains of East Africa to the islands of Malaysia.

Later on men can cuddle with the child, with his mother, and sometimes as a threesome. But they still can't nurse. Fathers just don't have that same bodily connection to the child that a mother does. Something's missing.

Finally, they're envious of the pair, of the madonna and child, of the relationship itself. They're not in the symbiosis. Maybe once they were—with their mothers—but not now. They're excluded—as they were from their parents' bedroom. They're not babies. They're not women. They're men, lonely men.

Ironically, it's in this surprisingly cruel fact of life that men at last find the solution—for themselves and for the threesome or more that is their family. As men, they invite their boys, who are already primed to do just this anyhow, to be like them—male. As men, not boys, they are able to make love to their wives, seducing them back into the erotic pleasures of adulthood. She has her baby, all right, a man such as Chuck tells himself, but she can have his penis, too.

• • •

That night they were to have made love for the first time in three months, Chuck and Simone.

The last time they'd tried it, those three months ago, it hadn't worked very well. The kid, six months old, was beginning to move about and pull at noses and earrings and look harder at the world around him. But Chuckie remained very much a "lap" baby. He was still sucking away at his lactating mom, whose episiotomy had been unusually slow to heal. Or so she said.

So Simone, that "sexy little French girl" of days gone by, hadn't been her old self. And though she wasn't ovulating again yet, the condom that Chuck had insisted on using "just in case" had further separated them from their pleasure in each other. So it hadn't worked.

On this night, Big Chuck found himself not in the bedroom but at the kitchen table in his bathrobe. He was just sitting flatly, sipping beer, puffing a cigarette, and chomping carrots (the last vain effort to melt away the tire that had been growing on his waist since the second trimester of his wife's very first pregnancy). Earlier that evening, they'd again started their *"amours"*—that's what she called them—only to have that bawling kid of his tear first him and then Simone away from their approaching embrace. She had then taken the child from its visibly irritated papa and fed him. Again.

Simone had returned twenty minutes later, and they'd started to settle into their sex once more. And again the kid had intruded with his wailing.

How did he know? How could he know that something was happening for a change from which His Highness was excluded? Ridiculous. The books said that sort of thing came later. Smart guy. Smart ass.

And this time, having fed him, Simone did not return. She fell asleep instead.

Chuck got up after the last angry gulp. He was feeling just a little high, he realized.

Intoxicated and resolved, he strode up the stairs two at a time and into Little Chuck's room. Madonna and child lay curled on the stained and friendly easy chair where so many of these feedings and naps had taken place over the three-quarters of a year that were Chuckie's life.

Big Chuck took them now. He took them one by one. Little Chuck he gently extracted from his wife's grasp and deposited in his crib—where he belonged. And Simone he simply lifted in his still powerful workman's arms, carrying her into the bedroom as he had so often before the baby was born.

And then he took her, rousing Simone from sleep, awakening her body over her protests until she groaned with desire and urgency. Chuck, it seemed to him, plunged into the welcoming womb from which their dearest love had come, where Chuck had been born. It was different, her body, now. There would always be another there.

These things Big Chuck did not tell Little Chuck later. He'd have to guess at them or rather learn them on his own when he became a man.

• • •

As the months unfold, a husband reestablishes his relationship with his wife. Simultaneously a father's tie to his child and sense of his paternity solidify. There's a threesome now. A triangle. Always a triangle. Destiny, it seems.

• • •

Around a year maybe, or perhaps fifteen months, Little Chuck seemed to have learned what a "man" was and that he was going to be one. Daddy was "Daddy" now, a word that could be spoken and a somebody whose "Daddy-ness" he could imitate. And in the year that followed this one, as more and more language poured into the boy's life and with it, as his ability to understand more about the people in this life grew, Little Chuck's excitement in his father and being like him took hold and blossomed.

Big Chuck had taken his son to a construction site to see how and with whom his dad worked and to show him off a little. For the "boys"! The souvenirs from the expedition had been a hammer and "Daddy" Dominic's hard hat, indistinguishable from that of his father. (All men were also "Daddy"—including Chuck's foreman.) For a day or so at least, these mementos became ever-present accoutrements in the toddler's life. He slept with them and trudged about the yard clad in diaper and helmet, dragging his bludgeon with him. After that, he still kept them in his room—the hard hat perched like some scarecrow on the bedpost.

Those were the days when Dad—such as he remembered him—was just marvelous, Charles, Jr., reflected later. All he wanted was, well, to *be him*.

• • •

But is life ever simple—even back then? It's supposed to proceed
on course if people are normal enough. But it never does. Nature
had conflict in store for this boy as for all others. His own conflicts,
that is, and those of the people around him.

• • •

Loving the shared joy of the beloved men who shared and still
loved her, nonetheless Simone was becoming depressed. Like others of her generation, she hadn't gone back to work after the baby
was born. He was still young, he needed her, and at last there was
no real need for money. Like a man inspired, aided by his newly
acquired educational smarts, her husband had dived into his business full speed ahead until it seemed almost to explode with pros-
perity. Men do that, she'd heard, become providers with a mission
when a baby's on the way and in the world. Necessity mothers
invention.

The trouble was, though, this mother was alone. Oh, yes, she
still had her boy and she had friends. And Big Chuck, of course.
But it seemed these men would be and were always already leaving her. And oddly, Simone Watson found herself missing her
mother and father, the family she'd lost so long ago.

"I want another baby."

She said it quite matter-of-factly.

Simone had been washing the dishes cleared by Charles while
Little Chuck, aged two and a half years, sat on the floor wiping off
his saucer again and again. There was no chauvinism, even then,
in the Watson household except for the work business. At home at
least, there was a de facto liberation of the sexes.

"Fine with me," Big Chuck replied, smooching a cheek to
prove his point and patting a fanny to remind his wife how it was
done.

"And me, too—*fine*," came the swaggering echo from the floor.

Except it wasn't. That night Little Chuck again couldn't sleep.
He kept coming into his parents' room, dragging his old hammer
with him. For the first time in months, they let him stay, thereby
deferring the making of the sibling.

He felt scared, it seemed. He'd had a dream about Tarzan and
how his mother, the ape lady, died.

Chuckie had been obsessed with Tarzan for the week since his
dad had taken him to see the movie—foolishly, his father realized
later. Chuckie had been trying to pound his chest like Johnny
Weissmuller and do the jungle yodel every few hours or so. Before

that it had been Superman from the TV show. And he'd thought that Big Chuck had powers like these since he went so high up in the sky each day. And he was beginning to get scared, too. Typical kid stuff, they'd been told—lions in closets and spiders in bathtubs. Thunder and lightning. Such things scare little boys. But losing a mother and bringing everything all together were new. And in the next two years it would get worse.

· · ·

As a boy develops his inner life, his parents respond with fantasies and irrational tempests of their own. Once his "core gender identity" is in place, the stage is also set for the drama of the Oedipus complex. It's this that is the subject of the next chapter in the story of Charles Watson, Jr.

12
...

Boys Will Be Boys

By two and one-half years, boys and girls know that they are one of two sexes. After that, sex researchers such as John Moncy have found in their studies of some of nature's more tragic experiments, one can't alter the sex assigned to a child by its caretakers. You can't convince a child with ambiguous or hermaphroditic genitals, or a boy, for instance, who happens to have his penis lopped off because of some accident or "human error" during circumcision, that he's anything other than what he already thinks he is. The die is cast and no amount of persuasion will undo what's done.

Still, these notions of what a gender is, of what it means for him to be a boy, remain unstable. During the course of life, they can be blown about by the wings of desire, of fancy, and of fear.

A whole big deal has already been made over a boy's penis as the sign of his sex and his future. Generally, he himself discovers its existence around ten months to a year, before he walks, when the nerves of the lower extremities are getting myelinated and beginning to function. He becomes aware of his erections around a year and a half, just about the time his identification with his father rises to the forefront. And when he sees a little girl's "crack," her vulva, he can get frightened and confused. Finally by three, the height of what psychoanalysts call the *phallic phase,* he's a little macho man, proud of the equipment he has and ready to extend it with all the spears, guns, and weaponry he can get his hands on.

The trouble is, he doesn't know what to do with the thing or just who is in possession of it. And the confusion gets scary. Why shouldn't women have penises, too? Little girls don't have one, a boy may learn, but then they don't have breasts either.

There are many variations, depending on cultural mores and individual family guidelines about nudity and exposure. In most households in our society, kids get to see their parents' bodies only rarely. Still at *some* time or another, they do get to see them. A little boy surprises his mother on the toilet or in the shower. Parents forget to close the bedroom door, and he wanders in on the "primal scene" in Freud's melodramatic jargon—mothers and fathers having sex. There are mating animals in rural areas or older kids' banter on urban street corners and at school. And the movies or cable TV these days leave little to young imaginations.

And when this boy finds out that his mother doesn't have a penis, he becomes deeply curious and troubled. Is it hidden in her pubic hair or tucked up her rear? Do penises come and go? Did she have one once and lose it for some reason—some choice, some bad thing, maybe? Do you exchange a penis for a baby, maybe? Or did she get it cut off as a punishment for doing or just thinking something wrong? Like him—the way he does sometimes, especially when it comes to sex. And for that matter, how are babies made? Do they come from eating something and pop out of the belly button or, more likely, from the behind? Just like BMs, which come after eating?

Gee, it would be pretty great to have a boy, or even a girl, of your own. You could feed it, take care of it, teach it things, boss it around—just the way your parents do with you. In other words, having a baby would make you big and strong like Mommy—and Daddy, too, maybe. But not if you lose the pee pee and ballies, which have begun to feel so good to the touch, and about which you're so proud! No, sir!

Maybe you better lay off. Don't touch. Otherwise somebody's gonna get pretty mad and do something!

Hey, Dad, he has a penis—still. And does he have anything to do with making babies? They don't grow in him, but does he do something somehow to help bring them into the world? And well, if there are two different sexes, male people and female people, then why? What's the difference and why? . . . Why? . . .

So run the child's thoughts in his effort to solve one of the first great existential dilemmas: the origins of life, the nature of the difference between the sexes, and the relationship between them. In his reading of the story of *Oedipus Rex* (see also Chapter 15), Freud referred to this primal mystery as the "Riddle of the Sphinx." Where other of the myth's interpreters stressed man's inevitable death, Freud focused on the child's inquiry into the nature of birth and of procreation.

"What," this mysterious creature, part woman/part beast, asked, "what walks on four legs in the morning, two in the afternoon, and three in the evening?"

"Man," the future King Oedipus answered her. Man, crawling on all fours or carried by his mother as a baby, then walking on his own two legs in the brief twilight of adulthood, and finally tottering with the aid of a cane in old age—lurching toward death.

And, Freud went on, a boy's attempts to solve the riddle of life itself coincided with a variety of equally disturbing wishes and fears, desires that defied the child's mortality. . . .

• • •

"What they didn't know," Dr. Chuck Watson told Dr. Peterson years later, "was that I was beginning to see things and understand. Maybe at two I didn't really know what they were doing in there, but pretty soon I could hear noises and stuff, and heavy breathing and groans down the hall. By three, maybe six months before Annette was born, I knew it had to do with sex. I'd listen and touch myself at night.

"Mom didn't like it when I flashed my dick in those days. She'd giggle, I could see, but then get mad. Dad—he didn't seem to mind my streaking. Dad seemed easier, even proud. And anyhow I got pretty uptight about these feelings I couldn't talk about. Damn it, she was so prudish at times—provocative, too, I guess.

"I couldn't quite get it straight, you know, thinking they were hurting each other when they were having sex, like a textbook maybe, like 'primal scene' stuff. And there was the night that Dad got drunk and slapped Mom, and she actually threw a plate at him. I was scared for real then. That was the time when I first got so quiet, I guess, and developed that damned fear about mad dogs in the woods—nutty. And I'm still scared of dogs. Only pets I never had. This analysis stuff hasn't helped yet. I guess it's just another tease, a come-on, right, Doc?"

"A tease?" Dr. Peterson asked.

"Yes, just like Mom."

• • •

Chuck Watson, Sr., impregnated his wife for the second time without a lot of effort. Her "belly swelled from their long embrace" as the Gypsies who sometimes wandered through the countryside of Simone's childhood used to say. It was with these very words that she'd answer her three-year-old son's insistent questions during the months of the expectation. Big Chuck tried to be a little more straightforward, but his son, cupping his ears or just looking about distractedly, seemed not to listen to the answers he'd asked for.

From his parents' perspective, their darling boy, so manly and definite as he had been in his assumption of his place in life, became quite impossible on the eve of the newcomer's arrival. And unpredictable, too.

There was the time when, like some crazed sex fiend or precocious Peeping Tom, he'd burst in on his mother in the shower. That got a reprimand for sure—and a good swat or two on a naked fanny unused to such indignities. Worse still was the time when he hit Big Chuck smack in the crotch. Yes, that's just what he did—walked up and slugged his father right in the balls.

He'd been cuddling and reading with his mother, whose body in its eighth month seemed about to burst, when his father came home and into the living room. He planted a kiss on Simone's cheek and invited his son, as he usually did, to put up his dukes and pretend fight. Only this time, rather than aim for fists or face, Little Chuck slammed his dad below the belt.

But the kid was also so confusing. Maybe that made him even more annoying than the mischief. One minute he'd be acting like some arrogant heroic hunk, and the next he'd literally hide behind his mother's skirts at the approach of a toy poodle. And not only was he suddenly such a scaredy-cat, he could be a downright sissy, too.

He'd be parading like a tough guy, trying to strut his stuff. But then, an hour later, Little Chuck would imitate his mother, of all things. Before Annette was born, he'd stuff pillows under his shirt—only to wonder an hour or so later whether his ballies could fall off. And after Annie arrived, "Poor Pooh Pooh Annie," whom he'd wanted to drop back in his father's cement mixer sometimes or in the toilet maybe, he'd asked for a doll of his own. *His* baby for once!

His skeptical parents relented. The doll lasted a week, during which interval he fed it baby bottles, hot dogs, and the lima beans he couldn't stomach. Later She-Pooh was simply discarded—tattered, soiled, and forgotten in a gutter by the backyard fence.

"I was driving them crazy; I was, as my mother put it, 'some holy *terreur*,'" Chuck went on, in another daily rambling. "You see, I had seen Mom's vagina, er, vulva, I mean, that time in the shower. I thought it looked like a gash, a wound, and I guess I thought making babies meant you had to lose your penis. Anyway, that would make sense, wouldn't it? I wanted to be included, and I still couldn't figure out what Dad had to do with the whole thing.

"And I was getting pretty mad on top of all this—at Mom and Dad. Mad and scared because not only was it my craziness—they were changing, too. It was about this time, when Annette was born, that their fighting started big time."

Chuck's impressions of those days as a three-year-old were fragmentary and confused, hard therefore to recollect much less put together later. "Islands of memory," the neomystical Swiss psychoanalyst Carl Jung called them in his memoirs. Chuck did remember: his sister's body, so different from his own, the slit in particular; his mother's spending less time with him; trying to take care of Annie, but being told most of the time he wasn't big enough; loving her but hating her, too. Wanting his mother . . . somehow.

• • •

Wishing to show off his body to his mother and to see hers, a four-year-old boy like Little Chuck also begins to desire her. There's a sexual edge to his curiosity, which in turn is linked to what Freud referred to as "obscure urges to penetrate" with a penis whose erections seem uncontrollable and incomprehensible. He wants her, yes, rather in the way a grown man wants a woman. He thinks and dreams about her, often touching himself, masturbating as he does so.

But what's involved in such a union? He doesn't quite know. But he does know that it has something to do with bodies both of which have become increasingly exciting to him—his, a male's, and hers, female. As Erik Erikson once responded when asked how little kids could understand such things, "Oh, they just know." And animals are simply preprogrammed instinctively to "do it," so why not human beings? Something has to be there to begin with—something instinctual, dynamic, impelling kids to do what "comes naturally."

There are complications. A boy this age is also aware of the bond between his parents. He needs the protection of his father, who not only shields him from a dangerous world but also stands between him and reabsorption by the woman in their life, mother and wife. On top of all this, despite his delusions of grandeur, a little kid recognizes that in fact he's "not man enough" for a full-grown woman.

If only he had a penis as big as his father's, well, then maybe he could manage.

These thoughts come together in the following conflict. Like the Greek gods Zeus or Kronos, the son wishes to castrate his father and use the bigger "phallus" he obtains in this way to claim his queen and throne. At the same time, however, he fears his father's retaliation, so he keeps his wishes to himself and develops his "superego" or conscience to safeguard himself from himself.

To keep himself from revealing or knowing himself. To keep quiet. Sssh! Yes, he'd better lay off. Even better, he'd better not even remember or know what he wants to do. Thus, his conscience leads him out of temptation by commanding him to repress his forbidden wishes. Now he sees them, and now he doesn't. Much of his thinking and imagining begins to take place unconsciously.

Moreover, a boy this age has been half in love with his father. He adores this man he wants to murder—a love that also takes on increasing sexual overtones. Having admired the mother he has hoped to conquer, he's also identified with her, too. With a growing awareness of the parents' erotic relationship, his wish to be a mother becomes a desire to be a woman—his father's woman. He wishes to surrender to him as he imagines his mother does in the dark of the night. And it also seems that only women have babies, which he wants. Avoiding punishment from the outside, he struggles against his wish to unman himself—to submit after all, make himself a girl, give himself to his father, and thereby have his baby.

Maybe that's the scariest part of all in the Oedipus complex, these "homoerotic" temptations. A boy (later a man) *wishes* to hurt, castrate, effeminize himself. Just like King Oedipus, who finally gouged out his eyes! Didn't Freud say everybody's bisexual?

The solution to all these competing desires begins to become apparent in a boy's growing comprehension of the facts of life. Toward the close of this so-called Oedipal phase, around six or seven, his intellectual capacities mature and he's able to put together the relationships between events in the world around him. With this intellectual capacity, as first described by the Swiss cognitive psychologist Jean Piaget, a boy is at last equipped to begin to understand that the father plants a seed of some sort in his mother's insides. This will then grow into a baby and come out of her.

Growing smarter, most boys begin to draw from images of their fathers as caring and tender. They come to see their parents as partners, mutually engaged in creating and sustaining a family. Having understood that fathers somehow help make and care for babies, boys can at last put together as one their parental aspirations and their ambitions as men. Now, around six, they want to be neither mothers nor *just men* but quite specifically fathers. That's how to have a baby, they understand at last; that's how to get close to mothers, to women. In biological and psychological fatherhood, imagined in childhood and then realized as an adult, is thus discovered the "sublimated motherhood" so essential, in Erik Erikson's terms, to the "identity of a whole man."

He doesn't quite know what all this is about since he hasn't ejaculated yet. He himself can't make babies. But he senses that it is his destiny to procreate as a man. He will become neither a mother nor simply his mother's lover—her darling, her favorite—but a *man* who makes babies. Yes, one day, learning from his father and making himself like him, the son will become a dad.

And so it was with Chuck, though like boys or men at any age, he needed a female—a Sphinx—to help him figure it all out.

• • •

He didn't know exactly when, but there was a time, maybe when he was six, when he got it: how she and everything else had been made. Then, too, Bonnie, the nine-year-old next door whose mother painted pictures with Bonnie in them, had started inviting him to play doctor. She also wanted to "do" it.

She'd lead him into the twilight of her room with the shades drawn while the adults were otherwise occupied. They'd take off their clothes and study their anatomies, their different "things."

Then one day she said she knew—yes, really—how babies were made. And having been told how, Chuckie touched the tip of his hard penis to her vulva, just touching, rubbing a little quickly and giggling before hurrying into his clothes again.

For a month or two he and Bonnie checked out her tummy to see whether she was getting any fatter. And then she lost interest in him when a bigger boy, another nine-year-old, a cousin of hers, came to live with her and her mom. And then she moved away. So he got interested in other things. Lots of things. He half-forgot it in the meantime—the idea that one day he'd be a father for real.

• • •

It is this conviction in his future as sexual, productive, and competent that anchors the sexual identity of a little boy such as Chuck. In the words of Erikson again, it is the knowledge of the human life cycle, fleshed out and realized later in the biological resources of an adult, that tempers the conflict between "initiative" and "guilt" of the so-called Oedipal boy and lends "purpose" to his life. He can't always get what he wants now, nor should he. But he can prepare to go after something rather like it in the future.

And unable to be "mama and papa," a man and a woman who have the ability to perform sex and make babies, the school-aged child determines to make things instead. The age of "industry" Erikson called the era; a period of "sexual latency," according to Freud and his followers. It's a time when incestuous and parricidal wishes are no longer expressed openly but emerge in disguised form. Beginning with the child's entrance into school at six and concluding with the biological changes of puberty at about twelve years or so, middle childhood is characterized by expanding energies and vigorous contacts in the world outside the family. "Sublimation," psychologists have labeled the process in which primal drives are redirected toward higher ends. It's a defensive maneuver but one that also helps a boy know and master his world and perfect skills with which to become a functioning member of his society. The sublimation of his most pressing wishes and a child's rapid intellectual growth fuel and enhance each other.

In his activity, a child plays out the reproductive roles of both parents together. His productivity is a symbolic expression in part of his fantasy of "parthenogenesis." A term borrowed from biology, this means that since he can't participate in really making babies, he imagines that he can do it all by himself. Long before his gonads have caught up with his ambitions or a real woman has become available to join him in his effort, his unconscious aim is to generate life all by and from himself.

And other forces, forces from the outside, also come into play molding a future man's identity during these years. Paramount among these is the mentorship of a boy's father.

It's not only the threat of the father's retaliation that moves sons to push away from their mother—and "girls" in general—at this point. It's also that getting close in any way to her threatens their newly established and still uncertain sense of masculinity and self-sufficiency. Possessing mother as a man might also mean "osmosing" and being "osmosed" by her. *Attached, dependent, reengulfed, entrapped, smothered, eaten up alive, effeminized, merged, fused*— these are but a few of the words clinical experts have used to describe a son's fear of sinking back into the psychological symbiosis and sexual ambiguity of his earliest days.

As I have shown and will continue to look at later, this specter emerges every time any woman opens her arms in welcome to a man. The fear of sinking back haunts and disrupts adult relationships. Later in life, "running scared" is probably a sign of trouble. But unless something's gone wrong with his development, *every* latency-age boy struggles not to remain a "mama's boy." And at this point, the need to get away is in fact adaptive, inducing him to grow up.

Playmates in the past, fathers now take over as supervisors, overseers, companions. Their boys turn to them both for help and as role models in making themselves into men and as a substitute for mothers whose caretaking and contact are now off-limits. Behind the shows of bravado on both sides lies a father's and a son's tender love for each other. They can effect a rapprochement now, a male bonding that makes up for the forsaken bond between mother and infant.

Ultimately, however, a boy's progress toward manhood will require forcefulness on the part of *all* the older males in his life. The first series of breaks from the world of women begins early on with the father as chief initiator. A second disengagement, this from the family as a whole, takes place later in most societies, around "age seven plus or minus one," to borrow from child psychiatrist Ted Shapiro.

In the old days, this turning point was ritualized into the concept of "the age of reason." Treated more as adults, as people who could think and make moral decisions, boys in particular were separated abruptly and forcibly from mothers and indulgent nursemaids. They were handed over to male tutors—Aristotle was one, his pupil Alexander the Great—who instructed them in the manly arts and ways of the world.

It's much the same in the Middle East or Asia even today. In India, for example, a "collective fatherhood" of fathers, uncles, cousins, servants, and hired tutors seizes hold of sons at seven years or so and begins their preparation for the rites of passage at the end of childhood. (See Chapter 13.)

And in primitive cultures, such as Papua New Guinea, the process involves a thoroughly violent disengagement. Even before puberty, women have become completely taboo. All sorts of sexual abuses are employed by the men of the tribe—for example, the demand that the eight-year-old boy drink in the semen of the older teenager—as if to inject masculinity into a boy taken from his mother.

Here, in the West, the process is more gradual and attenuated. For one thing, most elementary school teachers have traditionally been women. Yet the coaches are mostly male, father substitutes. Even dads such as Big Chuck have to give way—as a son moves further from home.

• • •

It was different in the Watson home. Annette and her mother never quite disengaged in the way she and her son had. Even after she became a girl Little Chuck could talk to, and not a baby anymore, mother and daughter remained connected in a special way through "girl stuff."

Chuck had the feeling much of the time that he was knocking at their door, trying to insinuate his way into a world—feminine, with long hair, brushes, party dresses, higher-pitched voices—a world where he didn't belong. He'd been there, in his mother's arms, and would get there again, but not now. He just looked on. Years later, in the presence of Dr. Peterson, he would speculate that in having a daughter Simone Watson had found her long-lost mother again.

Who knows what might have happened had Chuck been left to wait on his own in the corridors of his home? But he wasn't. He wasn't alone. He wasn't rapping anymore on the parents' bedroom door. Big Chuck was out there with him, too, shut out as well in a household where the lines, sometimes the battle lines, had been drawn between the sexes. This was male, this female, and as the gulfs grew, you stuck more and more to your own kind.

As Simone became more invested in her Annette, so named for her maternal grandmother, Big Chuck took on the role of mentor to his seven-year-old son. His avowed aim was to make a man's man of him. And so he let him in on the secrets of his craft, beginning with the carpentry that had provided the foundation for the building of buildings that was his stock and trade. He also taught Chuck how to throw, catch, hit, and run, how to make a football spiral, how to dribble, how to box.

Thus he imparted to his son the skills that a generally penurious and much philandering father hadn't given him. Busy with one scheme or another, the older Wysinski had little time left over for a kid. And so Chuck senior had learned the skills instead by toughing it out on the asphalt of the schoolyard, forcing others to father him and teaching himself. No son of his would ever have to fend for himself in these ways, Chuck had sworn, just as no wife would ever have to slave the way his mother had. No son of his would have to get shot at on the battlefields of France and Germany so he could get the dough he needed to educate himself.

Chuck fretted over his son's fretfulness at getting hurt and at his reticence in groups. Later, as a man who studied kids, this boy would learn that some boys are simply born shy from the start. His difference was in part "constitutional." At the same time, however, Big Chuck could marvel at the boy's deftness in acquiring and then exercising all the gifts he proffered him. As an athlete, Little Chuck was a natural. He was good at everything. But it was his speed and the grace of his stride that were most amazing even then, stunning to behold. Little Chuck ran like the wind. And soon, though not yet, his father resolved to hand the boy's tutelage over to a pro, a coach who could make a star of him. But no, not yet. He needed him still. The father needed the son. . . .

Son and father had turned to each other to glean what was no longer to be gotten from Simone. Yes, the love was there. She still loved Big Chuck's lovemaking, his bulging arms, and even his spreading middle. She attended her share of Little Chuck's meets and Little League games. She applauded with glee each time he brought home another trophy. But her heart and mind seemed to have receded somehow, and she glowed mostly in the radiance of her daughter's femininity.

In the past the boy had once been locked out because of sex. It was the fighting behind the closed door that now kept it shut to him. On one occasion, he overheard a terrible row and his mother's shouting something about a "whore Carolyn," but ten-year-old Chuck walked away before he could hear more. He went to the basement and fed his birds and fish, taking the coatimundi up-stairs with him and cuddling with it until he fell asleep.

Animals had begun to fascinate him—cats, of course, but also exotic ones such as this South American raccoonlike creature with its long snout. So the house, specifically his room and the base-ment, had become a menagerie. And it was all his—the felines, rodents, reptiles, amphibians, both domestic and imported from foreign climes. His parents acceded to the odors of musk and ammonia that inevitably wafted from these rooms through the rest of the house. Chuck could have his zoo so long as he kept his door shut.

Behind this, he was boss. Little Annie might be suffered to help out or taught a thing or two about the facts of life, but Chuckie prevailed here. Here he wasn't the one excluded now from his parents' embrace or the murmurs of women. Everybody else was—from Chuck's breeding place.

• • •

Though the days and weeks may seem long to a little kid, child-hood and its illusions are short-lived. As middle childhood comes to a close with the dawning of adolescence, the child's inflated and two-dimensional pictures of his parents begin to tumble. Nobody could be as perfect as he's made out to be.

By nine years or so, the child's intellectual abilities and wid-ening experience outside the family have enabled him to see the warts beneath the halos. He picks up his parents' individual flaws and the problems of their relationship to each other and to the family. A worker himself now, he begins to be aware of their professional and economic limitations and liabilities.

He compares his father, whose powers he may once have evoked as the ultimate protection (you know, "My father's bigger than yours"), with other adults whose defects he's generally less aware of. Alas, he finds that his old man comes up short some-times. There are teachers, coaches, other kids' dads along with sports heroes, rock stars, and other figures in the popular culture, many of whom seem to overshadow the guy at home. Somehow, like Doc Calise, they just know things a dad like Big Chuck doesn't.

• • •

Oh, yes, the facts of life. The boy especially loved breeding his creatures in one way or another—in all the ways, that is, in which the members of the animal kingdom get together to reproduce and nurture their offspring. He was a tender, supervising caretaker, too, when it came to the young, sick, or needy in his brood. Chuck proved ingenious as well in the contraptions he invented, the infrared lights warming the preemies and runts among them or reversing night and day for a South American honey bear, a kinkajou, recently torn from its mother.

He had his father to thank for his skill in constructing from wood and wire environments that simulated the real thing. But Big Chuck didn't know much about animals and only listened forbearantly as his son asserted his intention to become a vet one day. Predictably, the father reflected on the economically slight lot in life of Doc Calise in his shabby office downtown, the animal doctor who served as the boy's mentor in all matters "zoological."

"A doctor," he said to himself and sometimes aloud to his son. A people doctor. It would all come together—the mechanical skill, the caring, the school smarts, the low profile and generous style, and alas, the need for sufficient money one day. It would coalesce in the manly and prestigious practice of medicine. A physician— that's what his kid would be.

Again Big Chuck had wished he had a parent who'd pushed him along those lines. He was raking it in now, especially compared to the sums his mostly unemployed old man had plunked on the kitchen table every now and then. And he enjoyed the work. He loved seeing the structures he made grow before his eyes. Yet Chuck would always feel "lower class." *"Manqué,"* was how Simone put it.

He could admire but not understand the music made by the women in his house— Simone resurrecting a buried girlhood talent to help her daughter pound out Chopin on their Baldwin piano. Nor could he quite grasp the intricacies of the math and biology that his son, who had skipped a grade, was beginning to offer for his father's perusal and approval. Big Chuck was a Johnny-come-lately to the world of culture and mind, though he savored its expansion and refinement in his children. And his wife . . .

• • •

Ah, the facts of life.

On a certain rainy Wednesday afternoon, Little Chuck skipped the indoor football practice aimed at reviewing plays long ingrained in his easy memory and jogged home. He had needed to

hurry. The kitten he'd rescued from the bank of a stream behind
the bleachers was still ailing. Annette was in school. His mother
would probably forget to feed the kitten even if she got home from
her matinee in time. It would die without him, he reckoned.

Closing the door behind him, Chuck made his way not to the
basement but to his room where the frail thing was being kept out
of harm's way. Had he not been trudging upstairs to the second
floor, had he slipped instead through the door near the landing
and down into the basement, Chuck might never have heard or
seen anything.

But life is like that, injecting coincidence and the capriciousness of others into the timetable of development set to unfold
before us all.

So it was on the landing that Chuck caught the muffled laughter from his parents' bedroom. Just as in the dimmed days of
childhood gone by, when dragging his helmet or hammer with
him he'd felt drawn in unknowingly to intrude on their lovemaking, so now Chuck felt moved to know, to see. Had Dad come
home, he wondered, cut work the way he had school to tend to
matters of flesh and life? Were they getting closer again? Mom and
Dad. He smiled and proceeded in bounds up the steps to the
second floor.

But it was on this halting plateau that he discerned a difference in the sounds. His mother's voice, with its still-lilting accent,
was unmistakable. However, the deeper one was unfamiliar, lacking in the flat a's and guttural conviviality that identified his
father as a man from Massachusetts and a man of the masses.

And so, having intended to pass by that bedroom door with all
possible haste and decorum, despite the wish to do otherwise,
Chuck found himself drawn toward it in horror. It was, in fact,
ajar. And bending down, easing into the squat with the grace of an
athlete, Chuck looked in and on. The eavesdropper. The Peeping
Tom. Through the crack he could see all that needed, or needed
not, to be seen.

Simone was dressing, her back to her boy. Helping her in the
act was none other than Leonard Perkins, Annette's piano teacher
and a promising assistant conductor at the Boston. He was pretending to fumble with the snaps of her bra, to slip and slide with
those long and agile fingers of his. And they were laughing about
it. Fake, he realized, even then.

They were laughing, but Chuck saw, in the reflection from the
mirror into which his mother stared, a darkening slight scowl play

across his mother's mien. The corners of her lips sank in at the
close of each squeal and giggle of betrayal. The sadness and the
guilt. Sinking. And having thus seen her face, he wondered for an
instant whether she had seen his. Just for another moment, Simone seemed to squinch up her eyes in a further stab of silent
remorse. But neither she nor he discovered themselves each to the
other. Neither said a word.

Another kid, a child such as Annette maybe, might have announced herself and caught the adulterers in *flagrante delicto,* but
Chuck, shy soul that he was, quiet and kind from birth, simply
stole away. He slipped down the carpeted stairs and out the front
door and yes, never, never spoke about it again.

Chuck had forgotten the kitten. Two days later, Moses, Moses
of Medford, so named for having been discovered whimpering in
the reeds by that local creek, died.

• • •

"I guess she wanted to recover her mother," Chuck Watson, Jr.,
reflected rather despondently as he stared at the plaster peelings
and leaves of loosening white paint on Dr. Peterson's ceiling.

"But at twelve I hardly lived the examined life. All I knew was
how disappointed I was in her, how I felt first seduced and abandoned with Annie's arrival and then how betrayed we all were by
her—how the family had been dirtied or broken. You know, I
never said a word   to her, my father, to anybody. I don't know
whether he found out on his own somehow. But they did start
fighting more.

"Anyhow, that afternoon and all that was going on around it,
the sense of disintegration, changed me somehow. My concentration on animals, on growing things, softened—depression, I figure—though I kept my grades and sports way up there. If she was
gonna let me down, I sure wasn't going to do it to myself, too. And
there was Mr. Slavin, my track coach, to keep pushing me. It's
that I was more tuned in to people—to their moods, the signs of
sadness, uneasiness—like a regular shrink, even then. Dad, especially, became so sad.

"And well, I never wanted to be surprised again. I wanted to
pick up on people's motives before they put them into effect.

"But I was still too young to put it all together. For me, Mama
just began to fade away into silence."

• • •

As adolescence approaches and his parents are dimmed by their inevitable *de-idealization*, a boy's mind and body also begin to change. There's a sort of hiatus, a pause on the eve of manhood, when the eleven-year-old boy's hips widen for a bit, when fatty deposits make his breasts swell, ever so slightly, but like a girl's nonetheless. This brief pause in development, a girlish way station, is a last taste of androgyny before the male storm to come. A reminder maybe, nature's reminder about what he once was.

But even back then, he sees older boys with their muscles and brains, and so a prepubertal boy can envision himself being at least as much a man as his father. A man who can have sex with a woman. A welcome turn of events, the promise of this virile and independent future. Yet it's scary, too. The prospect of true masculinity begins to confront a boy with his essential solitude. It means he's now on his own. No matter what happens in his family. And again Chuck was no exception.

• • •

Charles Watson, Sr., could feel his heart swell as he watched his Chuck, a high school freshman yet only two weeks past his thirteenth birthday, surge across the finish line a good three strides ahead of his closest competitor. The boy was marvelous, running with the grace of a cheetah, sinewy and swift. He was everything Big Chuck had hoped he would be.

For these reasons, Big Chuck had hung in there a year ago rather than extend his three weeks' separation from Simone into something approaching permanence. And then, slowly, as Annie began to move away from her and into her own life, his wife had begun to return to him. First friends again, now once more they were lovers, husband and wife, parents and life partners.

Big Chuck made his way across the track toward the sidelines where he could see his son gasping for breath, his sides heaving, spent from his exertions. Hoping nobody could see, the father dropped his butt of a Marlboro, which brand had supplanted the nonfiltered Chesterfields that used to be his deadly favorites, onto the track. He covered it over with the chalk and black turf and proceeded on, coughing slightly.

When his father reached him, Little Chuck smiled and returned his hug.

"Great show, kid."

"Thanks, Dad."

Chuck shuffled and stared down and refocused his attention on Ray Slavin, his coach, who had interrupted the debriefing to

offer Mr. Watson a hearty but quick handshake. It was this coach
that had prompted Chuck to send his son on to Hadley as a day
student.

"Charlie."

Charlie? Nobody called Chuck junior Charlie. Or so Big
Chuck had thought, jogging his memory.

It was Harriet. Harriet Griffiths, the little kid who had lived
down the block until maybe two years ago. She was the skinny
little girl who hadn't needed braces because her teeth were perfect, but who still looked somehow as if she should have had them.
Except now her lips had become fuller, her jeans were tighter, and
the blond hair was combed across her brow in a way that reminded Chuck senior of Veronica Lake.

Chuck junior returned the greeting, shuffling some more and
blushing. The boy's father could see them inching toward each
other. Their pelvises tilted slightly as they edged into the future.

He remembered just then that he hadn't seen his son naked
for some time. And so he wondered, just for a fleeting instant,
what he was like "down there." . . .

Three A.M. and Little Chuck was awakened once again. Again
Harriet had seared his sleep. Again the mere image of their meeting had proved too much to contain. The first time he'd felt that
rush of warmth between his legs, Chuck had thought that he'd
pissed in his pants, like some three-year-old. Since then, he'd
learned what was happening to him and, on occasion, had helped
it along during daylight hours—a practice that was about to become an everyday routine.

By now, it wasn't all that humiliating or frightening, not pee
or blood, but "seminal fluid," as the books put it with their reassuringly scientific matter-of-factness. But still it was embarrassing and bothersome.

Each time he had to wash out his underwear and wipe off the
sheets in an effort to conceal himself and his sex from his mother
or the maid. Every now and then Loretta gave him some kind of
eye—as if she knew and, underneath her servile docility, was
laughing at him.

Chuck had gotten up and accomplished all this in the bathroom before getting to his own person—to the pubic hair surrounding his dick. Pretty good, he thought, as he surveyed his
stuff and then wiped the gook out of the curly growth that signaled
his manhood. All of a sudden it occurred to him. Sperm. It was
alive.

He had other lives in him now.

Even when his own father enjoys his son's growing power, others of the older generation are not so generous to a man in the making. As a boy such as Little Chuck comes of age, shedding the vestiges of his androgyny in the process, he finds that they're not so ready to give way. The passage ahead is a rough one.

13
• • •

A Boy Becomes a Man

In many cultures, a boy's coming of age is heralded by formal rites of passage. Some of these practices look quite dramatic and rather gruesome to the modern Western eye. They're hardly the tame bar mitzvahs, junior high graduations, and those other civilized ceremonies with which we mark a boy's entry into adolescence. And so anthropologists and psychologists, fascinated by them, have repeatedly tried to interpret what initiation rituals symbolize for specific societies and people in general.

Among the more primitive tribes of Africa, South America, New Guinea, and elsewhere, not only is a boy instructed in the mysteries of adult life, he's also subjected to humiliation, pain, actual mutilation, and the threat of further harm before being allowed to consider himself a man. Most often, the "collective fatherhood" up the ante of male dominance and take total charge of the initiate's life for a time, segregating him from women. At the end of these periods of preparation, the rites proper begin.

Typically, the older generation cuts the boy's penis. Usually, the pubertal boy is circumcised—as he is here at birth, when the nerve endings aren't supposed to be there, making the event an agonizing ordeal. In the Islamic world this occurs when he's five

or six. But in some instances, usually among the most aboriginal
of groups, the shaft may be "subincised." The urethra is slit at the
bottom so that the adolescent must now urinate in a squatting
position, thereafter referring to his male genital as a "penis-
womb."

Either before or after all these rearrangements of anatomy are
accomplished, the men-to-be are symbolically ushered into life
once more, this time by other males. In parts of New Guinea,
where the extended process begins even earlier (Chapter 12), the
older men pass the boys through their legs as if they were women
delivering babies into the world. Occasionally, the foreskins that
have been lopped off are sent to the women's huts where they are
devoured by the initiates' mothers and sisters. But even then the
feminine sex is excluded from the scene itself. Men alone have
life-giving powers now—when it comes to their sons' coming of
age.

The late Bruno Bettelheim, founder of Chicago's famous Or-
thogenic School for disturbed children, once suggested that we in
the West have oversimplified the meanings of these bizarre cus-
toms as we have the nature of the adolescent passage in general.
Yes, the boy is threatened by the big guys with castration, ad-
monished to stick to his turf and to women his own age, indeed
often to find wives outside the tribe altogether. That is, if he is
going to be suffered to join their company and assume the rights
of a warrior—indeed, if he's going to survive as a member of his
society. The violence and assertions of power are unmistakable.

But so, too, is the theme of sexual ambiguity, according to
Bettelheim. The need, that is, to come to terms with being but one
sex, male, and to give up forever the androgyny of childhood. The
cutting off of foreskins in circumcision is interpreted by him not
only as a threat of emasculation, but also as a means of relin-
quishing those folds of flesh that resemble a woman's labia. (See
Chapter 2 for the biological truth of this notion.)

In those cases where the boy's penis is subincised, Bettelheim
argues, the male role in procreation is not yet understood. Symbolically, these groups try to help an initiate make up for what
he's missing—a woman's womb and thus a place in the reproductive cycle.

It's hard to become a man, in fact, and many societies repeatedly brutalize their boys to rid them of their mother's imprint.
Once again the violence of males among themselves is used as a
way of exorcising the woman still inside them.

To some degree, girls are also abused in the service of solid-
ifying their sex-specific role in life. The notorious clitorectomy,
practiced by Muslims as well as more primitive tribespeople, is
the most dramatic instance of this—obliterating forever the part of
her that resembles a penis. But like the shaving of an Orthodox
Jewish woman's or a Catholic nun's head, this also represents an
effort to keep her sexual responsiveness and attractiveness under
wraps. Desexualizing her, the effect is to make a woman beholden
to her future lord and master whoever he may be. Nor is it women
alone who take charge of a girl's initiation. In some cases, an old
man inserts his finger into her vagina to rupture a girl's hymen,
once again asserting the older male generation's claims on a
daughter's virginity and sexuality.

The supreme irony is that those secondary sex characteristics
that provide the underpinnings of male adolescence and signal the
end of physical bisexuality—the muscles, genital development,
ejaculation, and procreative capacity—will eventually allow a kid
to get close enough to a woman to unite and feel at one with her.
It is this quest, albeit with many emotional diversions along the
way, that comes to dominate his teenage years.

. . .

As Simone Watson put it to Chuck junior: *"Cherchez la femme!"*

Like other teenagers in our culture, he hadn't been subjected
to such primitive ordeals. But he responded to the threats within
his mind, a mind that took a little time to catch up with a changing body. It would be a while before Chuck began to pursue girls
in earnest.

Adolescent boys have to find their heritage first, their father's
authority, and make this their own. In the modern world, they do
this mostly in their heads. . . .

"You know, I always knew my father loved me, really loved
me. It scared me—how much we cared for each other. Well, hell,
sometimes I thought I was a fag."

Dr. Charles Watson felt a little foolish acknowledging this fear
to Dr. Peterson. First as a camp-counselor-confidant and now as
a clinical psychiatrist, he had taken pains to reassure troubled
teenagers that these concerns were normal at their age and that
every kid had chinks in his sexual armor. That he himself should
have been troubled in this manner and that this "homosexual
anxiety" should have reasserted itself in his own analysis gave the
lie to his effort to achieve a Buddha-like tolerance for all matters

of the soul. Besides, having studied development, he knew how such conflicts come to be. And he thought he should—even then, as a kid?—have known better.

It's hard to give up your mother when you grow up, he told himself, and so even a normal heterosexual adolescent can't help partly identifying with her and her feminine ways. Any wish like this or any affectionate feeling for another guy is quickly labeled "queer" and banished from awareness. And this is so despite the fact that teenage boys often engage at the same time in thinly disguised *homoerotic* play such as "group jerks," "wedgies," and "sloppy seconds." (In many of these activities incidentally, women are also degraded and thereby implicitly contained and controlled.)

Ah, well, Chuck mused, life's full of contradictions and conflicts. And that's what makes it interesting, especially to a psychoanalyst. Besides, he went on, reflecting on his initial fear of lying down and spewing his guts out to a woman analyst, the idea of getting it on with a woman is terrifying at first, despite the teenager's bravado. That's why boys spend so much time masturbating or roaming with their buddies. They need to reassure themselves that they're whole men, that their balls won't burst when they come or something like that, or maybe disappear inside a woman during intercourse. That's why teenagers tell those jokes about *vagina dentata*, "cunts" with jaws, or getting stuck doggy style—you know, "Catch her, kid, quick, before she grows teeth!" They're scared to death!

Isn't that what the Elizabethan poets and the French called an orgasm—"the little death"? No wonder, with the loss of consciousness and the wilting of a detumescent dick. No wonder you need to keep beating the meat to make sure it's all there and still working afterward.

And women aren't just scary in their own right at this point. They're also off-limits—at least the ones at home, mothers and sisters. Incest is physically possible now even if it's still forbidden. So rather than threaten your old man's domain, you're tempted to submit to him, as in your Oedipus complex, and kiss his ass.

All this translates in your mind as being or feeling gay.

"I guess you could say you're big enough and smart enough to pose a real threat now? So, even just inside your own head, you are inclined to give in. Right?"

"Yes," Dr. Peterson interrupted her trainee's practiced and by now rather "intellectualized" disquisition on himself and the "manifold complexities of adolescence." Musing about having been an adolescent, Dr. Watson was also acting and thinking like one.

Teenage guys cogitate a lot, she thought to herself. They talk about rather than make love. They challenge parents by taking on their belief systems. Underneath the rebellion, they want to hear what the adults have to say after all so that they can rework it for themselves in their own ways.

"But apart from all this 'deep' stuff," his analyst now added, "you also loved him and wanted to protect your picture of him as your protector, 'your rescuer.' You saw how vulnerable he was—how he was hurting himself, his body, how he was probably dying."

There she went again, speculating about his parents' motives and problems.

"And you didn't want to give up him or your image of him and his undying tenderness, despite the fact you were fast becoming more than a match for him."

• • •

By his sixteenth year, Little Chuck was bigger than Big Chuck—well, taller, if not wider. His father had always been barrel chested, and the years of physical inactivity and the inevitable excesses of life had added pound after pound to his girth. Charles senior was by now a very large man, upward of 210, a man who wheezed when he walked too fast. His son, Chuck, in contrast, was at six feet two inches a lithe 165 pounds, an athlete still who had won the high school championships in the 440 as well as the mile. He was near the top of his class, too, and Harvard-bound, it seemed, and from there on to medical school.

It was a joke when they tried to play basketball or when they hit the neighborhood diamond with their bats and mitts. Big Chuck, at forty-seven, quite unlike his son years later as he neared this age, huffed and puffed his way about the court, unable to keep up any pace for more than a couple of minutes. He still had it in him to whack the hardball into the outfield and beyond, but in anything resembling a game, getting to base in time was another matter.

Prompted by his boy, intrigued by the kid's notion that they do a bike trip together, Chuck had tried to lose weight. Losing ten pounds was, however, quickly followed by putting on fifteen more. Both Simone and his kids had also begged him to quit smoking, what with his shortness of breath and hacking cough in the mornings. But their efforts were futile. And all he'd succeeded in doing for all his abortive attempts was to change brands some years back.

"It'll kill ya, Dad," Chuck piped in again. "I know it will. The Surgeon General's preparing a report linking cigarettes to cancer and emphysema. It'll kill just as sure as this lousy war is gonna get us."

War. For a couple of years at least, before Big Chuck came around to his son's point of view about Vietnam, the war divided them—the brash kid and the WW II vet. Only in private, Chuck hoped it would be over before his son came to his turn, unlike some of his cronies who felt it was their kids' duty to serve.

"Yeah," Big Chuck murmured into his jowls so nobody could overhear his lack of patriotism, "serve and get killed, too. I guess those guys never saw what I did in France—just young enough to serve God and country and get your balls blown away."

In the old days, men who were men went to war. Just that.

Chuck had—that's for sure—and come back with the stripes and medals that proved his manhood. But it was the absurdity of the first taste of combat he always remembered most. A week after the invasion he found himself on point on patrol. He entered a clearing in the woods at exactly the same time a German counterpart of his did. Turning in terror and seeing each other, they had lowered their rifles, backing off jerkily and shooting their guns in each other's direction. Chuck had found himself floating, numb, and so barely heard the short screams of a sudden and anonymous enemy as they found their cover simultaneously. Unseen by Chuck, his unknown rival had been hit—a kid like him, he later guessed. It was a minute or two before Chuck noticed the pile of crap in the backseat of his combat fatigues. In those prediaper days, Chuck Wysinski hated shit, and finicky as he was, heedless of who else might be on the prowl in the woods, he took as much of his time as he could to scrape the stuff off his ass before the rest of the patrol caught up with him.

Later that day, he thought he'd missed some of it in his shaky haze. But it was the stench of the corpses they had found by the road, not the odor of fear but the smell of death. Negroes, he thought at first, some special German colored outfit somehow, from Ethiopia maybe via Italy. But no, it was even these Aryans who had been darkened by death. Hitler's youth rotting into the pine needles of a France where they, and maybe he, didn't belong.

That was war. That was men at war—boys who didn't know anything being sent by old men to get killed.

Years later, when Little Chuck's Achilles tendon snapped, ending his running career, Big Chuck found himself reacting as he never thought he would. He sighed in relief. His son had had his share of glory, after all. And now Big Chuck was surer of his safety, the low lottery number and questionable premed deferment notwithstanding. Little Chuck was 4F at last. Big Chuck was reminded of his parents' stories about their unwanted wars, how his great uncle Lech had shot his index finger off so he wouldn't have to fight. Like his dear son.

During his high school years and the college ones that followed, it was Big Chuck who, in turn, occupied his son's thoughts. He loved this big, tough guy. Why, he'd even joined his protesting son for the anti-Cambodia march, replete in full tech sergeant's regalia and Distinguished Service Cross and an oak-leaf cluster earned when he, Big Chuck, was himself a mere nineteen (and only two weeks after that first meeting in the woods). He'd never talked about them either, sad about it all, mad as he was that they hadn't also given The Medal or even a Silver Star to Bernie Stein. Bernie had been with him all the way and more so, but he was a Jew.

Chuck junior ached for his father because, yes, as Dr. Peterson put it, he was now killing himself.

Why Chuck junior didn't know. Maybe, he thought later, he'd gone into psychiatry to figure out the answer. But he also knew he never would.

Chuck remained caught up with his dad and his dad's fate. That is, until he fell in love.

• • •

Fathers respond dramatically to their sons' and daughters' adolescence. Oedipus was sixteen when his father, Laius, challenged his right of way on the road to Delphi and was killed for it (see Chapter 15). King Lear struggled with the jealousy of a spurned lover when his teenaged daughter Cordelia refused to tender him all her love—reserving the better part of it for her husband.

It's in his children's adolescence and his own midlife that a man reacts most strongly to the challenge to his aggressive and sexual potency. If he's failed to establish his sense of "paternality" and hasn't put together the forces of femininity and violence within him, then he may enter the fray, often with disastrous consequences: tyranny, incest, heart attacks, unwise affairs, and more. If he's a decent and fatherly man, a man like Chuck senior, he savors his sons' and daughters' powers and exploits and vicariously revitalizes himself by taking in their youth. In all events, like the primitive tribesman, a man has input into his children's coming of age.

• • •

Big Chuck adored both his kids. Each day, it seemed, as age sapped or, more accurately, inflated him, their bodies seemed to erupt exponentially. Friday nights and Saturdays he'd hang out in his living room, relaxing from his work, which was booming then and running itself.

His belly spreading over his belt, he'd sip a Bud and he'd kid-watch—hazily surveying his son and daughter as well. He'd take in the girls and boys they brought home with them, first in groups and then as couples. God, they were gorgeous!

The budding of Annie's breasts was a beauteous, if also discomfiting, thing to behold. Tempting in an uneasy sort of way, of course, she was also a reminder that there was no longer any sort of baby at home and that her parents were indeed getting older. Then, too, Annie looked like him—more like her father than her mother. Or so everybody said from the beginning, but especially now. She had her mother's slim waist and long fingers and had taken as her own the way Simone—Simone *fille*, the girl of memory—had had of cocking her head and quizzically pursing her lips when speaking or listening, French style. But she had her father's black hair and almond eyes, the full lips and the round, forward-jutting, and friendly nose of a Wysinski.

So, Big Chuck concluded, she looked as he must have looked at her age, but with breasts and fuller hips, a bottom bigger than her waist. A girl's, no, a woman's body. And when she sat in his lap or snuggled, not only was there the awkwardness that came from the fear of being turned on to the child he had created and protected. Chuck also drew back for fear that he might get himself simply too close to her. Fleetingly, he was afraid that this big, fat, beer-swigging, chain-smoking construction boss (or so he liked to style himself) would find himself giggling, his wrists limp. Animated, he'd regress and transmogrify into a sweet sixteen in imitation of the fawn fatale that was his daughter. Little Annie. The girl he had, the one he'd never been. (See Chapter 14 for more discussion of a father's incestuous impulses toward his daughter.)

With his son, Chuck, and his girls, it was rather different. It was here that the competition came out, here alone that his father seemed to succumb to a certain selfishness, the son later concluded, here that easygoing Big Chuck lost control.

From the time he was a high school junior through the college years when he brought them home with him from Brown, Chuck, that shy superstar, managed to mastermind a serial harem, or so it seemed to his envious father. Girls, girls, girls. One by one, they drifted into the sunken living room, presenting themselves demurely or brashly and in all beautiful shapes and sizes—cream skin and auburn hair, gray-eyed WASPy blondes, ethnic black beauties; smart ones and sweet ones. And all were, once again, young—virginal in appearance if not necessarily in practice, on the verge or just over the brink.

It was now that Big Chuck began to worry about Little Chuck's morals. Was he taking advantage of them? Did his son know what love was—true love? And honor? Had he raised a reliable kid, a future family man, or some crass stud, "too well and unwisely" loved, after all?

Big Chuck lectured a little, and they fought a lot for a while. The son continued to date, to go out with a vengeance. He'd bring his quarry home, perhaps for approval, maybe to stir a little admiration and sour grapes, or to rekindle the dialogue, the flame, and all in the name of a closeness and ties that never seemed to stretch too far, loosen, or break.

The father ate, drank, and smoked a little more. He wondered whether he was out of it.

On one late May day, Little Chuck and Faith, his latest, the older girlfriend from Jackson College, closed the door behind them, en route to the movies. The last images Big Chuck caught were of Faith's tawny hair draping over a bare left shoulder and touching an open armpit—and the faded jeans, hugging and just revealing the crescent bottom of her left buttock. She was a philosophy major.

He emptied and rinsed out his glass and trudged upstairs. Little Chuck was sleeping in his own room and Faith in Annie's, who was away for the weekend. What they did was their business. But this was *his* home.

In the master bedroom, Simone was already half-asleep. Propped up, reading, eyelids barely open, she was still beautiful. But she wasn't nineteen.

Chuck smiled and walked into the bathroom. He brushed his

teeth, farted (privately, as he'd learned to do years ago at his wife's insistence), and slipped into his pajamas. But not before he caught sight of his nude form reflected in the mirrored wall that had proved so shameless in its reflections. Why, Chuck lamented to himself as he studied the reflection and reflected on who he truly was, his belly was now so big you could barely see his balls!

"To bed, to bed, to sleep off all the nonsense I have said."

He eased under the covers, pecked his wife, and proceeded with his new nightly bedtime ritual.

"Dominic told a great one yesterday."

Simone nodded and Chuck went on with this evening's joke.

Chuck punctuated this day's dirty joke with a laugh, a laugh that grew into a rasping cough. He quelled the cough with water and accepted his wife's chuckle and kiss on the neck. Then each rolled over to sleep.

And in the dark Big Chuck lit another cigarette, his last for that day. He sucked its smoke in, drawing it deep inside. He could feel the fiery comfort reach beneath his sternum, where it burned, oh so deliciously, into his right lung. Somewhere out there in the dark, Faith and Chuck were watching the movies, side by side.

And talking, he thought. What about? And feeling inside. But what?. . .

• • •

Maybe it was Little Chuck's aim to tease his father with his sudden prowess when it came to girls—women, that is. Consciously, however, the young man was proud of both his parents and his sweethearts. And beyond this, while they fairly obsessed him, "burning holes in his sleep," as Vladimir Nabokov had put it, Chuck couldn't stay with them for very long.

Harriet wasn't the first girl with whom he "fooled around." He'd never got there—made love. He only got to second base with her and touched third before getting tagged out in a rundown by Jack Jones. It was Jack, star pitcher and quarterback, who slid over Harriet's home plate.

Priscilla was his first. On a damp morning, on a Cape Cod dune, after a night of persuasion, Chuck entered Priscilla, and all other women, for the very first time. Again, reflecting on this milestone later on, he later searched the annals of Nabokov for the metaphor. Like the author, Little Chuck "parted the fabric of fancy, [he] tasted reality."

Except it wasn't quite like that. "Screwing Priscilla" was fun all right, and the sensation of their converging orgasms and the sand grinding between their pubes would stay with him forever. But the feeling died quickly, shrinking just as his penis resolved itself back into normal quiescence.

It took time to understand, but romantic that he was, Chuck realized later, he didn't know Priscilla and therefore couldn't love her. He *wanted* to love her, and certainly he was more relaxed and tender than were his agemates with the girls they dated and "balled," or so they claimed. But at sixteen Chuck just hadn't felt more. He couldn't. More accurately, each time a girl—Priscilla, Melissa, Suzanne, Betty, or Connie—yielded to his touch, surrendering to desire, well, some sharper resentment, a sense somehow of anger, vague at first, of disgust, even hatred, entered in to crowd out the pleasure of it all.

When they wilted away from each other, Chuck found himself *pushing* away as well. He'd try to hang on to the longing that had seized him at first, but he couldn't. So he'd either end these relationships or drift awhile, waiting for the girls to reject him instead and thereby ease his guilt over hurting them.

Beyond this, somehow he despised and distrusted women for their sensuality. There was the need, as ever, to dislodge from "her." Mother. Simone. And there had been her sexuality, thrust before him so rudely and so soon and for real, and the betrayal in it of all he had held dear. They had never been close after that. A sexy girl reminded him of what he'd seen *her* do.

Besides, there were Laiuses other than his father to deal with. Imaginary tyrants, and real ones, too.

As they filed through his life, lasting a month or two, Chuck's succession of girlfriends made him look like a stud to the outside world. He became the object of all eyes, and of their envy. Here Chuck was, this quiet guy with an obvious feel for women, mostly A's to his credit, a bunch of letters, and a chance even to break Gill's record.

Too much. He was the envy of his classmates and, alas, not a few of his teachers.

Neil Gill should have been Chuck's ally. At twenty-four, having returned two years earlier from Villanova to his prep school alma mater, Gill was an "assistant something" in just about every department—assistant track coach, assistant director of college admissions, sometimes science teacher. Like Chuck, he had been swift as a gazelle—swift of foot that is, but unlike him, a little slow upstairs. Cs had doomed him to a big jock school, rather than an

Ivy League college, much to the consternation of his Harvard-historian father. And even there he'd slipped into mediocrity, especially after being hobbled by a torn hamstring and badly pulled quad. Disgruntled, Neil had returned to Hadley, where he barricaded the boarders and kept an eagle eye out for contraband and other indiscretions on the part of the day students. The kids hated him of course, this prig who lived by himself and was never to be seen with a female of any sort. Was he a queer (gay, we'd say now), they wondered, or just asexual, or more simply still, a loser? It didn't matter in the end—Neil's personal life—as far as they were concerned. He was weird, and mean.

He showed a quick and special dislike for Chuck. When Slavin was out for a month with personal business (hospitalized for depression, actually, Chuck realized later), Gill even sidelined him for missing two practices. (It was the April week of Chuck's junior year when the first spots were found on the X rays of his father's lung.) In a physics course that Neil taught (badly), he seized on the fact that one 8 looked like a 3 to drop, yes, eight points from Chuck's grade, converting an A to a B+.

But it was in his position in the Admissions Office, with Chuck assigned to him, that he did the most damage. No, he insisted, Chuck was not Harvard material. Neil would have to throw his weight behind Skip Knight, on whose uncle's Beacon Hill home Big Chuck was then working. Skippy, he went on, had a special literary gift, the sort of thing the Cambridge crowd admired more than athletic skill. And there was also Babette Li, the Eurasian girl with those 1580 SATs. They could shoot for two, maybe, this year. Not more. Brown was a better bet. Duke maybe. Wesleyan, okay. Columbia. But not Harvard.

Under other circumstances even Chuck Watson, mild-mannered kid that he was, would still have been furious at having his dream dismissed in such a cavalier fashion. But it so happened, he found himself distracted by matters other than himself or his ambitions.

Big Chuck had a large part of one lung removed in October of Chuck's senior year. Cancer. Radiation followed. A sort of crash diet. After this his father recovered for a while—a remission, they called it. A parole. And after this "after this," he started smoking again. Nobody could stop him, least of all his son.

Besides, Ray Slavin, Little Chuck's substitute father figure, was never himself when he came back. What exactly had thrown him Chuck wasn't sure. His snooty son, Ray junior, had come out

of the closet, it seemed, a year earlier. It had been hard enough
having a nonjock for a kid, a literary type, but discovering that the
boy was, as they said then, "AC/DC" was the last straw. And
Slavin's wife had closeted herself in a happy farm to dry out. Well,
hell, that was enough, and besides he'd always been moody.

At any rate, there was now Gina to console Little Chuck—or
so it seemed for a while. The Italian girl, Dominic's niece in fact,
fresh from Napoli, had caught his fancy. Foreign, yes, like Simone,
he understood later. A reincarnation. But with her dark eyes and
blacker hair and that throaty laugh of hers, she had what no other
girl had. Not even Mom. Catholic still, she'd guarded her virginity. Also, like Annette and Simone, and rather incongruously for
a self-styled "peasant girl," she played the piano and treated her
date to an evening of petting to the strains of Toscanini recordings
of Verdi.

Chuck flirted with love. But he always felt he never really had
Gina. Then late in October, she called it off. A week later he saw
her at a fast-food drive-in with some Italian guy whom she introduced him to as "Johnny." She smiled, batted an eye, and when
she could pretend that she thought Chuckie wasn't looking,
squeezed the other guy's butt cheek. So Chuck himself sealed his
fate on those midterms: one A, one A−, two Bs, and yes, a C+.
No, he wasn't Harvard-bound, after all.

His father had been too debilitated to fight Neil Gill or to
admonish his son. Slavin hadn't pushed for him the way high
school coaches can. But in the end, not working, Chuck had done
it to himself.

"Guilt. . . .

"Gill screwed me. Slavin deserted me. Gina rejected me. But
I couldn't let go of Dad. I just didn't feel right concentrating on
myself and my successes when I knew he was dying."

Yes, Dr. Peterson mused, along with the revival of the Oedipus complex on the eve of manhood comes the guilt. It is this that
does many a young man in, at the very least shortchanging his
prospects. Still, the future's a long time coming and vanishing. It's
now time to find out who he really is and who the people are
who've made a man of him. Sometimes you have to get away for
a while though—first. So you can step back and look. . . .

So Harvard-bound Chuck went to Brown. And maybe, just
maybe, it turned out better for him. The school was fine. And the
hour's distance from Boston helped him forget his worry for his
father, who was doing all right for the time being anyway.

Even the snapping of his Achilles tendon his sophomore year had its up side. He'd run the race and won it, and well, on that final stretch in the locker room before showering, it just broke. Pop! No worries now about the draft, and the hours of immobility that the cast provided him converted a potential sophomore slump into an aced spring semester. And if he couldn't run for a while, he could walk, bike, and swim and begin to trot a little.

From then on, Chuck was on a roll, knocking off one premed course after another, with some literary and poli sci diversions thrown in to feed his soul. He was a sure bet for Harvard now, its medical school.

But Chuck didn't want to go there anymore. Instead, he wanted to get a little farther away. California, maybe, Chicago. New York—that was it. There were three med schools there at the same level, anyway. His friend Hy Bassin, who had brought Brooklyn to Brown and Chuck to New York, convinced him of the merits of Manhattan. Weekends they'd drive down I-95 to the city, ostensibly girl hunting. Years later, after grinding away together at Cornell Medical School and then internships and residencies in cities apart, the two buddies would diverge. But for a while, they were inseparable, Hy introducing Chuck to a world that he himself would leave behind.

Hy didn't follow in his uncle Milton Hurst's, the famous urologist's, footsteps exactly. He didn't want to spend his life dicing up glands. So he opted for sex and couples therapy in D.C. In the meantime in the Big Apple, Chuck took the plunge into depth psychology. Not just dicks and pussies and what they did. But what it all meant.

Chuck had thought his father wouldn't understand, self-styled hard hat that he professed to be. But he did. The books littered about (and there were even more of them now that he was working less and "semiretired") should have forewarned his son that Big Chuck would look favorably on the new adventure.

"Great idea. Fascinating. Like being a well-paid philosopher or practicing Shakespeare," Big Chuck—no longer so big—had responded to Chuck's announcement his third year in medical school.

"Why, I might've done it, if my time and place had been different," Big Chuck added, laughing, laughing once more into a bottomless wheeze.

• • •

There are critical moments in life, Chuck Watson, Jr., MD, board-certified psychiatrist, realized later in life. Or if they're not "critical" in the sense of dramatically changing a person in an instant, then they might be described as a sort of epiphany in which are distilled and articulated truths that were always there but had remained somehow unsaid and therefore unknown. Men especially like to hold on to these as aphorisms to make vivid life's ongoing ironies, to tell themselves about dialogues otherwise beyond words.

His father's words of approval for his opting for the "artsy-fartsy mumbo jumbo of headshrinking" was one of these moments of truth. It released his son, jarring him loose from conventions and oversimplifications, forcing the boy to see his father for who he was and to make himself his own man.

Chuck saw what he had always known. He was Chuck the elder's son. He had gotten his virtues and predilections from him. Social and economic circumstances, and his place within the generations, had demanded that this man be other than who he was, had required that he *do* rather than think. Well, Chuck thought, this tough guy might even have been "deeper" than his son. More literary. Soulful. Softer. Female even. Certainly, at their respective ages, he'd lived more. In making his choices, Chuck had defied the externals of his GI father's lifestyle only to unearth a hidden, a private tradition and then pursue it. In exchange the son had discovered a surprising continuity.

Only with all this in place, whatever you could call it, with your father inside somehow but made your own—only then would you feel free to wander through your own world, free also to love another.

• • •

The great psychologists of adolescence, Erik Erikson and Peter Blos (who were traveling companions and soulmates in their own youth), have reviewed moments like these in the lives of a son like Chuck junior. They have articulated for us some transitions that occur during the passage from dependence into maturity. Maturity, a man's emotional manhood, meant for them, in both reality and theory, a capacity to "love and work," as Freud had once put it.

First of all, work. Erikson, who had been some time in finding his own métier, laid the greatest stress on the choice of a profession or occupation in concretizing a man's identity. Especially among more gifted individuals in our modern Western world, he elaborated, where work roles aren't fixed ahead of time and where an array of opportunities presents itself, a "psychosocial moratorium" may be required. Between childhood and adult responsibility, many pause.

In our society, this interim has been sanctioned and ritualized as the period of college and graduate study and training. These make for an apprenticeship before a young man enters the world and his journey through time as a real-life worker.

It is a time when an individual such as Chuck sorts out his old identifications, looks for new role models, and finally emerges with a sense of "wholeness, sameness, and continuity" and the conviction that his image of himself matches the picture others have of him. A good deal else takes place during this moratorium, changes that not only have to do with the ways in which one will make one's way in the world but with one's sexuality and identity and with matters of the heart.

Love. Others, such as Blos, place a greater emphasis on the shifts that take place in the primary objects of a late adolescent's affections. They concentrate on the people in a young man's life and the values that go along with these passions and personas. Bound to the person and picture of his father, a youth finds himself clinging at the same time to the feminine in himself, whatever his outward shows of machismo and bravado, which are more quietly aimed at garnering a father's approval. Independence requires that this relationship be given up and "transmuted" into what psychoanalysts call an "ego ideal." By this is meant a set of internal standards, values, personal principles, which have become more or less immune to external influence.

Instead of seeking approval from others, the young man now looks to himself.

When this internalizing of a personal ethic is accomplished, according to Blos, a young man can be guided by his own lights. Experiencing himself as a more complete man, his father firmly in place, the son is further freed at last to love a woman. That is, to find a woman outside himself and to complete his life and himself with her, ironically, by being a heterosexual man.

Lots of men fail in this achievement. (See Sections II and V.) And most of the time, falling and then staying in love are stormy processes. (See Chapters 1 and 2.) As the great love stories tell us, they are fraught with feelings of both joy and despair, ecstasy and remorse, the sublime and the depraved. And the emotions passionate love calls up derive from the overwhelming conflicts in loyalty that befall men as they struggle to give up their fathers and their more abstract allegiances in favor of their devotion to a woman.

A man's romantic love of her lies beyond and above the comforts to be found in conventional morality. It moves him to seek out and expand himself through something and somebody altogether new.

Or does it? Having fought so hard to escape a woman, the mother he once clung to, a man finds himself drawn to her persona once more. He's got to be pretty sure of himself, if he can weather his passions. Indeed, Erikson has gone so far as to assert that "ego identity" must be secured before a man becomes capable of sustaining intimacy rather than running away and hiding—distancing and isolating himself. Otherwise, closeness with a woman will threaten to plunge a man into roles he can't handle. He may feel like a little Oedipus—a pretender, inadequate, or at risk. Or he may fear regressing even further, becoming like a dependent child perhaps, a kid whose selfhood and sexuality aren't clearly defined.

But does the passage into manhood always work that way? In adulthood, when biological growth gives way to cultural influences and existential choices, does life always unfold in predictable phases?

• • •

It was a question that Chuck, by his late twenties, had begun to ask himself quite directly—a question for which, both then and later, he couldn't find an answer.

First of all, Chuck had had it in mind, "you" weren't supposed to fall in love and then marry in medical school. But *he* did. And as a freshman doc-to-be at that, and over a common corpse, of all things. Why, he would've lain down on that slab along with "Brendan," the old Irish tramp they were slicing up, just to be touched by her, Sylvia Cushman. And for a while at least, it seemed that was what he'd have to do. Sylvia was still besieged by her college boyfriend, Ira Scher, who was Jewish like her, and who was at this point a first-year law student uptown. She and Chuck would sip coffee, study, and talk together. And he'd content himself with mere images of nestling into her neck or the quick outline of a breast through her shirt. But that was all. And it went on through the whole first year of school.

But then one night, "it" fell into place, as Chuck and Syl just fell into it—fell in love. They had been cramming together in her apartment and decided to break for twenty minutes to catch their breath. Sylvia slipped into her kitchen and was fiddling with her coffeemaker when Chuck slipped in behind her and, on impulse alone, slipped his hand around her waist, finally planting its palm on her belly between her T-shirt and jeans.

Just impulse, a fleeting indiscretion. But Sylvia spun around to meet his gaze. Instead of pushing him away, she kissed him hard and deep, as if sucking him into her. Impulse again. Never had Chuck felt suffused with a touch—her hands were all about him now—and a scent that were so electrifying and soothing at once. For a year they'd danced about each other, chatting, working side by side, afraid to get close—and now the pull was inescapable. No equivocation now. Something greater than a wish. They made love all night—these conscientious physicians-in-the-making—while their textbooks lay open and unread in the next room. That exam and others to come would not see the efforts of earlier days.

It would not prove to be their "best" semester, though their performances and evaluations hardly seemed to matter. More wrenching by far was Sylvia's fitful leave-taking of Ira—especially that horrible night she made love to him for the last time.

Chuck had sat in the coffee shop across the street from the Scher guy's apartment, torturing himself. When it was all over, at five the next morning, and Sylvia exited the building at last, he walked up to her and caught her before she'd even gotten out from under the awning. Then and there Chuck slapped her—twice—across the face. He'd never before hit a woman and would never hit one again.

Sylvia forgave him. Making up, she promised never again to hurt him: "Never, never!" An impossible oath, of course.

A year later, they married—over the objections of her chauvinistic parents, if not his. In fact, Simone and Sylvia got along famously. Too well, Chuck thought at times, especially as the wedding had approached. Their series of strictly *entre nous* and tête-à-têtes recalled the exclusivity of his mother's immersion in Annette and evoked in him another order of jealousy. Sylvia, who was also headed for psychiatry and had already had her course of therapy, explained that his mother had replaced her own. Mrs. Cushman had emotionally and otherwise long neglected her, favoring the more beautiful Nissa, her firstborn. She now threatened to disinherit a daughter who had defied the Jewish tradition and her wishes, finding a moral pretext for her long-lived diffidence.

"Cushman, née Capulet," Big Chuck had mused. "Juliet and her mother. Watch it, 'Romeo.' Cover your ass!" But marry they did, with all major relatives physically present at least. It would be some years before they'd start having kids.

"Love and marriage" going together like "horse and carriage" and "living happily ever after" were myths Chuck had long ago dismissed given the tremors and near quakes in his parents' relationship, one of the minority these days to survive. Sylvia's promises were inevitably overly optimistic and false, and hurt and fight each other they did at times, sometimes through no fault of their own, but just because life's like that.

For one thing, Syl proved to be smarter, a better student than her husband—and that took some adjusting to. For another, there were the simple strains of living together without squeezing each other out, of standing up to the stresses of hard training on little income and getting something from another person without being suffocated oneself. Being there and being whole—was this what was meant by intimacy? In any event, intimates he and his young wife were and remained—lovers, friends, partners.

• • •

As Chuck continued to muse later on, this time in the presence of Dr. Peterson, the milestones of manhood do not present themselves as a smooth progression of stages. With Sylvia, unlike the women before, whose charms he'd resisted in the end, he had indeed *fallen* in love.

There were also the passionate rivalries that, he'd come to realize, were visitations from the past, intimations that like all men, Chuck had had an Oedipus complex once upon a time. And still did in fact. And on top of this understanding of the surges of hostility and pugnacity he could feel, Chuck couldn't help wondering whether all this aggression didn't have something to do with staying male. Despite his love for Syl and oneness with her, he remained a man after all—a fighting man, like Dad.

As their years progressed and inevitably Chuck felt inclined to be selfish or was even tempted to stray, and as their first passions cooled to some degree, his wife also figured as someone to whom he felt dutiful and loyal. Someone whose advice he sought, too. "My God," he realized, "at times my wife became my father."

"Yes," Peterson interjected. " 'Revenants,' Freud called the people of our later life, 'those who return.' And as Erikson put it, there's this back and forth flow. One life phase or crisis always recapitulates everything that went before it."

"Yes, but"—and this was another of Charles Watson's objections to adulthood or the theory of it—"you're not supposed to lose your father so young. But I did!"

Life's unfair.

• • •

It would take Big Chuck over a dozen years to die after they cut out a half of one lung. He'd just about reached the magical five-year mark when they discovered another "site" and did some more butchery on the other one. It would be another few years before they found ugly invaders in yet another place, and then another, and another until at last everything began to give out. Chuck wasn't even sixty.

But even at this age, made old before his time, the war hero and contracting emperor yearned to give away his weapons and scepter. Like King Lear, he said, he hoped to "set my rest" on his children's "kind nursery." Like all hopeful or expectant or actual grandparents, Charles senior longed to assure himself of his redemption, to be idolized and humored by his grandchildren, to see his future in theirs. At the same time he looked forward to being tended, nurtured by his children in their turn, making "my daughters—and uh, sons—my mother."

Annette had been the first to oblige him, and with a son, too. After all, Chuck junior reminded himself, she hadn't had the years and hours of school to contend with. Still, Isaac was the first boy, the first kid of any kind in his generation, in the Wysinski family.

Indeed, he was the firstborn for her in-laws as well, salving their wounds at learning that their other child, Annie's sister-in-law, had been married to a homosexual who in the end had come out of his closet and left her for the gay world. The Blaines had been frantic about the possibility that Karen might have been infected with AIDS, and so little Isaac was proof "positive" that their life would continue. Life everlasting for them as for Big Chuck.

Formerly the firstborn of families that had been destroyed, scion of the New World in the aftermath of Europe's devastation, Chuck couldn't help feeling displaced by his nephew and beaten to the punch by his sister.

Silly, he thought, selfish.

He also felt that once more he'd let his parents down. Here he'd had his father invest half his pension money with Paul Mandell, whose name he'd gotten from Marv Landsman at Blustein, Landsman, and Stein, respectable enough accountants, only to have the kid broker blow most of it and get himself fired on top of that so that there was nobody even to complain to. He felt like the "thankless child" indeed, unable to repay his father in either cash or flesh.

But, he reasoned, he and Syl had to wait. And when they could—nine months before the end of Sylvia's residency, with a deferral of her psychoanalytic training—they started trying to get her pregnant. Twelve months later their daughter was born. The Wysinskis were a fertile lot. . . .

In the months before Agatha was delivered, Chuck senior had begun to slide downhill. They'd thought to let him die at home, in the rambling house he and Simone still inhabited, where his children had been born. But these children were living in New York now, with one of them working at one of the city's best hospitals. And so at their kids' urgings, the Watsons moved, leaving Medford really for the first time since they'd come back from the war.

Sylvia and Chuck had found them an apartment in their building where they stayed until it became essential to put Big Chuck in the hospital. His son was a junior attending physician there and able to look in on his father daily. For the first days of these two weeks, they'd still been able to chat and laugh. By the end, however, the son and the father simply held hands.

On the morning of November 29, Chuck was in the hospital for another purpose. Agatha had been born the night before, and now he was wheeling the gaunt figure of "Big Chuck" to see her. Up and down elevators, through basements and swaying double doors, from one building to another, the caravan made its way— Little Chuck, Big Chuck, Simone, and Annette, and a quivering IV stand. At last they found themselves positioned before the glass window of the sixth-floor nursery. One of the nurses had raised the little red girl to the glass for their inspection.

Big Chuck's eyes, unblinking now, seemed almost unseeing. Or so his son thought, until he felt the bony index finger tap the top of his hand. His father was whispering something, and Chuck bent down to hear him. After a moment or two, he could make out the faint and rasping words:

"A look-see."

Chuck returned the smile his father managed with a deep

laugh, a laugh that sobbed inside. But again Charles senior motioned his son closer, asking again that he attend him.

This time he raised his hand as best he could and pointed at his son as he spoke:

"My father."

• • •

Sigmund Freud once called the death of a man's father, occurring usually during his middle years, the most significant event in a man's life. At the time it seemed it was—both expected and unanticipated in its impact. But as Charles Watson, no longer the "Little" Chuck, was now beginning to see, often to his dismay both for himself and for others, life is full of surprises.

Being a man, a man in full authority and en route to wisdom, his own father figure now, Dr. Charles Watson would look for no more rescuers, no easy answers. There were unwanted truths to be found in his own and in everybody else's lives, he now realized. These had to be integrated somehow, however ugly or unhappy they might be, put together with what is whole and beautiful.

Men at
Their Worst

For all their foibles and missteps, the Charles Watsons of the world (senior and junior) are uncommonly decent men. As they grow into manhood, their morals reshape their elemental desires, making them want what's good for others as well. Deep down, such good men may want to merge with their mothers in bizarre and lascivious ways and want to kill off their beloved fathers—and sons. Yet higher values have also entered their hearts, transfiguring the most primitive and unacceptable of impulses into more sublime aspirations—romance, mystical union, fatherhood, initiative in the service of the common good. Sublimation, a process from which everybody benefits.

But no book on men and their wants could be complete without attention to men at their worst. Women and children must also contend with men who happen to become fathers but for whom this transformation has failed to occur. And they aren't so lucky. In such men, men with "sociopathic" or immoral features, compunction and concern are missing. They are capable of a more naked lust and brutality, exploiting the weak and the helpless to ventilate their frustrations and satisfy themselves. They violate their sons and daughters, compromising their freedom and trust for the rest of their lives.

How, you ask, could these "monsters" either do such things or even want to do them?

In the chapters to follow, I will address these questions, first of all underscoring the moral failings of incestuous and aggressively abusive fathers. With this, I will note as well their terror of exactly those wishes that trouble all men—their urge to unite with a mature woman and their fear of fair fight with men who are their equals or betters. And I will show that their impulses to do harm are themselves expressions of fear. Finally, as we enter the minds of these utterly "bad fathers," I will suggest that, sad to say, there's a little of them in all of us.

And lest you still think that such crimes are rare events, then consider the following simple statistics. According to the National Committee for the Prevention of Child Abuse, reports of child abuse and neglect have risen from 1 million instances in 1980 to 2.1 million in 1986 to 2.4 million in 1989. In 1986, the last year of complete data collection, 42 percent of the reported cases were absolutely substantiated. Most of these kids had suffered more than one kind of maltreatment: physical assaults, sexual violation, and malignant neglect. In 1989, 1,237 children died as a result of murder, "man"-slaughter, and lack of care—more than were killed by leukemia. Since Joel Steinberg battered to death his adopted daughter, Lisa, and the world looked on in horror, but too late, psychologists, physicians, teachers, dentists, and others have been required by law in several states to take courses on the legal imperatives of recognizing and reporting maltreatment of children.

"The evil that men do lives after them," and the "sins of the father shall live on unto the third generation of them that hate." Once again then, I'll begin with a woman's point of view—not just as the object of selfish cads or imaginary demons this time, but as a survivor of greater hurts. One of the unexpected legacies that these guiltless men leave in their wake, we shall see, is the irrational guilt suffered by the victims of their real crimes, even long after they've been perpetrated. And in the process of understanding such questions of responsibility, we'll learn a little more about what a doctor such as Little Chuck Watson does for a living now that he's become a big man.

14
•••

Incest: An Evil That Men Do

Incestuous fathers are greedy, insatiable men, infantile in their impulses to eat up alive everything in their path—including their kids. Losing control of themselves, they need to control everything and everybody around them—though outside their homes they may find themselves in all-too-impotent positions. Scared children find themselves helpless to say no to such molesting fathers' demands. Though he may be tender at other times, and thoughtful, too, when he wants something, when he's in what observers of animal behavior call an appetitive state, his daughter (or son) becomes an object of his need, without a life of her own, used but unseen. Like a baby, the sexually exploitative parent would feed when he will, and he usually does.

And like Oedipus, the daughters of these men try to blind themselves to their fathers' misdeeds. Incest survivors deny and forget, sometimes even repressing seductions and rapes occurring later on in childhood or adolescence when their memories should be continuous and unimpaired. Unearthing the facts, and indeed separating them out from those immature fantasies that are retrospectively mistaken for fact, is a difficult, uncertain, and often lonely undertaking. A terrible true-life detective story.

• • •

"It felt so real. Was it?"

"Was what?"

"The dream."

"Dreams aren't real. They're dreams."

"This one was."

Chuck—Dr. Charles Watson now—didn't know how to continue.

Ms. Pritchard—Molly—had reported that the night before she'd had another of "those" dreams. In it she turned on the tap to get some water to quench her burning thirst. She cupped her hands to scoop it up, then wanting more, positioned her head in the sink, mouth under the faucet, to gulp down the flow of clear liquid. But instead of water, the pipes spewed forth a red and salty substance, like V-8 juice. It poured into her with a relentlessness that she could no longer control, and rather than slake her thirst, it whetted it all the more. Nor could she free herself from the grasp of the white porcelain basin.

Molly Pritchard had awakened from this nightmare gagging and sobbing. She'd run to her bathroom and thrown up. The vomit and then the dry heaves had hurt, as if gouging out the inside of her throat. All alone at two in the morning, twenty-four years old, she had wondered to herself whether she was all right after all, whether she wasn't sick inside, whether tumors or something like diphtheria hadn't invaded her mouth and gut. It hadn't helped that she was having her period and ached all over or that she was alone—as she felt she had to be.

Dr. Watson's buzzer sawed into the momentary silence between them, and Molly, lying on his couch, flinched. He reached over to push the button that opened his outer door, and overhearing the rustle behind her, she flinched again. Having been startled, Molly swallowed, even whimpered a little.

"What's the matter?" Chuck Watson noted that his shock and his surprise, the undertone of alarm in his voice, hardly sounded sage or even professional. Infected by Ms. Pritchard's anxiety, he found himself frightened, as if his movements in answering the intercom amounted to some dangerous breach of the rules.

"I don't understand it," his patient continued. "I'm just all nerves. I didn't know what you were doing, and I could've jumped out of my skin."

"Ms. Pritchard, I don't think we understand everything yet.

But this much is beginning to be clear: the dream wasn't 'real,' but something else was. Something happened and you forgot it."

He remembered reading something about how when dreams call up intense sensations, they may point not just to wishes but to actual events, to forgotten traumas of some sort. But he couldn't recall just where he'd come upon that notion. Anyhow, he'd have to think about it.

It was their "time for today." Announcing the session's close, Dr. Watson found himself particularly, perhaps unduly, careful in rising from his chair not to make any sudden movement. Not to get too close. Not to intrude in any sphere.

Molly's face seemed frozen as she left. She hurried across the little room, not daring to look at him, hunching over so as not to be looked at by him. Besides she had to rush back to pack and catch her train. Her father, the venerable Master Pritchard, hated it when she was late. So missing its departure was out of the question.

• • •

"Gentleman," Carter D. Pritchard had concluded his speech, "on Monday the nation has seen fit to celebrate at once the birth of two of its presidential midwives of liberation. Enjoy the break in the long winter, but remember how hard-won freedom is." St. Luke's School chapel had hummed vigorously with the boys' departure, punctuating the headmaster's words with the scraping of chairs and feet and indecipherable words of exclamation. Now the din and the boys who had made it were gone. The chapel was empty.

It was five o'clock on Friday afternoon, and darkness had begun to blanket the campus of "Dr. Pritchard's" New Hampshire prep school. Having given his scrupulous instructions to the buildings and grounds supervisor about the cleaning of this and other buildings during the break, Dr. Pritchard locked the giant door to the assembly hall himself.

Making his way home across the expanse of lawns, frosted over for February and probably March after it, Dr. Pritchard thought of his own weekend ahead. His wife, Samantha—his second one actually—had planned a visit to her mother that weekend in Greenwich. The Cummings matriarch had been ravaged by Alzheimer's, and it had been decided, therefore, that Samantha would go alone from now on, sparing her family the ordeal. Their four-year-old son, Colin, was to be left in the care of his father for a night. Then the boy's half sister would be coming up on Saturday from New York. During her visit, his daughter, Molly, would be able to take over most of the childcare duties while Carter started to prepare for what remained of the semester before spring break.

Up ahead on the path before him, Dr. Pritchard had eyed an unbroken patch of ice. Reaching it now, he savored the sound and sensation of it cracking as he pressed down on it with his heel. Ever since his first school days as a lowly lower-middler, he'd loved this crunching and breaking through, the sounds of ice underfoot.

This was the least of his compulsions. Others dogged him, dragged him down. He felt mired by his "silly" needs at times. Yet their pull, their suction, had been with him ever since he was a boy. And so there was precious little he could do about them except to forget what he could and hide what he could not. He gave in, but then in his mind's eye made them not happen. He'd had to live with his secrets indefinitely, trying now and then to give to these private ghosts a certain dignity.

And now he opened the door to Amis House, the headmaster's residence. Angela Robinson, the housekeeper, greeted him, described the day, and together with the au pair, Erica, then departed for the weekend, their mistress, the young Mrs. Pritchard, having preceded them. A hard hugging of the knees had been all Carter had gotten from his son before Colin raced from him and returned to his favorite TV show blaring away in the den down the hall.

Alone again, in his living room now, Carter settled in. First, he poured himself a scotch. Then he swept away the remnants of reading material from his wing chair before sinking into it. Gazing ahead, he thought and drank, catching now and then the strains of the cartoon whose noises reached him from the other room. If the truth be known, this master of boys, never having been allowed to be much of a child himself, didn't quite know what to do with children when they were close at hand.

Raising the tumbler to his lips, he noticed that the ice was jiggling now against an empty glass. Carter rose to make another drink, crunching what remained of the frozen cubes in his mouth. He could hear Colin laughing. . . .

She wasn't quite sure, but Molly felt like a character in a scene out of either *The Turn of the Screw* or *Jane Eyre* as her train made its approach into the Gray Landing depot. It had been three years since she had visited St. Luke's, her father actually. Now that she'd been in psychoanalysis for two of these, she sensed that she was nearing something uncanny and rather evil, ghostly in fact, but also strange and inviting—all in the person of her father.

And Molly Pritchard now knew just how prim she was. She saw herself sitting there—her suit, the careful and unflamboyant makeup, the containment of her small, regular features and unblinking expression (not your typical graduate student). She should have had a hatbox in the overhead compartment, she mused. That way, when she arrived, she could've handed it to the carriageman. Ten minutes later she was there—carryons, shopping bags, and all—and Carter was helping her maneuver her way to his aging Volvo.

"God, you look just scrumptious," Pritchard said as, in greeting her and taking her bags, he slid his open hand over her shoulder blades, down her back, and to the upper edge of her neat hips.

Flinching imperceptibly, Molly bent over to kiss Colin, then took his pudgy little hand in hers. The boy hardly seemed to see the "big sister" he'd met only two times before. Now he spun circles and diagonals as the three of them made their way to the parking lot, leaning into her outstretched arm and pulling her about. By the time they got to the car, the four-year-old boy was wild.

"Stop it now, Colly," Carter snapped as he shoved Molly's possessions into the trunk. With this the boy froze, ending his mayhem. "Why didn't you drive instead of this anachronistic nonsense of trains!" Carter then snapped at his daughter, who got into the front seat beside him.

"You know I don't drive."

"Yes, sorry, I forgot—strains of primary parenting." And trying to ease out of his irritation, he patted her knee.

Easing away from his touch, Molly noticed the extra strength Tylenol on the armrest between them.

They chatted and then drove in silence for five minutes before Colin tapped his father on the shoulder.

"What is it, Colly?" Carter said, snapping again.

Unable to speak, the boy in the backseat merely gestured frantically toward his distended lips. He was pale. Evidently he had to throw up.

Stopping the car abruptly, Carter got out, opened the door, pulled his son out and onto the shoulder of the road. He held the child's hand while he vomited, but stared off in the other direction, Molly noted.

"Here, I'll help," she said, though she was hardly familiar with children. And fetching her Kleenex from one of the totes, she cradled the little boy as he finished heaving a little in the end, shaking and shivering, as Molly wiped the throw-up from his chin and the tears from his cheeks. All this done, their father ushered his two children into the car again and whisked them home.

Molly said her good-night and went up to the guest room that used to be her own. Tomorrow she would go back to her own place. . . .

People, Carter Pritchard reflected, had always seemed to drift through this house that wasn't really his, the domicile provided by the school. Leda, his first wife, had lived there but now resided in Cleveland again, where she'd been born. Number two, Samantha, would return tomorrow after his daughter left. Colly would still be there for a while, he guessed. So would he.

History repeats itself. And indeed it *had* seemed much the same when years ago he had been the child of the house. Except that he had been expelled from it rather than left behind. Well, that wasn't quite correct, not altogether true, since his real father had left before memory set in to be followed by two more of mother's husbands. The second of these had remained in the inebriated haze of the home after his stepson Carter had been sent off to school, English style. His departure had been heralded by a tinkling of tumblers it had seemed, and a brief gesture of farewell before Mother and Mack ("Dad") sagged back into their over-stuffed love seat.

Pritchard now sank a little deeper into his chair and pressed the cold glass to one of those eye pouches that gave the lie to an otherwise boyish and wholesome face. Tonight he was drinking martinis. In deference to his daughter, he'd restrained himself relatively, and even at the late hour this was only his fourth. He would have liked a cigarette, too, but had last year broken at least this one addiction at the insistence of wife and doctor.

Time for bed, he murmured to himself, and rose, swaying a little. Pritchard deposited the emptied glass in the sink of the wet bar and suddenly spun about in a private but gleeful pirouette. Then, retrieving *the* magazine from under the pile of periodicals—he couldn't believe he'd left it there—he trudged upstairs. Past the girl's and boy's bedrooms, Pritchard shuffled into his own. Having undressed, he walked into the master bathroom and locked the door behind him. . . .

Colly had lain awake, the bedclothes tucked up to his chin,

sucking on a corner of a sheet, absently cupping his crotch with his hand and missing his mother. He'd started to fall asleep at last, dreaming of Dumbo again. But then he'd started at the sound of his father's footsteps coming up the stairs and past his door. The boy thought of going to find his daddy but ended up searching out his sister's bed instead. He'd opened the door, marched in, and quietly snuggled in. He'd hoped she wouldn't get mad at him the way his mother did at hours like these when he woke her.

Molly had also remained awake all the while. She'd never been able to sleep in Amis House as a child—especially for the last two of her teenage years there, the years before she left home. She'd been thinking of her mother, so far away now it seemed, when Colly came in. Warming to his presence, the smooth skin, the lingering scent of milk even on a child that age, she'd wondered about his mother. Was the new Mrs. Pritchard just as remote—unseeing, unfeeling—as the old had been? Probably. She pretended not to notice his arrival. When she felt him fall asleep, so did she.

At one o'clock the next day they were preparing for Molly's departure. A short visit.

Having cleared the dishes, Molly answered Pritchard's irascible cries from the car outside to get in it, and in her turn, she called for Colly. Silence. She looked about, finally traipsed upstairs. He wasn't in his room so she searched out hers. He wasn't there either.

Finally, she entered her father's bedroom, having recoiled at first from this, the inner sanctum. It was still dark in there with the curtains drawn.

The boy had burst from the bathroom in a roar of sibilant hollers. "Gotcha!" he yelled again. And here, too, she nearly jumped out of herself again.

Colly had held in his hand a large and rather green banana left over from the offerings of fruit at the end of lunch. He now proceeded to place this in his mouth and whir around, arms outstretched, like wings, she thought. In a moment he was careening about and pretend-flying, jumping on and off the bed.

Again and again Colly hurled himself at his sister and butted her—in the pelvis and belly, the breast and the buttocks. Then he swooped down and tried to swoop up from between her legs underneath her skirt.

Dizzy, Molly found herself frozen in place in that room. And she began to gag. Again, just as on Thursday night. Or like Colly the day before. Sickening, she moved herself toward the light of the open bathroom. Shutting out the boy's clamor, she vaguely heard yet another voice, a deeper one behind her.

She was just inside the door when she heard the words and felt the hand.

"Dumbo." Carter Pritchard's forearm had inserted itself between Molly and the toilet. "Dumbo—his favorite cartoon. He's always playing the part."

He steered her out of the bathroom, out of the room, into the hall.

"Colly," he added unequivocally, yanking the boy away as well.

But it was too late, she later recalled with a vindictive moral pleasure. Her gaze having gotten in the bathroom, Molly had seen the magazine.

. . .

"Discovery," Dr. Watson had said. "Discovery is the first route to cure."

"Discovery," she had repeated to herself, then added, "You mean scientifically and *legally?*"

"I'm not sure I follow."

"I mean discovering it for myself and then also discovering it to other people."

"Oh, you mean the truth. Knowing and telling the truth. I'm not so sure about the latter." Dr. Watson was thinking his own thoughts just for a moment . . . remembering himself at twelve . . . his mother.

"Well, I am!" She corrected him harshly and unhesitatingly. Then, softening, remembering who *he* was, she went on.

"What I mean to say, and I'm not sure you can understand this, is that you can't know something if nobody else does. There are some secrets that become so secret that it makes them unreal."

And it *was* different—his brief horror and her hell.

They had, two weeks later, begun to understand the dream she had dreamt the Thursday before that weekend—the one she had dreamt in order to use that weekend to remember. And understanding this, they had at last understood her. And knowing, she would have to tell. Molly Pritchard, she and Dr. Watson had discovered, had been a victim of incest.

She had always known that her father, the eminent and respected Master Pritchard, had been unduly seductive with her.

He was also an alcoholic. In the privacy of his home, he had let down his, and her, hair. "Republican" in most other respects, when it came to bodies—the family's bodies at least—Carter Pritchard was an avowed libertarian. And in this climate, Molly remembered being surprised in the bathroom by her father's naked form or in her room by his unannounced intrusions. Yes, surprised, again and again. Once, and she wasn't sure whether this was a figment of her imagination or an actual event, she seemed to recall her father standing there next to her impassive mother, both unclothed, while, swaying slightly, he carefully pointed out their anatomical features and differences to his five-year-old.

Following her lead and her father's disclaimers before this, Dr. Watson might have written off these displays to the legacies of the Auntie Mame and Summerhill mystiques. According to this rationale, it's good for children and parents to see one another "completely" and speak "frankly" about sex early on. Though psychologists now know that the ethic of overexposure is usually a cover-up of more selfish wishes to show off one's "superior" anatomy to a little kid, and that overstimulation leads not to liberation but to sexual inhibition—still it needn't have gone any further than this.

Indeed, his patient might have drawn from these experiences the stuff from which she then fashioned her forbidden fantasies before finally numbing herself altogether to escape her guilt over her wishes. This would have made her a severe but still "garden variety" neurotic, yet another casualty of what Freud called "modern nervousness." Like all of us.

But there were telltale signs to the contrary, signs of something more, something sinister, not just of desire but of events that carried the Pritchards beyond the bounds of expectability and respectability. Like so many men's, Carter's secrets were laid out in concentric circles. Even he couldn't know where the center was, where it all finally stopped. Not in the imagination only, but in reality: where would he stop?

For all the talk of sex at home, Molly had always suspected that there was little taking place between her parents. By the time she was nine, her father and her mother, who was as inwardly icy as she was obviously diffident, were sleeping in separate rooms. With this arrangement, his breath stained with Players, scotch, and as it came into vogue, vodka, Master Pritchard got into the habit of getting into bed with Molly in the early-morning hours. Colly's creeping in from what used to be her father's room, she further realized, had reminded her of their father's first nocturnal visits a dozen years earlier.

"Just for a cuddle," he'd said in a North Country accent, "a little touch of Molly in the night . . . to warm me outta the cold, girl." And truly, nothing much happened. He'd simply wrap himself around her from behind, "like two spoons snuggling in a felt-lined silver chest." He'd say something vaguely coherent about how he missed "both our mommies" and how this was the only warmth to be gotten—this "body heat." And then, burying his hot snout in her hair, he'd snore himself into sleep.

But as Molly got older, got her period, saw her breasts grow from unformed buds into a woman's bosom, the visits became more frequent. The Pritchards were fighting more often now and nearing divorce, or so she understood after the fact. Her mother left more often than before, going home to Ohio and her mother for weekends that began to extend into weeks. So he was lonelier. And maybe she was, too.

Pritchard would get into her bed now and slide his hand under her as well, reaching out to probe her bodice with the absentminded knuckle of an index finger as he exhaled into her. Once, after a particularly ugly brawl between her parents, the one where he hit her mother, the one that finally prompted the marriage's end, Molly thought that she had felt his erection—something hard, brushing, just for a moment, through the cotton flannel and touching her backside. She couldn't be sure, though.

"You see, nobody knew," she explained to Dr. Watson.

Carter Pritchard was a "pillar of the community." A classicist teaching at the secondary school level, he had returned with his doctorate to his alma mater and taken over its helmsmanship at thirty-one. Almost unheard of. And then, fund-raiser par excellence, he'd made more money for the place than any of his predecessors. There were no successors. Pritchard hung on to that headmastership, forever it seemed, becoming a fixture at St. Luke's, a man equated with the institution itself. A man for all generations.

Nobody knew he drank even. They knew nothing about his family. They'd never seen his parents, who appeared somehow not to have existed. And they only understood that Mrs. Pritchard and her daughter were shy. He was affable, elegant, often charismatic, while they were quiet and removed, leaving him alone. Carter Pritchard was to the eyes of the world a man in perfect control.

Not a soul knew about the magazines, of course. Molly had found them when she was fourteen while cleaning out the study one Saturday—just to help in a "special" way while her mother was away. There they were, unmistakable. Only one had pictures of adult couples performing sex. The others pictured "nubile young things," with pink mounds for breasts and hairless vulvas displayed for the camera—groups of girls stripped for view, captured chatting as if they were wearing cardigans and carrying their books to class.

Catching her as he had that Sunday two weeks earlier in the bathroom, Pritchard had then told Molly that he was doing work on "unrequited love." *Lolita* by Nabokov. The great literary critic Lionel Trilling had called this tale of Humbert Humbert's love for his teenage stepdaughter the last possible romantic tragedy. As always Pritchard had wanted to get underneath convention and mere words to the experience itself. Not to worry.

Worry she did, however, as always. Still Molly said nothing, knew nothing. College was approaching anyway, and soon she'd be free of the hideous ambiguities. Besides, her father's divorce from his wife and her mother had, unexpectedly, begun to free her from him. Mr. Pritchard had begun to date "Sammie," a twenty-three-year-old English teacher who was remarkably composed for her years. His interest had turned elsewhere for a while.

But then there had been psychoanalysis, the dream, the truth insofar as this last was possible. Molly had begun her low-fee treatment at twenty-one at one of New York City's psychoanalytic institutes to cure her of her extraordinary sexual inhibitions. A graduate student in comparative literature, pretty and gifted, she had never dated.

No sex. No dates. Oh, except once, and when he kissed her, pushing his tongue down her mouth, Molly had thought she was drowning or being hanged. She couldn't wait to get away. Molly was always throwing up. She never felt comfortable, for her throat seemed to be perpetually constricted. Around men especially, she found herself choking.

As a result of her analysis, Molly had tried out masturbation for the first time in her available remembrance. She'd reached to touch herself down there—hardly knowing where and what "there" was. But just as she'd felt that little tingling, the pictures of those girls had inserted themselves into her consciousness. The tingling had abruptly stopped, and again she'd rushed to the bathroom to throw up. . . .

The dream, the dream, these days it always came back to the dream. As he prepared to deliver his interpretation at last, from behind the couch, Dr. Watson found his head swimming. Chuck Watson was still a student, a psychoanalytic "candidate," to whom Ms. Pritchard had been referred by the institute's treatment center to fulfill the clinical requirement of his training. Though he'd already worked with many other people in different kinds of therapy, she was his first to come four or five times a week and lie on his couch—the first of three or four such patients he would treat before graduating, the first of many to come thereafter. And here he was about to break the rules, to make one of those dramatic reconstructions of the past he'd read about, the sort of thing no longer in fashion in clinical circles. Well, Watson did what he did because he believed in truth, even when it hurt.

When he thought about it afterward, Dr. Watson could imagine what Molly must have gone through in her young and unprotected life. As far back as *Oedipus Rex,* incest has always been about unwanted truth, he went on to himself. Just as Oedipus is about to get to the heart of the crime, about to discover that he has killed his father and married his mother, she—his mother, his wife, Queen Jocasta—tries to warn him off the truth. "All men have dreamt such things," she says. Sort of like a psychoanalyst telling his patients it's in their imagination. Or a parent with a guilty conscience.

Dr. Watson cleared his throat before speaking into the twilight of the room. "When you were very little, Ms. Pritchard, perhaps three or four years old, the evidence suggests that your father forced you or even seduced you into performing fellatio on him. For a kid it doesn't much matter—it's coercion either way. It was both exciting and scary, and it took place at a time when it's easy to forget things that make you too guilty or afraid, and so you did forget it. You covered it up in your mind just like you did with everything else he did in reality, and you bore the blame."

He stopped himself there. His pulse was racing as, he imagined, his patient's was. The two of them were utterly still as he sat behind her in the fake Eames chair (he'd get a real one someday), she on the couch before him. As Dr. Watson spoke, Molly had had to struggle to grasp hold of his words, fighting her effort, yes, to forget them on the spot. Yet with the terror they spread before her, there came relief as well. She could feel the envelope of her body easing palpably in the aftermath of his words of understanding. The tight darkness in her head began to open or fade, she wasn't sure which, letting in more light and a little feeling.

And there, she imagined or remembered, suddenly there *he* was before her. A memory or an idea, a plausible image at last, a truth nonetheless. Headmaster Carter D. Pritchard was standing there, and not in the august black robes he wore for commencement either. He was in his pajama tops only, reaching to grab hold of her head and pull it toward him. There before her eyes, little then, she realized in retrospect, and uncomprehending, his erect penis seemed huge, bloody, demonlike. It was getting closer and closer, and soon there was nothing more to be seen except it—no porcelain sinks nor white tiles nor Pritchard even, just a huge monster of flesh and desire. Then it was in her, and there was nothing. The world of the child turned black.

Molly Pritchard wailed into the silence of the consulting room and then collapsed into tears, deep convulsive sobs that came from her whole life. She just lay there and wept.

She was Chuck Watson's last patient for the day. So once again he broke the rules. Spent in a way that reminded him of his days running track, he let her cry herself out. Another whole half hour.

• • •

Maybe Molly isn't typical. Only 10 percent of the incest victims interviewed in a recent study by Boston psychiatrist Judith Herman were sexually abused by their fathers before the age of five. Girls seven to ten years in age, at a time in life when most children should expect a period of relative "sexual latency" (see Chapter 12), are about twice as likely to be sexually molested. So are female adolescents from about thirteen years on. And according to more official estimates, the numbers provided by survey data and the inferences made about the population at large, only about 1 percent of women have suffered incestuous sex of any sort.

But this mere 1 percent translates into the following absolutes, asserts David Finkelhor: 1 million American women have had incest with their fathers at this time with 16,000 new victims each year. Other investigations find such estimates far too forgiving. Psychologist Susan Foward, for instance, has declared that at least one in ten women has been molested as a little girl by a close family member, making for a total of upward of 10 million such survivors.

And according to this expert, these are still conservative figures at best. Surveying children from the white and mostly middle classes, systematic incest studies also omit the disadvantaged families where, ironically, such deviations seem more commonplace.

Nor could any large-scale poll possibly take into account the myriad *unreported* instances of sexual abuse. Incest is like adultery in this respect—only more so. These breaches of the biggest barrier of them all, the universal taboo against sex among blood relations, are sources of endless shame and burning guilt. Threatening the family as they inevitably do, they are shrouded in mystery.

It's not even clear just what is meant by *incest*. Some researchers restrict the term to include only acts of genital intercourse between family members. Others place under this heading any untoward exhibitionistic display, voyeuristic snooping, or verbal innuendo on a caretaker's part, even where there is no question of arousal or climax and no blood tie between the participants.

But however incest is defined by the outside observer, its victims and perpetrators sense when it has occurred. Father and daughter, child and stepparent, know when they have crossed over the boundary. They know on their pulses when libidinal pleasure and violation have undone the trust between parent and child and, whether in a moment or over many years, have made their relationship into something other than it should have been. Forever.

No, father-daughter incest is not even the most common form of sexual abuse. Other adult males are more likely perpetrators. Stepfathers, who are without biological ties to the child, are more apt to violate the proscriptions of a paternity that for them is artificial, short-lived, and tenuous at best. Brothers and sisters may have more sex than fathers and daughters, since, while trespassing within the family, they are not at the same time threatening the generational hierarchy.

Still, incestuous acts on a father's part—toward his girls and, occasionally, toward his sons—are far more common than similar transgressions by mothers. Thus after reviewing the five largest studies of parent-child incest, totaling 424 cases, Herman concluded that 97 percent of the abusers were male. Boys, other researchers have noted, are generally far less likely to be victimized by adults than are girls. However, even when they are found to have been similarly assaulted, whether by parents or others, in 84 percent of the cases the "aggressor"—a word we shall come back to—is a man.

Whatever its place in mythology, in reality mother-son incest is a far rarer occurrence than sex between fathers and daughters. There are probably many reasons for this paradox.

Until recently at least, it is women alone who have been charged with nurturing young children. An act of frank incest with a child would amount to a violation of a mother's almost sacred trust, one that, because of the parent's ongoing familiarity with her child, she couldn't fail to acknowledge. Conversely, a woman's greater contact with a son or daughter, born of her body, has already permitted her to take physical liberties with that child's body, intimacies of the sort mostly denied to male parents.

Indeed, much of what passes for normal mothering has gratifications and even seductions built into it (see Chapters 3, 4, 5, and 11). Some observers have suggested that many women derive an almost orgasmic pleasure from nursing. Through no fault of their own, mothers may exude the scent of sex—pheromones—to which their sons respond. Their presence thus makes for the sort of mixed messages only psychoanalysts learn about after the fact, when adult patients lie back and reflect on what they experienced so long ago at a parent's hands.

Actually crossing the bridge into an acknowledged sexual transgression—that's another matter altogether. For a son certainly, and for his mother as well, to do so would mean to challenge not only that trust between parent and child but the generational order and the sociology of power that goes with it. Mother-son incest defies the dominance of the older male. For a younger man, especially a son who has to count on a father's protection and goodwill, to violate the incest taboo is to risk exile, death, and worse still perhaps, castration. From any son's or mother's perspective, even now when women are no longer considered chattel, such are the specters conjured up in the face of incestuous temptation. And so it's only when either or both such participants are entirely crazy or maybe—*maybe*—utterly desperate that incest between them actually takes place.

Not so fathers, and the younger females in his household. For a father, an act of incest—penetration, fellatio, looking and showing, fondling and being fondled—is a more natural extension of his male supremacy. An exploitative one to be sure, nonetheless it's a behavior that expresses rather than threatens the traditional ordering of power between the genders and the generations.

Still, the sociopolitics of incest fail to explain how it is that a man would *want* to have sex with a young girl, especially when she is also his daughter. Why does he not pursue women who are older, more voluptuous, and clearly responsive? And granted that his *motives* may be understood, still how can he defy the strictest ethical code of all? How can he bring himself to act on those wishes that other men (men such as Big Chuck in Chapter 13) may glimpse but banish from awareness long before any untoward action becomes possible?

Clinical researchers have been trying to pinpoint and further categorize these fathers for some time now. Often they try to link certain personality types with the forms the abuse takes and with the daughter's age at its onset. What, they wonder, is it in his personality or background that permits a man to cross the bounds of decency and trust? From what class, race, and religious background is this molester of his own child most likely to come? Is the incestuous father a weakling or a tyrant? Is he typically a sociopath or otherwise ethical and upright, even a stern moralist whose rigidity merely conceals his felt human frailty? Is he self-indulgent or generally deprived and needy? Is he crazy or normal like you or me? What about Carter Pritchard—what do *you* think?

• • •

"Ahhhhgrhh," Carter Pritchard groaned into the night.

He was alone. The second Mrs. Pritchard, Samantha née Cummings, had left him so. And she had taken Colly with her. She had complained of his alcoholism, his excessive control, and the magazines, which she, too, had found. She, too, was gone for good.

There could be no more explaining everything away as with the last time. Not a second time. This time they'd see that something was very wrong.

Having comforted himself as was his wont, especially on this loneliest of nights, Pritchard staggered from the bathroom toward his bed. He stood at its foot for a moment swaying. Then, spread-eagle, he let himself fall forward onto the mattress with its mound of blankets, linens, and comforters. Just like a little boy, he chortled, no, a little he-she child, bouncing and quivering into gradual immobility.

Pritchard remembered himself before he went away to school, an all-boys school, falling into the piles of dry autumn leaves. As then, he was now reminded of a famous photograph from *The Family of Man* of a little girl lying just like that in the leaves of fall. She was facedown, like him now, and like him buff naked, and, he further imagined, scratchy on one side and, on the other, airy and tingly all over.

Maybe if Master Pritchard had been a little girl like his half

sister Tracy, they would have loved him. No, *she*, his mother, she
would have loved him and kept him at home, too. Maybe she
wouldn't have been so remote—sober or drunk. A Freudian might
have thought this, he thought, seeing in Carter's "eccentricities"
and his choices of wives, even his drinking, efforts to draw Mother
into him. Oedipus. Nonsense, he sputtered into the pillow, feeling
the bedsheets under his belly and genitals below. How did
Nabokov put it? "Psychoanalysis was fine for those who liked to
have Greek myths applied to their private parts." Nabokov—now
he understood. He envied her, the little girl in the leaves. And
envying her, oh, how he wanted what she had. How, therefore, he
"loved" her!

Barely awake, he indulged in mute fancy. There was something quite glorious, Carter felt, about a denuded vulva. He'd
asked the first Mrs. Pritchard to shave off her tangled forest—just
to give it a try, to spare him, through playful enactments between
consenting adults, the need to turn elsewhere, somewhere forbidden, to gratify his illicit desires. Alas, Leda had refused her swan.

Illicit wasn't right really—*innocent* was more apt. Nabokov had
savored this paradox. Young girls seemed so and made him feel
young and unformed again—naive, naked, expectant. No darkness, no juices, no risk of pregnancy . . . so many meanings. No
commitment to manhood. Power but no commitment. A way of
not being alone. Also, young girls made Carter feel strong and
young. He could have an impact on them, as he hadn't on his
parents, or even the family he'd created. Touching them, he could
feel pleasured, caressed as he never had been when he was a boy.
He could teach, helping them discover the resources of sensation
and transport abiding in their bodies—even their delicious fears.

Like flowers opening and growing. Everybody young, expectant, emergent. Everybody coming alive, coming alive. Not so
women, and not with boys.

Oh, love me, "little" me!

Carter Pritchard lay there for a time, breathing into his pillow
and nestling into the wetness his breath left behind until, sucking
in darkness, he embraced the forgetfulness of sleep, not owing
anybody anything.

• • •

Attempts at generalizations about incestuous fathers break down,
it seems to me, and are remarkable more in the exceptions than in
the rule. But certain patterns, themes, do emerge nonetheless.

First of all, a great many, maybe a majority, of incestuous abusers are alcoholics like Carter Pritchard. The demon rum bribes their conscience, lulling it into sleep and permitting such men to take liberties that shame or guilt (those guardians of civilization) might have put a stop to.

As in the enactment of many other perversions, the incestuous father does his terrible deed in an altered state of consciousness. Aided and abetted by intoxicants, he forgets who he and his child are. And he expects others, the children he exploits, to do as he does—to put it all behind closed doors. For the moment at least, he is mad.

Consciences not only protect the people around us, they also keep us sane. And so an act of incest reflects what clinical psychiatrists have called an "encapsulated or transient psychosis." When he does what he does, the sexually abusive father has abandoned his humanity along with his child.

Not only this, the fact of the addiction tells us something more about the motivations and personalities involved. In his child, a man who abuses her sensually also sees his childish self. His female or sexually ambiguous self, that is. Though they may not admit it, men like this ache to be children, "oral" and dependent and without any clear definition of their gender.

Unlike Carter, many of these fathers are also violent, with their children as with their wives. (Sometimes the wives are as well.) At one level, this tells of faults in their personality. Under certain circumstances at least, incestuous and destructive fathers cannot control impulses of any kind.

At another, the connection says something about the sexual abuse itself—about its motives and consequences. The sexual overstimulation of a child is hardly an act of love, erotic or otherwise. While to some extent and in some instances it may also be motivated by regenerative desires—to become vicariously young again, to capture the emerging femininity of an innocent little girl—the violence and destruction are always there. The incestuous father's spiteful aim is to overwhelm, to master and destroy, to violate and betray, to hurt and devour, to seduce sexually and abandon emotionally, and through demonstrations of "phallic power," to pretend that he is not so insecure about how much of a man he is.

He also seeks to get revenge for all the insults he has suffered as a child at the hands of his parents and other caretakers entrusted with his emotional protection. Like all hard-core perversions, then, incest represents an "identification with an aggressor." It is a dis- and mis-placed vendetta. To borrow from sexologist Robert Stoller, it is an "erotic form of hatred." The abuser is a heartbreaker and crusher of innocence, a violator who runs roughshod over the bodies and consciousness of others in his life. Carter Pritchard is a spoiler, a destroyer. Yet he knows not what he does. And *his* disavowal makes it all the more difficult for others to know as well.

Most incestuous fathers have bad relationships with their wives, adult women who are often said to be either too sick or depressed or absent emotionally and physically to fulfill their roles as mothers either. A lot has been proposed about the mother's role in incestuous families, about how they condone, encourage, or deny the incest. And there have been further assertions about the parents' sex lives—good or bad, too little or too much. Once again the variations probably defy classification. If the truth be told, many such assertions on the part of incest researchers (most of them male) seem subliminally aimed at partly exonerating the fathers involved.

But this much is clear. The fathers in question *experience* their wives as being unfit to meet their needs—whatever the reality and whoever is to blame. Either they are not women enough for them and are felt to be withholding, critical, or allied to others of their sex; or else, far from seeming inadequate, these wives seem too much for these men to handle, scaring them off, prompting their husbands to look for females they can manage, for girls who are not yet full-blooded women.

And another pattern is also clear. Whether or not they have explicitly colluded in the committing of incest, turning blind eyes and deaf ears to the obvious, these mothers are once again *experienced* by their *daughters* as having failed them. Not only have these mothers left their daughters unprotected by not intervening to stop the crimes occurring beneath their very noses. Not only have they failed to satisfy their husbands' sexual needs. These mothers have deprived their daughters from the start. They are often depicted as cold and withholding, forcing their children, like their husbands, to turn elsewhere, and then in sexualized modes, for motherly warmth and affection. And they, too, practice disavowal, knowing and not knowing at once.

An atmosphere of abandonment, evolving mistrust, and deception thus permeates a family of incest. Something—adequate parenting—is missing at the core. And with this void, and the lack of essential protection and the duplicity, all hell can break loose. An incestuous household is a home without parents—mother and father.

. . .

"Still, how could he do that!" you exclaim. That's indecent, immoral, creepy. No parent in his right mind has feelings like that. No *sane* father wants to have sex with his daughter!

Really, nobody? Isn't there a distinction to be made between doing and wishing, between an act of abuse and those fleeting thoughts to which we all succumb? Are we so childish and timid that we must banish from awareness the truths of the heart, whatever we then do with them?

What about the times those sweet little toddlers wriggle in your lap, and after a minute or two of growing uneasiness, you extricate yourself somehow from the disquieting intimacy? Could you feel yourself getting aroused? Oh, "Nonsense!" you say?

And remember Big Chuck (Chapter 13). Yes, what about those teenage daughters as their breasts begin to bud and still they walk about in their pj's or underwear, heedless of the womanliness coming upon them and its effect on you? Why are you averting your eyes from the body of the child you once diapered? Why do you snap at your seventeen-year-old as the two of you sidle past each other half-dressed in the corridor in the hour before work or school? Why do you criticize her bralessness and her miniskirts? Why do you check out, critique, and disapprove of her boyfriends?

Why is your wife feeling so neglected these days?

Another of Freud's ingenuities lay in his discovery of the universality of the Oedipus complex and its derivatives in everyday life. Present in the imagination of the child and of the father, who was after all a child himself earlier, incest is everywhere. It is there when a little girl shows off, and her father admires her delicious body and emerging femininity. It is there in the schoolroom, with the flirtations and crushes of teacher and student, a playfulness that is not infrequently consummated in a real erotic encounter. Father-daughter incest is to be seen in the proverbial mutual fascination of dirty older men and younger women for each other, the one in search of youth, the other seeking a Pyrrhic victory over her mother. You can find it in the sexism of the workplace. Most sadly of all, incest exists as an omnipresent threat to the therapeutic contract, with some so-called healers exploiting their attractive patients' longings—based on their yearning fatherly transference love and their idealization of men whom they do not really know—to prove their power and perfection. Or to make up for what's missing in their real lives.

Incest is everywhere that men envy women and girls their femininity. Everywhere that they can exact their revenge and prove their power through shows of pride and dominance. Yes, incest is everywhere.

Not that we can turn faintheartedly from the "psychic" implications of these manifestations of the real thing. Analyst and patient must tolerate and talk about the latter's guilt-ridden desires, using these in the service of understanding. Teachers, whether they know it or not, bank on their students' "transference loves" to motivate their desires to learn and to get them to take in what is taught. And fathers, too. As I've noted in the very first chapter, fathers have to let themselves be seduced—up to a point—to reflect back to a daughter her feelings of beauty and worth. "Optimally" or "minimally" seduced is how Robert Stoller once put it. As always, it's a matter of realizing how far to go and when to stop, of empathy, of sensing when pleasure and the stimulation of body and soul have crossed over into the realm of pain. Of knowing, that is, when the erotic has become what one psychotherapist, Ivri Kumin, once called "the erotic horror."

• • •

Dr. Chuck Watson was thinking to himself.

He had told himself that he had never been tempted by his women patients. Failing to reciprocate their attraction to him, feeling either "clinical" or "paternal" toward these women, he'd found himself also nagged by a sense of guilt. It was as if he were being patronizing or superior (qualities he hated), as if he were wounding them by not "loving" them as women.

Perhaps they intuited the genuineness of his reserve and got angry at it. One or two had left therapy because of it, he guessed in retrospect. Like that rather "wild" woman who came one day, announcing that she wasn't wearing any underpants, embarrassing him and making him avert his eyes, hoping she wouldn't uncross her legs. She was one who never came back after the summer's break.

After the epiphany with Molly, and as his own daughter, Agatha, started to grow up, it began to change. Dr. Charles Watson didn't feel guilty like this anymore. The tensions with the women he was treating eased, and he wasn't sure why.

He'd keep such thoughts to himself for the time being. Or rather, Chuck would save them for the privacy of his own personal training analysis. They weren't the sort of thing you discussed with a supervisor. Too private, he figured.

So now "Dr. Watson" simply closed his notebook and started to rise, concluding his weekly session with Dr. Bernard, the training and supervising analyst charged with overseeing his "control case." The latter rose in response and, rather untypically, Chuck thought, came around his huge desk, emerging from the halo behind it.

He was really a small man, the supervisee tried to remind himself, kindly in an effortful sort of way, a supervisor who had worked hard to establish a collegial relationship with his student.

"Remember, Dr. Watson, it's not so much what happened to Miss Pritchard as what she made of it—inside, psychologically. That's analysis."

"Yes," Dr. Watson murmured his assent, reflexively extending his hand to shake the one Dr. Bernard had offered him. But squeezing it, he reminded himself that Ms. Pritchard had taught him something quite to the contrary. What had happened, the fact that it had happened, had mattered very much indeed and needed simple acknowledgment as much as any analysis of its inner meanings.

Dr. Watson still had a lot to think about. The truth did matter. For a daughter such as Molly, it did, a daughter of incest.

• • •

Daughters of incest. How ambiguous this phrase is, almost suggesting that the victim of a father's advances was conceived herself in just such a union.

Again, researchers can pinpoint no single kind of sufferer. A father's or perhaps other older male relative's abuse of his little girl may have all sorts of consequences later in her life. She may become promiscuous, making sexual her search for love while repeating her loveless past. She may turn from men altogether, fleeing them for women perhaps, who don't threaten her. Or she may opt for nobody at all, making the most of her own person instead.

Or perhaps, unprotected by her parents from the arousal of sexual feelings that as a child she had no way of fulfilling, and irrationally guilty as well, such a woman may numb herself and succumb to all sorts of *hysterical* symptoms. Frigidity, sexual anesthesias, crippling anxiety, and other psychosomatic disturbances represent covert means of expressing her desires, the conflicts they call up, and the traumatic events that set them in motion.

These are the sort of women, women such as Molly, who more readily seek out psychotherapy to cure them of ills they've otherwise tried to forget. They are the "guilty" ones, guilty because unconsciously they have assumed the responsibility for the parent's indiscretions and because they have seen what everybody says they should not have and therefore "have not." When a man approaches them, when they imagine any kind of sex, flashbacks intrude to give them pause.

The victims of incest forget, remember briefly, and forget again, punishing themselves all the while because of the most terrifying truth of all about incest. Its victims have fulfilled their dreaded desires, their unwanted wishes. "Wishes," Freud said in his book on dreams, "forced upon us by nature" yet "repugnant to morality." They have had their fathers sexually, something *all* little girls both want and dread. They have had them and for a few erotic if brutal moments, torn their demon "lover's" attentions from the other rivals with claims on him.

Participants in real sex, incestuous daughters are rendered guilty of psychological murder. They've committed imaginary matricides and fratricides, themselves killing off what remains of their parents and siblings in a world already shaken by their absence. They are plunged into moral and emotional confusion. Depravity has been thrust upon them.

Where most of us innocents merely imagine the illicit, these girls have had to create their own innocence. They've had to deny what it was they and their fathers did. And they've done it by finding these fathers in all men, seeing their sex as inherently lewd and lascivious, by pretending that men don't exist, by becoming homosexual, or by repressing their sexuality altogether.

In the end, then, there's not much difference in the purposes served by the sufferers' inhibitedness or their impulsiveness. Both are responses to a profound mistrust in the goodness of men. Even where the daughter has sex with them, sometimes with the vengeance of promiscuity, she doubts that anything good will come of it. Choosing badly, she fulfills prophecies based on past betrayals. There's no difference, she tells herself, between her father and these "fucks"—between the childhood she lived as a victim and an adult world in which she has become her own agent. She's still a slave of her past.

It takes a long time for people to discover what happened, and even then they don't get at the whole truth. The biggest Pritchard secrets, for example, remained in the family.

• • •

"Quite simply put, it is the end of an era."

Having concluded his farewell, Roger Pace, '49, chairman of the board of St. Luke's Preparatory School, gestured behind him on the dais to the slightly slumped figure of Carter D. Pritchard, outgoing headmaster. Straightening immediately, Pritchard rose with a broad smile to return the accolades and say his good-bye. The assembly hall burst into a roar of applause, infusing the now elder statesman with a final shot of glory.

What they didn't know—this assemblage of teenage scions, their parents, teachers, alums, and friends—was that the board, through observations of the faculty, had become dismayed by Pritchard's behavior since the departure of his second wife a year earlier. It was the drinking that got them, moving them to suggest that it was time for a change. A change for all concerned.

Still they didn't really know and never would. But now Molly did. And Dr. Watson. And Jeremy Hurst.

• • •

"Yes," Pritchard sighed after some moments in answer to his daughter's question three weeks later. He was on her territory now, at McHenry's Tavern not far from the vicinity of Columbia where Molly studied and lived. Her home. The only thing familiar was the vodka martini, his fifth that long evening, in his bony hand.

"Yes," he repeated. "We, er, did 'fool around.' How shall I put it—well, yes, I had you suck me off several times when you were very little"

There, he'd said it at last, Molly thought.

"Uh-oh," he groaned, looking away. "Thought you'd just forget it—no harm done."

She knew what it had done to her but had no interest in telling him, now.

"I know I tried to forget it. God knows how guilty I was." Was he?

"But the guilt only made it worse. I tried to wash it away with feelings, sensations, and . . ." He gestured toward his glass.

He couldn't believe she had remembered it, he thought to himself in a panic. And he'd never imagined that one day they'd *talk* about it, branding it into memory, making history of a dream. Realizing that all this was a nightmare, Carter importuned Molly with his gaze.

"And I was so lonely—lonely my whole life."

Pritchard reached across the checkered tablecloth and flickering candle, straining to touch his daughter's cheek. But she had sat farther back into the darkness, removed from his fumbling.

Hoping she was unseen altogether because of the blur of his inebriation, Molly looked at her father. An observer, at last. Fighting off her compassion, drawing back from the love that had proved so dangerous to her, she thought about her own loneliness.

"Well, anyhow . . ." And he took another swig, sloshing out his mouth with the vodka and the aftertaste of the olive.

Molly knew what had happened to her. She and Dr. Watson knew for sure. She was beginning to tell Jeremy, who had two months earlier laid more proper claim to her adult virginity. Now she had had to get *him* to confess, to know, to lift her guilt. But there was something she still didn't know.

Piercing her father's stupor, she continued to probe, half-happy at her temerity and not a little remorseful at the pain she was causing now that her father was down and out, the boy wonder turned premature pensioner.

"And Colly?"

"What!" he rejoined, and reddened as regret gave way to sudden rage. "What do you think I am, a damned fairy?"

The language was so uncharacteristic, she thought.

"A pederast? A pervert? A *monster!*"

Again Pritchard and his daughter stared at each other in silence. Now the one, now the other averted his, her gaze.

All the while he was thinking to himself.

Molly should understand that he loved her because she was a *girl*. Nothing else moved him so. But he was confused. It hurt. He had hurt her. He knew it. But he didn't know whether he'd wanted to or not. Yes, he was addled—befuddled, feeling the fool. He didn't know what he wanted.

Besides, the mere accusation could now make him a perpetrator just as once the pretense and deception had cleared him of the actual crime. Under such pressure, reality can be what one wants it to be. But what *had* he done? He lost his train of thought. And knocking over his drink, Pritchard rose, only then to look about distractedly and make his disoriented way not to the front door but to the men's room.

Looking at his back as he receded into the rear of the bar, Molly saw that it was shaking. She couldn't tell, however, whether he was laughing or crying. This was only the beginning, she now reminded herself, echoing Dr. Watson yesterday. "Discovery" was only the beginning, and there still was much confusion to be cleared away. But at least in that haze of a West Side bar, two people had begun to agree on something terrible that one had done to the other and to know its truth. Two people—the one a mystery to the other still, the other a mystery to himself. . . .

• • •

Hardly an act of love, then, men's sexual abuse of children does violence to them and has at the core of its meaning the *wish* to do harm. For men such as Carter Pritchard, sex is the form his destructiveness takes. And for victims such as Molly, it is her sexuality, and the love and trust expressed in it, that is most at risk. For other men, the aggression is more direct, the physical destruction more palpable—though for them, too, their sexual manhood is also at risk. But this takes us to fathers such as Christy Davies and sons such as his boy, Pat, and to the next and final chapter of *The Male Paradox*.

15

...

Sins of the Fathers: Abuse

Men's aggressivity, unfamiliarity with children, and deep doubts about their masculinity make them vulnerable, moving them to brutalize their sons and sometimes their daughters. When the abusive father doesn't get what he wants (which is often the case), he avenges himself with a fury too dangerous to express toward a worthier adversary—an equal, a superior, or simply the forces of nature and society over which this petty tyrant in his own poor home has little or no control. His helpless children then bear the brunt of his cruel quest for power and the fears that drive it.

And what are the effects on his dependents of a father's "intimate violence"?

Far from being beaten into submission, these kids get mad and turn bad instead. They can't concentrate and so fail in school. They present disciplinary problems. They commit crimes—such as stealing. Later on, they may torture their offspring. Above all else, they fight. They spend their lives fighting—people and property, at home and in school, on the streets, and eventually within the homes of the families they in turn produce.

In fact, there resides in the heart of every parent on whom a

little child depends for his very survival the impulse toward filicide. All men, and men especially, want to live and prevail forever. And to the extent that they don't see themselves living
through their legacy, they are moved to subdue or even murder
those destined to take their place in life.

Thus, like incest, the more crude forms of child abuse serve to
remind us about the unwanted truths of every man's heart. The
derivatives of a father's hostility toward his children are to be
found everywhere: in the demands authorities make for absolute
obedience and devotion; in the imperiousness of parents who try
to dictate their children's lives; in the resistance of the older generation to change, and sometimes simply to truth; in the readiness
of old men to send young ones to war; in the murderous "envy,"
as Freud put it years later, having discovered the "dreaded impulse" in himself, the "envy of those who are growing old for
youth." Above all, the reciprocal rivalry between fathers and sons
colors men's dealings with one another, calling up the specter of
self-serving violence each time males of any age and relationship
to one another get together.

And so it was that Pat Davies found himself sprawled on the
gym floor of Great Neck Elementary School.

    • • •

Pat had stared over his fist at the knuckles and signet ring rock-
eting toward him. When he thought about it afterward, he realized that he could have blocked that punch. Maybe. But he didn't.
It was as if Pat had welcomed Stein's fist into his face. Even before
he could feel or see the damage, Pat had known somehow what
had been done to him. His head and neck snapped back from the
impact, and his feet shot out from under him, landing him on his
coccyx and expelling the air from his lungs.

Sprawled there, he remained conscious through the spinning
images spiraling through the sudden haze. Ironically, it was his
backside that hurt first. As the fragments of impressions coalesced
back into whole forms, the room and the people in it regaining
their meaning, Pat stared down at his shirtfront and lap. Red
rained down on him, blood pouring out with a relentlessness he
couldn't even have imagined. In the hot liquid he saw little white
bits, fragments. Oh, shit, his teeth!

And before he felt anything like pain, nature having numbed
him to absorb the blow, Pat staggered to his wobbly feet and
lurched toward the locker room. There, above the sink, a mirror

told him what happened. The right half of his upper lip was hanging by a ribbon of flesh, torn off, he realized, by the ring. The canine behind it had been smashed in half. His gums were bleeding profusely.

It was then that the injury began to throb, jolting Pat with agony and terror. Awash with blood and tears, he rushed out of the bathroom. He overheard himself through the daze, weeping and wailing just like a child, he noted afterward, like a little kid having a temper tantrum.

Stein stood before him, fists lowered but still threatening, ready for more if necessary—as if waiting for the ref to count out his vanquished opponent. Except that when Pat hurled a folding metal chair at him, he did nothing—nothing except to make a gesture of dodging the projectile, which had in fact missed its mark by that proverbial mile.

Pat Davies had hit Stein's kid. Eric had run into the woods behind the playing field earlier this hot July day, and when Pat, charged with his supervision, had come to fetch him, the seven-year-old boy, giggling from his perch in a birch tree, had poured Orangina on his counselor's head. Pat had yanked him down, scraping the boy's thigh against the branches as he did so. He'd slapped him twice across the face, pulling down his shorts to add two whacks for good measure across his backside. It was all over in a minute.

No broken noses, just a black eye. "But 'twas enough," or so the Bard might say, " 'twould serve!"

For vengeance. The wounded father had burst from his office to his home in the moments following the phone call and from there to the school grounds in which the summer day camp was also housed. He'd swept past the director and counselors and into the gym where, he was told, the "punk" was to be found.

He'd insulted Pat, hoping to provoke the first blow. Happily, the "mick" had lunged at him to no effect. Now they'd all have to live with the results.

The visible results—because for Pat it had begun long ago behind closed doors.

• • •

In 1962, Henry Kempe, in collaboration with Brandt Steele and others, described "the battered-child syndrome." They called the attention of schools, health-care professionals, and a growing number of local and federal agencies to a crime of more than epidemic proportions. Hidden from view for so long, "intimate violence," as it has been called, now became an object of all eyes—legal, journalistic, sociological, and professional.

Based on a variety of differing criteria, estimates on child abuse have ranged from half a million to 4 million incidents per year. Perhaps most revealing—certainly more so than studies making use of abuse reports after the fact—are the family violence surveys conducted by Gelles and Straus in 1975 and then a decade later, in 1985. These researchers showed that physical violence toward children could not be considered apart from a context of aggression within the whole family (including sibling violence, abuse of the elderly, etc.). They also found that the nation's growing awareness of child and wife battering had had an impact in reducing their incidence during the ten-year span between their surveys.

Still, in 1975 and to a lesser degree in 1985, roughly 3.5 percent of the parents who responded to their questionnaires reported that they had committed an unmistakably abusive act toward their children that year. And this excludes the myriad instances of what these parents might call "normal discipline."

All this says nothing about who does the beating. With their children as with their wives, men have stopped battering as much as they used to, more fearful as they are of the public eye. In contrast, the numbers of assaults on their own bodies and sometimes their very lives by the women and children in the house have remained constant or maybe even increased in the last decade. Husbands are somewhat more apt to be hit by their spouses, Straus and Gelles discovered, and fathers are the most likely of all to be murdered by their children.

Figures from other studies—and these seem fairly consistent—have slightly more mothers and women in general beating young children than their male conterparts. How does this finding square with the image of the domineering male ready to erupt in violence toward his dependents? Well, who, after all, spends more time with children? Women, of course.

The trends may have changed somewhat over the years of the so-called new fatherhood, but in the 1970s developmental psychologists observing father-child interactions found that most male parents spent only minutes, sometimes just seconds, a day with their offspring. Usually it's mothers who take care of the kids all the time, mothers whose nerves can be worn thin, exposing their resentment toward those who need them.

So, men are around kids much less than the children's mothers, but when they are, they're far more prone to strike out. According to one report, for instance, 42 percent of the children abused were beaten by men, who have so little to do with them, while another 48 percent were assaulted by women, with 10 percent unaccounted for. Typically it's a father or maybe a father substitute (a stepfather or boyfriend) who does the damage. And while abusive mothers are less discriminating, when it comes to paternal violence, it's boys who more often than not are the butts of their fathers' rage.

The demographics are only a prologue to the whole story, of course. Once more it's up to the psychologists to ask the whys and hows of child abuse. Why would a man *want* to crush his kid? And how could he bring himself to act on such an impulse?

While it's by no means an invariant pattern, many of these men are unemployed, immature, miserable, otherwise dejected souls, angry at the world for their downtrodden lot in life. They have no one to blame for their failures, no one on whom to exact their revenge—except the innocent children who happen across their aimless paths. Abusive fathers of all stripes—classes, races, social setting—attack their children because they themselves feel inferior. They make a last-ditch attempt to achieve an illusion of mastery through causing pain and fear—through *sadism*. It's the oldest trick in the books, and one of the worst around.

Psychoanalyst Brandt Steele, one of Kempe's collaborators, has profiled these men, to the extent that they lend themselves to generalizations. Some child abusers are clearly psychologically "sick," psychotic or pervasively sociopathic. But not all fall under these headings of severe psychopathology.

Most men can act pretty aggressively, after all. Indeed, the one consistently demonstrable sex difference, borne out in research study after study, is that the males of our species are more aggressive in their behavior. And many abusive fathers are *young* still, jolted by the male hormone, testosterone, untried and unaffirmed, unsure of themselves, and prone therefore to prove their masculinity. Many are not yet mellowed out, except perhaps with the help of drugs, Steele continues.

What most child abusers have in common are some of the following characteristics: an uncertain sense of identity; poor self-esteem, sometimes compensated for in exaggerated displays of self-assurance; feelings of emptiness and mistrust; social isolation and the sense of being persecuted; a lack of empathy; and as if to rationalize their abiding rage and proneness to violent behavior, a moralistic conviction in the value of corporal punishment.

Others have taken issue with the assertion that most child abusers were themselves abused by their parents, or at least with the inevitability of "generational transmission." Steele argues that the vast majority of these men have "identified with the aggressor" who humiliated, hurt, and enraged them when they were too small to fight back. They *project* images of themselves onto their children and act as their parents did. Whatever their resolve may have been to the contrary, they end up aggressing against them after all.

From a different perspective, unconsciously they confuse and even at times reverse roles with their children. They see in them their parents reincarnate, the parents who failed and hurt them, the ones who should now take care of them. Such fathers expect more of them than any little boy (maybe girl) is capable of. And they come down brutally on kids when they fail to measure up to the adult standards that are beyond the parents themselves. They are ruthless and unforgiving in meting out their unjust justice. Without knowing it, these men are also punishing their parents each time they attack a child.

Once again, the secret is that it's the father who "won't grow up." Underlying the picture he presents of imperious cruelty, behind the tyranny lurks his image of himself as puny and damaged, hardly a man at all. Because of this, such a man and his child are particularly at risk when a father is slighted by another adult or by the more impersonal misfortunes his flesh is heir to. It is then that he comes to expect redress in the unwavering and unwarranted respect from the child. His child should reward him as others fail to do and be his far better *alter ego*. And when the child doesn't, he gets punished.

The abusive father thus resembles the "authoritarian personality" described by psychologists—submissive to his masters, oppressive to his subordinates. Only more so.

Many of these men drink. And a good number also molest their children sexually. So they have much in common with incestuous fathers. Yet there are notable divergences.

Actually, many purely physically abusive fathers tend to deny themselves and their children any pleasure in life, and their wanton cruelty—perhaps the one arena in which, ironically, they grant themselves satisfaction of any sort—can go hand in hand with a reflexive moralizing when it comes to sensuality. They have little time for pleasures of the flesh, and their children shouldn't either. Not all, of course, but many.

Finally, as I've noted in the previous chapter on sexual violation, men have a harder time bonding to their children than do women and are less tuned in to their feelings and needs. And to repeat myself here, acting on violence seems to be more in their nature than in a woman's. So it doesn't take quite so much to trigger a destructive outburst in any father when compared with a mother.

Fathers must rely on their morality and "access their tenderness" to restrain themselves. But some men, abusive men, may fear that feelings and displays of affection toward a child will only further unman them. So when they are tempted by such love, they strike out defensively to achieve distance and mastery. They hit rather than hug in order to prove to themselves that they are men, after all.

And so it was with Christy Davies.

• • •

"You fuckin' little shit, you asshole," Christy Davies snarled, "How could you be so dumb to do a thing like that?" And menacing as usual, he raised the back of his hand to strike out at his son. In a rare moment of restraint, however, confronted with the picture of the face before him, a face almost cut in half, the "elder" Davies—actually a mere thirty-nine, a kid himself still—re-aimed his assault, smacking instead the less fragile shoulder to the right of it.

Pat shivered with relief. Not that he imagined it was anything like compassion that had stayed his father's arm. No, he thought to himself. It was the specter of the lawsuits he was probably savoring, and he didn't want to mess up the evidence. Either this, or the bastard was scared that with his son in the public eye now, he'd get caught in the act at last. But hit him or not, how much had Pat come to hate him!

Aching and maimed, out of commission for a month or more, Pat looked up at his angry father and back on their growing up together. It had always been like this, he thought. Always the pain—till he'd finally gone numb.

Stein's crushing blow had done more physical damage than the whole of his father's clumsy battering over the years, the scars on his skin from these assaults having faded and flattened out with time. But it hadn't hit his heart as hard. Indeed, Pat had felt oddly relieved in having been bludgeoned, as if the whole family's guilt were being expiated by this one act of a father's just revenge.

Not so, Christy's assaults. They had driven into him, penetrating him with a virulence that he then made his own. Far from being cowed, Pat had finally turned bitter and hostile. The little kid with the tousled hair and puckish face had hardened over the years of innocence lost early, breaking his own laws now. Beating his son, Christy had gotten inside him.

It seemed as if there hadn't been one day in his life, one hour, when Christy hadn't hit him. Rationally, Pat—who was far less dumb than he tried to be—realistically, he knew that this couldn't quite be true. His mother and older sister had further told him that Dad —"Dad"?— hadn't abused him until Pat was four and a half. It was then that Christopher Davies lost the job of his life.

Christy had gotten himself kicked off the force. Like his father before him, Brendan Davies, no saint in his day but eventually a police captain in Chicago, he had been a cop. As a kid himself, Christy had migrated all the way to Long Island to escape the shadow of competition and control of his father, only, five years later, to do himself in. "Drinking on the job," "excessive force," and last but not least those "hints of extortion" that brought Internal Affairs nosing around had been the accumulating sequence that culminated in his dismissal.

Life had never been the same after that. Not that home had been great to begin with, but now it took a quantum leap beyond worse. In fact, Davies probably ended up making more money selling cars than he ever could have as a cop. But his spirit was slashed, the gashes salted by his father's "told ya so's." Between the oddly eloquent lines of his father's letters, Christy could picture the splotchy face purpled with rage, the invectives spewing from Brendan Davies's distended lips, the gaze that never saw him but left him filled with hatred and loathing nonetheless.

The letters arrived from Chicago in roughly monthly bursts of venom until the oldest Davies died of liver cancer at fifty-two—old and dead before his time, looking like the bum he was at last! Yes, Christy had his own scars to contend with. The sins of the fathers, the first book said.

Brendan Davies died, and Christy's beatings of Patty had gotten worse. His wife had tried to get in the middle of her men. But smacked herself for her efforts at intervening, Mary soon retreated to the background, nursing her son's wounds after the fact. Besides, when she showed Patty love, his father got even hotter, hotter than hell.

He was jealous, she came to see, an overgrown kid himself, too young to be a real father—why had she rushed him?—and too possessive of the wife who was servant and mother to him. And this at least was his house. Here nobody could kick him out.

Mostly, the attacks were rationalized as discipline. Pat had done something wrong and "deserved" to have the "badness" beat out of him. Which was bad enough. But worse still, sometimes the father's violence was gratuitous. Causing pain pleased him.

At five years old, Patty would walk into a room and trip over an outstretched leg. At seven, he'd been forced into a boxing lesson. Or at nine, having been caught smoking a cigarette the week before, he'd be "smoked" by that cigarette himself. It'd be crushed out on his scalp, searing him until his skin smelled like a hot dog on a grill. But beneath the hair, so nobody could see. And on and on the torture went, monotonously horrifying.

And still Pat loved his father. Even as his initial promise in school dimmed and the social trouble started, the boy hungered for the man, pursuing him like a little puppy. Once Pat sneaked upstairs and into his father's bedroom closet where he found the blue hat and empty holster (no badge, no gun anymore, thank God), all of which he put on. But boy, did he get it for that.

It was only at fourteen that his rebellion found its true target. Once or twice, Pat had thought of hitting Christy back or just talking back, but stopped himself from doing it. Instead, he didn't do anything. Anything, that is, his father asked. Or better, he only did what his father did.

So Pat didn't study. He drank. He did some cocaine. He fought. The kid with the 125 IQ dropped out, came back, and while his nursery-school classmates began their college careers, found himself a high school (rather than a college) junior grudgingly taking advantage of a second chance to right himself. But at least he was trying now, trying to reclaim a life.

His uncle had gotten him this summer job as part of the younger Davies's resuscitation program. And for three weeks he'd done okay—more than okay actually. Pat liked kids, he realized. He had a short fuse still, and they could get on his nerves. But he liked them and wanted to do well by them. He had been a good jock and knew how to teach. It's just that that spoiled little Stein brat was too much. The day before, his father, Big Stu himself, Great Neck's Little Big Man, had come to cheer on the kid in his baseball game. In his BMW 750i. Eric's father was always there. Hovering. Kissing and loving.

The Stein kid wasn't any too good at that sort of thing, either—at sports. But when he managed to hit the rag ball off the batting tee, the old Yid—Christy's kind of word, drummed into Pat from the time he was little Stein's age—went wild with cheering. It was revolting, embarrassing. And what about the other little guys? The brat didn't deserve it. And for a fleeting instant, Pat saw later, he'd felt jealous. He would've wanted a dad like that. Unconditional love instead of unconditional hate.

Anyhow, the next day, the boy had run wild. Pat had chased Eric into the bushes with all the other kids clamoring and running about. It was three forty-five P.M. and school buses were waiting in the lot to reclaim the campers, and here was Pat, like some oversized sissy nursemaid, rushing about and screaming for the kid helplessly. And he'd gotten dumped on, too, literally.

There was an instant after he looked up into that tree before he pulled the boy down from it. There he was, himself, staring back down—"I mean me, looking at myself," Pat later told his counselor, Mrs. Dolly Goldsmith, a social worker at Long Island Jewish Hospital. It was as if he had become Christy all of a sudden—just like that, crazy. Now it was Pat who went wild. He'd had his share of fights, but he'd never hit a kid that little before.

"Identifications with the aggressor" are like that, Dolly's supervisor, Dr. Sylvia Watson, had told her. They're sudden, compulsive, and yes, oh *so* complicated underneath. It had all started at least two generations ago when Captain Brendan Davies went on the rampage.

And then Stein again, an avenging angel, a Jew, now he ran amok. No, Pat reflected, he may even have let him get that punch through—at least in its full force. But who could've known! Dad, who could have known? Who could have known an old kike could hit so hard?

. . .

Spare the rod, spoil the child? Hardly so. Not for Patty Davies. Yes, discipline is necessary in rearing a child. But as far as a growing conscience is concerned, in the end love proves to be the most effective weapon. Children have to *want* to love parents and be loved by them if they are to live up to ideals and demands that become increasingly their own, developing a superego. When a parent tries forcibly to co-opt the superego's job, it's counterproductive. He or she nips an unfolding conscience in the bud, so to speak, squelching a child's moral development. Like spinach or liver, it's hard for a kid to take in what he or she hates. Abuse tastes bad, and it can't be consumed as readily as care and love. The child comes to rebel all the more against anything that, in his mind, smacks of oppression. At best, he or she swallows the aggressive parent wholesale without digesting him, without quite making the aggressor with whom he's identified his own. Plagued by a foreign body, a pernicious psychological parasite, he becomes sick for life.

Psychoanalysts call these ugly little beings inside people "bad introjects." They resemble demons that are very difficult to exorcise indeed. They're not real—not flesh and blood or supernatural spirits. They're imagined. But in a way that only makes matters worse. Introjects can't be found and removed.

It's this failure to integrate a set of internal ideals along with the rage evoked that end up making the victim of abuse both so unsure of himself and so unable to contain his own violence. Chronically stressed, living in internal and often external disarray, he falls apart all too easily, erupting in anger. And given what he's been through, why should he be moved to do otherwise?

At war with memory and the bad dad inside him, a boy and later a man like this is always getting himself into trouble. Aware of how their parents have savaged them, victims of parental violence, like incest survivors, try to forget what has happened to them. But they can't help remembering—sometimes in neurotic symptoms, but most often in destructive actions that look simply impulsive to the outside observer. Momentarily forgetting where all the violence comes from, the abused son strikes out at people, at everybody he can, as if they were the father who had violated him. And he does so in ways and in circumstances that further often invite retaliation. Apparently remorseless, "sociopaths" such as these—defined as such because they are asocial and lack a reliable conscience—replace the tensions of felt guilt, restraint, and inner torment with external action and consequent conflict. They "act out."

In the act of violence, the abuse victim identifies himself with both his tyrant father and the object of his aggression, his victim. Having injured his symbolic or would-be self, the angry young man such as Patty then adds a double whammy to the destruction and self-destruction he has wrought. The authorities—schools, courts, irate parents—come down mercilessly on these sufferers who have made themselves into such obvious criminals.

In so doing, many of these children of violence are also unconsciously protecting the parents they both hate and love by putting themselves in jeopardy. In a certain sense, many of these kids—not all but a goodly number—are closet martyrs. Placing themselves in harm's way once again, sacrificing themselves to safeguard the picture at least of a grossly imperfect parent, they are also acting to reassure themselves that there's still justice in the world after all. Bad guys get what they ask for. And if they behave badly, then they must have deserved what they got from the very beginning.

Even at its most horrible, the abused child's abuse later on serves as an expression of love toward the father who hurt him. First of all, it says "I love you. . . . I love you so much that I will be just like you." Second, it pays homage to the parent's self-esteem: "You were right all along. I was the bad one." And finally, it is testimony to the great Christian edict, namely, "Greater love hath no man than to lay down his life" for another—for his hard father.

While Christy and Pat Davies represent the extremes (alas, the all-too-common extremes), I doubt there's a parent alive who hasn't struck out at his or her children at least once in his or her life out of anger, helplessness, desperation, or fear—and sometimes because he or she must. And we all can't help demoralizing our children now and then. Leading them on. Belittling them. Demonstrating our superiority. Enjoying their littleness and their pretenses at bigness.

Sometimes the violence seems more gratuitous. With men especially, children can provoke attacks that start out as playful but become downright serious as the ante gets upped. Women are appalled by these spectacles, yet even so they can tend to egg them on: "Those men!" (*"Les hommes,"* as Simone declared in Chapter 11, referring to her thirty-year- and six-month-olds!)

Nevertheless, most of us don't aim to break our children's bodies and souls, though we are all of us human. There's a continuum when it comes to aggressive abuses just as there is when we consider the sexual violation of children.

Yet there is a critical point when this intergenerational violence takes a quantum leap into the stark, the unnatural, and the immoral. And this leap occurs when the adult's intent is to injure and to harm, and when this intent is clearly evident in his or her behavior, even though both the perpetrator and the victim along with the world of colluding adults may try to disavow it.

On the other side of the coin, overpermissiveness and bending

over backward to "do anything but" can also have dire consequences. Depriving boys of an important rehearsal for the real
competition of adult life amounts to a sin of omission. Men were
fated to be aggressors, fighters. And fight they must—sometimes
even when it comes to their kids. Otherwise they might just kill
them with kindness.

It was a hard lesson for Stu Stein to learn, the need to "access" his formidable power in setting limits for a son and protecting him in the long run.

• • •

His vengeance spent in that gym, Stein had been horrified at what
he saw before him. Causing harm wasn't in his nature. Not anymore, he'd thought.

In fact, any onlooker, such as the building custodian and
assistant coach who had actually witnessed the event, would have
found the spectacle before him not only frightening but altogether
unlikely. The kid who had been bloodied and was flailing about—
clearly the loser in the duel of the generations—was Black Irish
and big. At nineteen and a half years and six feet two inches, Pat
was in his prime and fit the stereotype of the brawler.

In contrast, Stu Stein, the winner, was at fifty-nine years old
short, bald, and potbellied. He was wearing a gray business suit
and a shirt with a monogram. And the only thing about him now
in disarray were the glasses that had fallen from his face with the
shuddering aftershock of his blow to Pat Davies's jaw.

But had anyone with a sports reporter's eye looked a little
closer, he might have found the telltale signs that swept away
disbelief: the slight indentation at the bottom of the bridge of Stu
Stein's nose where it had absorbed a not dissimilar blow forty
years earlier; the stubby, meaty paws for hands with their ever so
slightly misshapen knuckles; the bulge of the forearms and biceps
that had not dwindled even after the belly had begun to sag. Stu
Stein was not the "pussy" a kid such as Davies might've figured
him for. Far from it, in fact.

At Pat's age, in the Navy, Stu had been a boxer, an achievement he'd regretted until this day. And not for any lack of success,
either. A welterweight at a mere five and a half feet, The Stub had
packed a wallop that was the envy of the taller and heavier men
who trained with him. Predictions had him moving on to the
championship of the armed services and from there, maybe, an
Olympic gold, and perhaps a professional fight career beyond

that. Not bad—for a Jew in a world dominated by immigrants of other nationalities and ethnicities and the first-generation Americans they had produced.

The trouble was, Stu hadn't had the heart for it—not for the hurting. In the quarter finals, he was up against the guy purported to be his most serious competition, Jimmy O'Hara. It was over in the second round. O'Hara had pounced on Stu, finally catching his squat opponent with the right that broke his nose. Staggered temporarily, The Stub had found himself summoning up pictures of the gangs who had tortured his brothers, sisters, and himself as a boy, of the kid who had once nearly raped his sister Ethel, of the tough who had driven an ice pick through his kid brother Amos's hand. Maybe that's why Amie turned out to be such a prick—or so he'd wondered later on.

Stu had reared up from O'Hara's blow and hurled all the anger he and his family had ever had through his shoulder and into his fist and, it seemed, through Jimmy's face. Jimmy hadn't gotten up afterward. Blood poured from his crushed nose while his eyes remained closed, staring, The Stub had imagined, back into his own brain.

Stu had retired his gloves the next day and resolved never to hit anybody ever again in his life. Not that a man such as Stu could simply wipe away either his temper or his wish to win. Suffering her husband's "mouth" no more, his first wife, Lenore, had left after nearly twenty years of driving irritability.

More happily, the pharmacist's mate had become a pharmacist, subsequently upping the ante even further to acquire a chain of drugstores on the Island. He had become a father figure, caretaker to the community, and people as remote as his wife's cousin Jake Mandell were indebted to him as a benefactor.

Stu had married again, and late in life this time, very late, producing a second set of kids, the two of them objects of his tender joy. No punishing for these kids, a boy and a girl, Eric and Jenny, and no hitting either. And he didn't give in. Ever.

And now Stu stood in the gym of one of their schools, just as he had in that ring two generations earlier, and the streets of Brooklyn before that, knee deep in blood and pain. Yes, another kid had fallen. He hated what he had done.

• • •

It seemed that Sunday would never come. But it did. Sinking into the living room sofa at last, Stu was trying to read the Arts and

Leisure section of the paper. Each time he turned a page, however, he caught sight of the scab forming on the second knuckle of
his middle finger. Stu was thinking about the spasms that had
ushered in that weekend and the protracted aftermath no doubt to
follow. He was preoccupied with these images, those just past and
those to come, when Eric jumped him.

For an instant, his perspective dimmed with the thud of pain
and momentary blackness, Stu felt his nose being sliced as his
glasses tumbled from it. Regaining his interrupted consciousness,
he saw two drops of blood on the *Times* before him in his lap.
These were hardly the torrents he had opened up two days earlier,
but once again they were nonetheless enough to tell him that some
violence had been done.

It was Eric's habit these days to bombard his father, yes,
never taking no for an answer. But this time, shod in the precocious baseball spikes his father had bought him, he'd given his old
man a good one indeed. Eric had smacked the unsuspecting Stu
across the bridge of the nose, driving cleats and tortoiseshell into
its flesh and opening a wound that had been made and then
healed a generation ago.

In the instant before he recognized his assailant, Stu found
himself overtaken by the old white heat from within. With a
sweeping gesture of his right arm, he grabbed at the T-shirt beneath a face he didn't see yet and lifted the little-boy-missile from
him. Straight-arming Eric, Stu stared at his son.

Eric's eyes had an undaunted glaze, and the rest of him
seemed frozen into some shivering smirk. It was the look of a kid
who simply feels entitled to do anything he wants even when he
senses that he is wrong somehow. But a kid who's scared of himself, of going too far.

Usually Stu could tolerate being pounced on and invaded
hour after hour by this child. But this time, and under these
circumstances and with the effect of hurting his father there, on
the nose, reminding him of the hurt he had caused on that bratty
kid's behalf—at last it was just too much. And so, to everybody's
surprise in that room, to the shock of wife/mother Sara, sister/
daughter Jennifer, and pet cocker Lady, and not the least that of
father and son, Stu shouted at his son and simply dropped him on
his backside.

"That's enough, Eric!" he yelled. And smacking the boy with
these words of reproach, he then let go—that's all, releasing him
from his grasp. Eric fell the two and one-half feet to the plush

carpet below him. Not enough to smart really or do any damage, but with an unmistakable bump to his rear end that shuddered up into his skull and, hopefully, the mind within. The wind wasn't even knocked out of him. But still Eric looked about him, shocked and indignant. Nobody moved to help him.

Quite the contrary, surprising himself, Stu continued, "Eric, you ought to be ashamed of yourself! Look what you did."

Eric turned from the father, who rose to retrieve the shards of his glasses and clean off his dented and bloodied nose in the bathroom down the hall, and sought redress from his mother instead.

Sara also surprised herself when she continued, "Your father's absolutely right. That was terrible."

"Yeah, terrible, you dunky crap," Jenny chimed in.

And crying, Eric ran to his room.

• • •

Though they may resort to it in order to ward off any felt weakness, most men also hate the violence that comes with their being male. They're prone to buy into sexual stereotypes. And so they are apt to see themselves as loutish and cruel just because they are who they are, men—who are moved to possess and protect their boundaries and their turf. And seeing themselves so, they may act out of guilt to unman themselves.

When in particular, a child, especially a boy child and potential competitor, threatens or invades these domains, he evokes even in the most loving father the impulse to fight back—and to the death, if necessary. That is, if he is to prevail in his basic territorial claims, his right to life itself. This survival impulse is immediate, instinctive, swift, and ruthless. It is checked mainly by the forces of guilt, love, and common sense. And at times, by a certain defensive posturing of a different kind: the tendency of certain fathers is to submit, overindulge, surrender their authority.

A man such as Stu, for instance, fearful of his own strength, retreats in the face of his son's inevitable challenge to his authority. As sure of his strength as he is of himself, such a man has no need or desire to oppress his boy. At times, out of love he just lets himself be used as a punching bag. Moreover, he wants to give himself over to his son and heir, to make life easy for him—too easy. He can even find himself acting like a "woman."

Frightened of abusing Eric, Stu ends up depriving him and

leaving him at risk. He fails to set limits. And he omits to offer a true-to-life testing ground for confrontations in the real world, rehearsals that might provide his young son with a more accurate measure of himself. If he had thought about it harder, Stu might also have recognized just how much toughing it out—instead of riding the crest of a parent's achievement—had helped him out in life. Helped him grow strong, resilient, realistic.

Patty thus became Eric's and Stu's avenging angel, providing a rude awakening for son and father alike. But Patty's father's awakening, Christy's recognition of his impotence, proved to be ruder by far.

• • •

On this his forty-first birthday, Christopher Davies glowered at his twenty-one-year-old son, Patrick, with whom he shared the anniversary of their coming into being. That generation ago, "she, that bitch," his wife, Mary, had spent the day birthing her whelp on what should have been celebrated as his first birthday of their married life. Instead of Christy's poking it into her, that kid of his had stuck his head out of her twat and said, "Hello, world, here I am! And by the way, move over, Pops!"

Stupid maybe, but Christy had never forgiven either of them for the coincidence. He'd never bought "all that stuff about Pat's being my gift, like she said." So now he stared down the younger man across the half-eaten cake, his sights seizing on the white web across Pat's upper lip. Over a year old now, the scar had come to remind Davies of an affront to his person, his family honor, his father's heritage, the "race" itself.

Undaunted, the son returned the father's fierceness in a feral and unrelenting look of his own. Maybe it was the girl who now loved him whose presence gave him new courage. Chutzpah, Gloria called it. Yeah, she was Jewish! Having been distracted by his images of her, Patty tuned in at last to his father's voice as it hammered into his ears. "No," he answered. "No!"

"What do you mean 'no'? You gonna let that aging beanie boy slap you around and get away with it? Besides that, and your mother's grief, we've had fifteen thousand dollars plus in surgical and dental bills."

"The insurance paid—"

"Eighty percent—"

"Stop it, damn it. You can just eat the rest!" Pat gestured toward the cake.

Christy found himself shocked, stunned. Never before, no matter how wild he'd run, had the boy spoken to him like that. So, once again, reflexively he raised his arm to strike.

No words now. In silence, Pat simply reached out to meet it, grabbing Christy by the wrist, staying the forearm. He had grown stronger than his father, they both realized, as he pushed his father's oncoming blow back slowly into a crooked elbow of helpless surrender. For a moment, Christy tried to struggle, to wriggle free, but relented in the face of greater force—as, indeed, he always had.

Pat looked at the overwrought and small-minded man before him. All those years, he'd been so awed by the pummelings, and he thought, all evidence to the contrary, that they had something to do with him. What he did or was. Even that he deserved them. Now he saw that his father, a kid himself when Pat was born, was simply striking out at everybody bigger than he was. It wasn't only Pat whom Christy'd been beating up but the Steins, the Jews, the rich and the famous, the higher-ups all over. All those "others" who towered over him, who in the end were simply stand-ins for *his* father, the commander who had cowed him.

Nobody was human in any of this violence, Pat saw. They were all things. Furniture to be broken. Even the enemies weren't people, just objects of destruction to a guy like his father. And Pat realized, he himself wasn't a person either. Like other races and religions, Pat wasn't human. Yeah, the whole of Christy's world, victims and persecutors alike, merely existed as figments of his violent imagination.

Time to get out of it.

"No, I'm not gonna sue or anything, and now that I'm legally my own man you can't either—on my behalf. And no, you're never going to hit me again."

Pat hesitated and added, "You see, Dad, Stein's more powerful than you. More powerful in spades. Through and through. I want my chance. I need him. In fact, I want his guilt and his goodwill. And one reason you've been hitting me is you got nothing to give."

Christy sat back, silenced. He watched his son's back recede as he walked away, and then he watched the door close behind him. A roach ambled out from under the kitchen table.

And he crushed it.

• • •

These Christys and Pats—they're the sad truths of our times. Throughout history, across cultures and in myths and legends, men have always murdered those they should have loved. As I have said in earlier chapters, the Greeks, whose mythology is our Western heritage, were no strangers to filicide. Maybe we remember more easily those instances when ambitious sons rose up to overthrow the fathers and tyrants who stood between them and the throne. Yet each such rebellion was foretold in the older generation's earlier and usually successful attempts to contain or even kill off the rivals they had fathered.

King Oedipus is perhaps the most famous patricide of all. However, like Sigmund Freud himself when he first interpreted the myth at the turn of the century, we still tend to remember only that Oedipus killed his father and married his mother. We forget what led up to these crimes on the son's part, to his acts of vengeance.

Oedipus the King, paradigmatic parricide of the Western world, also figures as its prototypical victim of child abuse on the part of the man credited with "inverting pederasty." The universality of the son's story and the "complex" named after him tells us that, like incest, filicide is everywhere.

There is one myth that expresses *The Male Paradox*. And this one must be told, retold, before coming to a conclusion.

• • •

In his analysis of Sophocles' tragedy in *The Interpretation of Dreams*, Freud described how Oedipus' relentless inquiry has revealed that the evils that initially seem to lie outside himself really reside within. Having learned that a plague befalling the city of Thebes will be lifted once the murderer of King Laius has been found and banished, Oedipus begins his inquiry, hoping to conquer the truth as he did so many years ago when he solved the riddle of the Sphinx and rid Thebes of her reign of terror and thereby won his queen and throne. However, to his horror the king now discovers that it is he who has slain King Laius, who further proves to be his father—he who has married his mother, Queen Jocasta.

The Greek hero is Everyman, Freud went on. Like the patient in an analysis who starts out blaming others, ultimately he finds himself. Freud concluded that, like all men, Oedipus is guilty— either of actual misdeeds, or as with ordinary men, of sins of the heart. Psychologically, it doesn't much matter which; reality and psychic reality. Except that it does.

Blinding and exiling himself, Oedipus punishes himself hideously. He berates his dead mother for abandoning and seducing him. But he says nothing about the guilt of the father whom he has killed. Yet, is he, as this paradigmatic patricidal son, the only or even the central culprit in this family tragedy? Not when one thinks about it, certainly not when one knows the whole story.

Having heard the terrible prophecy that his son would kill him and then replace him in his wife's bed, it was Laius, the adult, who had first acted to set the tragedy in motion. It was Laius who, fearful of being a lover of a woman and becoming a father of a son, Laius who refused to have sex with his wife. That is, until she got him drunk one night and conceived with him their "avenging angel" of a son. It was he who commanded that Jocasta hand her infant over to a servant, who then pierced his feet (Oedipus means swollen or club foot) and left him to die. It was Laius, the premeditated and would-be infanticide, who later added insult to injury by trying to drive the adolescent boy off the road, grazing his already crippled foot with the wheel of his chariot.

Rising to the challenge and killing his father, Oedipus the son reacted out of preordained, or as the psychoanalyst would say, an "unconscious" vengeance toward the man who had ironically made himself a stranger to his son. Even strangers—the servants who rescue him from the mountainside and the king and queen of Corinth who adopt the foundling—even they prove to have been more paternal than Oedipus' own parents. In the end, blinded and cast out again, Oedipus must depend on his daughter Antigone to care for him.

Moreover, as texts other than Sophocles' play reveal, not only had King Laius tried to have his baby boy killed, not only had he tried to run down his teenage son. Laius had originally been condemned because as a displaced prince fleeing from the uncle who had usurped his dead father's throne, he had kidnapped and sodomized Chrysippus, the young son of his host and protector, King Pelops. Pelops joined with Queen Hera in condemning Laius, decreeing that Chrysippus would be avenged by another young boy, none other than Laius' as yet unborn son. Oedipus' later rebellion was thus an inevitable response to his father's pederasty and to his tyranny—to Laius' sexual exploitation of other children and to the attempted murder of his son and heir. No wonder Laius failed to solve the Sphinx's riddle, failed to understand that man is mortal and must be moral, that he can't always get what he wants.

Thus *Oedipus Rex* is an allegory not only of parricide but of intergenerational rivalry. As it had earlier in Freud's early theory, the Oedipus myth again sheds light on the dealings between real-life fathers and sons. To Freud's Oedipus complex there has to be added a "Laius complex." The son's terrifying patricidal wishes find a counterpart in his father's even more horrifying urges to commit pederasty and filicide—the impulses not of a weak little boy but of a grown and powerful man. Male aggression is reciprocal and deadly serious.

As I've said, such aggression isn't all that terrible at times—a father's need to aggress against his sons and daughters. People have a way of making a virtue of necessity, and the normal as well as "sick" influences on a child's emotional development of the "Laius complex" are many. They range from the exciting games that fathers play with toddlers and that help them to escape the mother's softer and more enveloping hold—the scaring, chasing, the pretend fighting—to forthright paternal discipline, to outright and often bizarre acts of violence. And as Stu's sins of omission reveal, bending over backward not to be tough can be a form of paternal deprivation. Boys need their fathers' toughness to get away from their mother and to prepare for real life. For better and for worse, endowed in this way, a father serves as the "disruptive caretaker."

A hard lesson to learn.

And behind it all lies that other elemental fear of a father for himself and for his son. The fear of loving each other, that is, and in this love, of being left womanly. Or ambiguous and monstrous like the Sphinx herself. The fear of love of any kind. The other inner battle of the male sex, the fight to remain a man.

Conclusion:
The Pleasure in Paradox

Men, most of all, want to be men. And they think they want a simple formula to tell them what makes a man. Such a formula may help guide a boy as he grows up and tries to become a man. But what I have learned is that in the long run there is no simple formula, no truthful role model, and that tenaciously holding on to a spurious ideal is itself the single greatest impediment for men to become men. It hinders them from knowing and thus having what they truly want.

In the preceding chapters I have tried to describe what men want and don't want, what they think they want, what they think they ought to be. I am myself struck by the repeating patterns of self-deception, the repeating need to deny what is disturbing in themselves, what is contradictory, strange, and mysterious. In denying ambiguity and mystery, men become alienated from themselves. They fall prey to illness and are prone to accept the most life-denying and self-annihilating stereotypes.

Men, I have found and as I've attempted to show, struggle against two felt dangers—the danger of succumbing to their feminine nature and the danger of affirming their masculine integrity through repeated acts of aggression. What leads men to discomfort and disease is not the struggles themselves but rather that they define these struggles as life-threatening contests. They need to win them. They feel they must banish femininity in themselves, must assert themselves aggressively. If they could define these struggles not as contests but as play, they would be far more comfortable and content. If they could allow their femininity to take them over from time to time without fearing they were becoming "pussies," if they could allow their aggression full and well-directed expression when necessary without fearing they were becoming "killers," they would lead fuller, happier lives.

Being an accomplished lover and becoming a successful father, the fullest expressions of a man's masculinity, require that he use both his identification with a woman and his full masculine power. Loving and fathering call upon him simultaneously to succumb to another and to assert himself. To please a woman and to raise a child he must use both parts of himself. And the more at ease he is with both parts of himself, the more pleasure he will give a woman and the greater love and power he will impart to a child. The more whole he will feel, and the more content, as a man, he will be.

Toward this end, I have tried to describe the ambiguity and paradox that are at the heart of all men's maleness and by so doing make paradox familiar and, I hope, acceptable to men. I have tried to warn men of the dangers of the comfort of stereotypes, which seduce them with easy choices but finally rob them of their full humanity and happiness. It is my hope to make men more comfortable with themselves (and thus more comfortable for women and children to be with). I want to reassure them that all men's lives are filled with mystery and contradiction, that they are not alone. I want men to experience the mystery and variety in their maleness and find pleasure in paradox.

A Selected Bibliography

Bergmann, Martin S. *The Anatomy of Loving*. New York: Columbia University Press, 1987.

Blos, Peter. *On Adolescence*. New York: Free Press, 1962.

————. *Son and Father: Before and Beyond the Oedipus Complex*. New York: Free Press, 1985.

Blumstein, P., and P. Schwartz. *American Couples*. New York: Morrow, 1983.

Bly, Robert. *Iron John: A Book About Men*. New York: Addison-Wesley, 1990.

Brazelton, T. Berry. *Toddlers and Parents*. New York: Delacorte Press, 1974.

————. *Doctor and Child*. New York: Delacorte Press, 1976.

Cath, S., A. Gurwitt, and J. Ross, eds. *Father and Child*. Boston: Little, Brown, 1982.

Erikson, Erik. *Childhood and Society.* 2nd ed. New York: Norton 1950, 1963.

Farrell, Warren. *Why Men Are the Way They Are.* New York: Mc-Graw Hill, 1986.

Freud, Sigmund. "Some Psychical Consequences of the Anatomical Distinction Between the Sexes" (1925). *Standard Edition,* vol. 19. London: Hogarth Press, 1961, pp. 243–58.

Gay, Peter. *Freud: A Life for Our Time.* New York: Norton, 1988.

Gelles, Richard J., and Murray A. Straus. *Intimate Violence.* New York: Simon & Schuster, 1988.

Herman, Judith. *Father-Daughter Incest.* Cambridge, Mass.: Harvard University Press, 1981.

Hite, Shere. *The Hite Report: A Nationwide Study of Female Sexuality.* New York: Dell, 1981.

———. *The Hite Report on Male Sexuality.* New York: Dell, 1986.

Kakar, Sudhir, and John Ross. *Tales of Love, Sex and Danger.* New York: Basil Blackwell, 1988.

Kernberg, Otto. "Mature Love: Prerequisites and Characteristics." *Journal of the American Psychoanalytic Association* 22 (1974): 743–68.

Kinsey, A. C., W. B. Pomeroy, and C. E. Martin. *Sexual Behavior in the Human Male.* Philadelphia: W. B. Saunders, 1948.

Levine, J. *Who Will Raise the Children? New Options for Fathers (and Mothers).* Philadelphia: J. B. Lippincott, 1976.

Levinson, D. J., C. N. Darrow, E. B. Klein, M. H. Levinson, and B. McKee. *The Seasons of a Man's Life.* New York: Knopf, 1978.

Lewes, Kenneth. *The Psychoanalytic Theory of Male Homosexuality.* New York: Simon & Schuster, 1988.

Maccoby, E., and C. Jacklin. *The Psychology of Sex Differences.* Stanford, Calif.: Stanford University Press, 1974.

Malcolm, Janet. *Psychoanalysis: The Impossible Profession.* New York: Knopf, 1981.

Nemiroff, R. "A Review of Adult Development." In R. Nemiroff, *Race Against Time.* New York: Plenum, 1985, pp. 11–24.

Osherson, S. *Finding Our Fathers: The Unfinished Business of Manhood.* New York: Free Press, 1986.

Person, Ethel. *Dreams of Love and Fateful Encounters.* New York: Norton, 1988.

Ross, John Munder. "The Development of Paternal Identity: A Critical Review of the Literature on Nurturance and Generativity in Boys and Men." *Journal of the American Psychoanalytic Association* 23 (1975): 783–817.

————. "Toward Fatherhood: The Epigenesis of Paternal Identity During a Boy's First Decade." *International Review of Psycho-Analysis* 4 (1977): 327–47.

————. "Fathering: A Review of Some Psychoanalytic Contributions on Paternity." *International Journal of Psycho-Analysis* 60 (1979): 317–27.

————. "Oedipus Revisited: Laius and the Laius Complex." In A. Solnit et al., eds., *The Psychoanalytic Study of the Child*, vol. 37. New Haven, Conn.: Yale University Press, 1982, pp. 169–200.

————. "Beyond the Phallic Illusion." In R. Liebert et al., eds., *The Psychology of Men*. New York: Basic Books, 1986.

————. "The Darker Side of Fatherhood." *International Journal of Psychoanalytic Psychotherapy* 11 (1986): 117–44.

————. "The Eye of the Beholder." In C. Colarusso and R. Nemiroff, eds., *New Dimensions of Adult Development*. San Diego, Calif.: University of California Press, 1990.

Sheehy, Gail. *Passages*. New York: Dutton, 1976.

Stoller, Robert. *Sex and Gender*. New York: Science House, 1968.

————. *Sexual Excitement*. New York: Pantheon, 1979.

Stump, Jane Barr. *What's the Difference? How Men and Women Compare*. New York: Morrow, 1985.

Tross, Susan. "Psychosocial Concomitants of Survival From Adult Onset Testicular Cancer." Ph.D. diss., Ferkauf Graduate School, Yeshiva University, New York, 1983.

Vaillant, George E. *Adaptation to Life*. Boston: Little, Brown, 1977.

Wallerstein, Judith, and Sandra Blakeslee. *Second Chances: Men, Women & Children a Decade After Divorce*. New York: Ticknor & Fields, 1989.

Index

About the Author

A practicing clinician, John Munder Ross has been a pioneer in the study of men for the past twenty years. He teaches psychoanalysis and human development at the institutes and medical schools of Cornell, Columbia, and New York University and is a member of the New York Psychoanalytic Society and the American and International Psychoanalytic associations. He is the winner of an Outstanding Book Award from the American Association of Publishers. Dr. Ross has a sixteen-year-old son and lives in Manhattan.